POET IN NEW YORK

POETICS OF WORK

POET IN NEW YORK

Federico García Lorca

Translated from the Spanish by Greg Simon and Steven F. White

Edited and with an introduction and notes by Christopher Maurer

NEWLY REVISED AND EXPANDED BILINGUAL EDITION

Farrar, Straus and Giroux   New York

Farrar, Straus and Giroux
18 West 18th Street, New York 10011

The Library of Congress has cataloged the previous edition as follows:
García Lorca, Federico, 1898–1936.
   [Poeta en Nueva York. English & Spanish]
   Poet in New York / Federico García Lorca ; translated by Greg Simon and Steven F. White ;
edited and with an introduction and notes by Christopher Maurer.—Rev. ed.
     p.   cm.
   Poems in English and Spanish; introduction and critical matter in English.
   ISBN 0-374-52540-4
   I. Simon, Greg.   II. White, Steven F., 1955–   III. Maurer, Christopher.   IV. Title.

PQ6613.A763 P6313   1998
861'.62—dc21

                             97049953

Paperback ISBN: 978-0-374-53376-2

www.fsgbooks.com
www.twitter.com/fsgbooks • www.facebook.com/fsgbooks

20 19 18 17 16 15 14 13 12 11

Contents

Note to the Third Edition

This third edition of Lorca's *Poet in New York* draws on a new edition of the Spanish; recent biographical and textual research about the poet in America; new critical readings; and some second and third thoughts about the meaning of certain lines in the Spanish original. Greg Simon, Steven F. White, and I have revised every part of this book. Thanks, as before, to Mario Hernández, María Estrella Iglesias, and Andrew A. Anderson for their advice, criticism, and help. I am also grateful for research support provided by the Fundación Federico García Lorca and Boston University.

Introduction

Federico García Lorca would remember his stay in New York (June 1929–March 1930) as "one of the most useful experiences" of his life, and in fact the year that he spent in New York, Vermont, and Havana changed his vision of himself and of his art.

This was his first visit to another country, his first encounter with the racial and religious diversity of a democratic society (Spain had been ruled for almost six years by the dictator Primo de Rivera), and his first, frightening glimpse of urban crowds. The importance of all this for a poet who had always been deeply interested in social problems can hardly be underestimated.

New York also served him as a great school of the theater. His own career as a playwright was just beginning: only two of his works had been staged in Spain, and a third, *The Love of Don Perlimplín*, was in rehearsal when it was closed down by government censors. The trip to New York gave him the opportunity to distance himself psychologically from the Spanish theater of his day and to judge it as a whole. Two important experimental works, *Once Five Years Pass* and *The Audience*, were begun in the New World. "One must think of the theater of the future," he writes to his family. "Everything that now exists in Spain is dead. Either the theater changes radically, or it dies away forever. There is no other solution." He must have been greatly interested in the way the theater was organized in New York. He had had no previous contact with a viable tradition of university or repertory theater, and it is likely that American groups like the Neighborhood Playhouse (who would later produce one of his plays), the Theatre Guild, and the Civic Repertory Theatre served as models, after his return to Spain, for the drama groups he himself founded during the first years of the Spanish Republic. He was fascinated by the black musical revue, as much perhaps by African American audiences as by the performers, and he must have remembered all this after his return to Spain as he sought to save the Spanish stage from the expectations of middle-class audiences. What plays he saw in English no one knows. The language barrier would not have prevented him from absorbing what seemed interesting or novel about the nonverbal aspects of drama.

Few critics have written about Lorca's life in New York without insisting that he felt depressed and isolated. The Spanish poet Rafael Alberti tells us that *Poet in New York* was written by "a lonely poet . . . lost amid docks and avenues and skyscrapers, returning in nostalgia and anguish to his little room at Columbia University." This may be the impression given by the poems, but the letters that Lorca wrote to his family show that he was surrounded and affectionately cared for by Spanish-speaking friends, old and new, who were either living in the city or passing through. Because his command of English never advanced as far as syntax and grammar—he was a simple collector of "English" words, from *spaghettis* to *shishpil* (sex appeal)—his only American friends were those who already knew something of Spain and of Hispanic culture: the editor and book critic Herschel Brickell, the journalist and translator Mildred Adams, and an adventurous young writer from Vermont whom Lorca had met in Spain, Philip Cummings.

The trip to New York and Cuba took place at an extremely difficult moment in Lorca's life. In August 1928, the thirty-year-old poet confessed to a friend that he was going through "one of the worst crises" he had ever known:

> I now realize what it is that the erotic poets mean by the fire of love, and I have come to this realization precisely when I need to cut it from my life in order not to go under. It is stronger than I suspected. If I had continued to nourish it, it would have done away with my heart. You [say that you] had never seen me so bitter, and it is true. I am full of despair and feel listless and crippled. This has made me feel extraordinarily humble. We'll see if I can accomplish what I

want to with my poetry, and if I can finally cut these terrible bonds and return to the happiness I once felt.[1]

He is alluding to the end of his affair—one of the most important of his life—with a Spanish sculptor, eight years younger, Emilio Aladrén. The poet's love had not been reciprocated: Aladrén seems to have played cruelly with Lorca's emotions and used him to further his own career. The affair was a subject of gossip in Madrid, and Lorca's disorganized, impulsive way of life was now a source of worry to his parents, who hoped that in New York he would learn to administer his time, and their money, more wisely.

The poet would accompany one of his former professors at the University of Granada—Fernando de los Ríos—to the New World. This was a close family friend, a distinguished liberal politician and thinker, and a mentor to Lorca; the person who had persuaded his parents, years earlier, to allow him to study in Madrid. He would leave Lorca in the hands of friends in the Spanish Department at Columbia University. In New York the poet would study English and prepare a book about his American experience.

The "emotional crisis" to which Lorca refers in several letters of 1928 had been strangely aggravated by the critical success of his third book of poems, *The Gypsy Ballads*. The *Ballads* had drawn national attention to his poetry for the first time, and had made him known as a "gypsy poet," a term that had once amused him but which he now found revolting. The contrast between his public image and his private self, both as a writer and as a man (for Spanish society could not accept his homosexuality and several of his closest friends chose to know nothing about it), was becoming ever more grotesque and painful. The beginnings of fame made it all but unbearable. As early as January 1927, more than a year before the *Ballads* were published, Lorca told a friend how irritated he was by "the myth of my gypsiness":

1. Letter to José Antonio Rubio Sacristán, in *Epistolario completo*, eds. Andrew A. Anderson and Christopher Maurer (Madrid: Cátedra, 1997), p. 573.

People confuse my life and character. And this is the last thing I want. The gypsies are nothing but a theme. I could just as well be the poet of sewing needles or hydraulic landscapes. Furthermore, this "gypsy" business gives me an uneducated, uncultured tone and makes me into a "savage poet," which you know I am not. I just don't want them to pigeonhole me. I feel they are trying to chain me down.[2]

Salvador Dalí, who had been Lorca's close friend since 1925, but from whom Lorca had now become estranged, sensed the anguish the poet was feeling. Soon after the *Ballads* appeared in print, he wrote to reassure him:

I love you for what the book reveals you to be, which is just the opposite of the reality that has been invented by putrified people everywhere: the dark-haired gypsy lad with the heart of a child, etc.: that whole decorative, unreal, nonexistent Lorca . . . who could only have been dreamed up by "artistic" swine who know nothing of the little fish and the little bears and the soft, hard, and liquid contours that surround us.[3]

But Dalí's opinion of the *Ballads* themselves only deepened Lorca's depression. In the same letter he reproaches Lorca for having written a book that is "bound, hands and feet, to the old poetry," one that "cannot move us and cannot satisfy the desires of modern readers." The indictment goes cruelly on for several pages. The *Ballads* are filled with clichés and stereotypes, "all the usual ideas about things." The book's imagery only serves to reinforce a "traditional" view of reality, in which things are compared with one another or evoked sentimentally, but never allowed to be *themselves*. The minute hands of a watch, Dalí explains,

2. Letter to Jorge Guillén, in *Epistolario completo*, p. 414.
3. Federico García Lorca and Salvador Dalí, *Sebastian's Arrows: Letters and Mementos of Salvador Dalí and Federico García Lorca*, ed. Christopher Maurer (Chicago: Swan Isle Press, 2004), p. 104.

only begin to acquire real value when they stop pointing to the hour and, losing their *circular* rhythm and the function assigned to them arbitrarily by our intelligence, . . . *escape* from the watch and become a new bodily joint, in the place that corresponds to the sex organs of bread crumbs.[4]

Another old friend, Luis Buñuel, had complained, rather less eloquently, of the *Ballads'* traditionalism:

The book has a certain dramatic quality for those who like that sort of flamenco dramatism. It captures the spirit of the classic ballad, for those who want the classic ballad to survive from one century to the next. There are even some magnificent, extremely original images, but there aren't very many, and they are all mixed up in a plot which I find unbearable, one which has filled the beds of Spain with menstrual blood.[5]

Buñuel was writing to Dalí, whom he had long hoped to separate from Lorca. That winter the painter invited Buñuel to Figueras, where they wrote the script of *Un chien andalou*, shown in Paris in the spring of 1929. Although he may not have seen it until much later, Lorca knew of the film, and believed that Dalí and Buñuel were conspiring against him. In New York he is said to have told Ángel del Río: "Buñuel has made a little shit of a film called *An Andalusian Dog*, and the 'Andalusian dog' is me."[6]

All this forms part of the biographical background of *Poet in New York* and helps to explain Lorca's abrupt departure from the poetic manner of his earlier works. For many reasons, *Poet in New York* marks a turning point in his poetry. It is his first book inspired by the city, rather than the country, and the only one not tied in some way to Andalusia. The New York poems are also the first that directly address social injustice. The

4. Ibid.
5. Luis Buñuel, *Obra literaria*, ed. Agustín Sánchez Vidal (Zaragoza: Ediciones de Heraldo de Aragón, 1982), p. 30.
6. Ibid., p. 33.

book is as innovative formally as it is thematically: although there are several poems in hendecasyllables, and "The Birth of Christ" is written in fourteen-syllable alexandrines, free verse is used more extensively here than previously. The major stylistic change, however, lies in the nature of Lorca's poetic imagery.

By October 1928, Lorca was aware of having entered a new stage in his development as a poet. Dalí's observations on the *Ballads* seem to have provided the stimulus for a lecture entitled "Imagination, Inspiration, Evasion,"[7] in which Lorca discusses two types of poetry, the first of which he thought he had now transcended. There is, he writes, a poetry that is content to discover unsuspected relations between objects and ideas: this is the poetry of "imagination," whose eternal symbol is the great baroque poet Luis de Góngora. The "imaginative" poet follows the laws of "human logic, which is controlled by, and cannot break free of, reason." It is imagination, Lorca explains, that has "discovered the four points of the compass and the intermediate causes of things." The poet uses it to explore and describe the universe, and to "construct a tower against mystery and against the elements." But there is a second type of poetry, the poetry of "inspiration," which permits poet and reader to *acknowledge* mystery and to "evade" reality. In "inspired" poetry, the traditional metaphor yields to the *hecho poético*, the "poetic event," or "poetic fact," or "poetic deed"—an image that seems as inexplicable as a miracle, for it is devoid of any analogical meaning. Based on the *hecho poético*, and bound together by *la lógica poética*, the poem becomes a "self-sufficient entity without reference to any reality outside itself."[8] *Poet in New York* tries to take the reader to a place where (in Lorca's words) "things exist *just because*, with no explicable cause or effect."[9]

The book has often been read as an example of surrealism. Lorca had known of that movement at least since 1925, and, like all the major Spanish poets of his generation, was familiar with André Breton's first manifesto. One of the movement's forerunners, Comte de Lautréamont, had

---

7. Dalí, *Sebastian's Arrows*, pp. 153–62.
8. Derek Harris, *García Lorca: Poeta en Nueva York* (London: Grant and Cutler, 1978), p. 12.
9. Dalí, *Sebastian's Arrows*, p. 160.

seized his imagination at an early age, and it has often been observed that *Poet in New York* owes much to the hallucinatory quality of *Les chants de Maldoror.* It should be noted, though, that in his lecture of 1928 (repeated several times in New York and Cuba), Lorca explicitly rejects the surrealists' use of dreams and of the subconscious as a technique for "poetic evasion." Such an evasion "may be very pure, but it is not very clear. We Latins want sharp profiles and visible mystery. Form and sensuality." In *Poet in New York*, Lorca would avoid the automatism that Breton had advocated in 1924. The critic Derek Harris has written that Lorca "exploits the surrealist freedom from moral, aesthetic or rational constraint, but only as a means of production for his imagery. He does not seek to establish the condition of surreality where conscious and subconscious experience combine."[10] The "surreality" of *Poet in New York* is not an end in itself, nor does it have much to do with the epistemological impulse that lies behind the work Dalí was doing in 1927–28: Lorca could not have shared Dalí's longing to discover "reality" by liberating things from their usual "functional" meaning and emotional charge.

In *Poet in New York*, as, to a lesser degree, in the *Ballads*, traditional metaphors appear, in a disconcerting way, among hermetic images. The windows of Wall Street, for example, are compared to a *columbario* (literally, a dovecote or cemetery niches). Roses bound together for shipment to the city are "manacled" flowers, and the rage of the blacks is "fire [that] slept in the flints." A "harp of living tree trunks" lines the shore of Havana, where the poet hears the "rhythm of dried seeds" (sound of the maracas). Clouds are herds of bison driven by the wind. These metaphors are not very different from those that occur in the *Ballads* and in earlier works. But a far greater number of images can be elucidated only after patient study of their semantic connotations throughout the *entire cycle* of New York poems. Much of the imagery is quite resistent to rational "explanation," and some critics have responded, perhaps a bit vengefully, by dismantling the poems one by one, charting Lorca's "poetic universe," and trying to puzzle out which images are "positive" and which are "negative." These critical approaches,

10. Harris, *García Lorca*, p. 14.

which often pay lip service to the multivalency of Lorca's images, have led to wildly divergent readings of certain poems. "Abandoned Church" has been said to deal with the lost promise of the blacks of Harlem; with "the drama of Christian hypocrisy"; with sexual frustration; with the horrors of World War I; and with the loss of religious faith. Reference to other poems does not lead us much closer to knowing why that poem is included in a section of *Poet in New York* entitled "Los negros." The funeral service alluded to in the poem, the "dead fish beneath the ashes of the censers," are examples of the sort of poetic "evasion" mentioned earlier.

Poet in New York is both a condemnation of modern urban civilization—the spiritual emptiness epitomized by New York—and a dark cry of metaphysical loneliness. Lorca once considered entitling the book *Introduction to Death*, and the "death" alluded to is both spiritual and physical, both that of the poet and that of the world around him.

The central and most dramatic death is that of the poet himself; not the author of the book, but the first-person "subject" of the poems: a protean, self-conscious figure who has been aptly described as "Prometheus, prophet and priest."[11] The difference between this figure and Lorca himself, between the "empirical author" and his poetic persona, must not be overlooked. The family letters presented in this volume will remind the reader that *Poet in New York* cannot be read as a lyrical autobiography. The boyish, carefree writer of those letters and the tragic "self" or "subject" of the book of poems are two of the masks, or voices, of one of the most complex spirits of modern European poetry, and one of the themes of *Poet in New York*—and of *The Audience* as well—is precisely *that*: the quicksand of identity and the struggle to transcend societal masks.

Lorca died without seeing the book published, but in the 1930s, as he searched for ways to organize the unpublished poems he had brought back from the United States, he presented many of them in the form of a lecture

11. Penne J. Laubenthal, *Prometheus, Prophet, and Priest: An Interpretation of Lorca's "Poet in New York,"* Ph.D. dissertation, George Peabody College for Teachers, 1972.

to audiences in Spain, Argentina, and Uruguay. In this reading, in which he creates an autobiographical and political framework for the poems[12]—"that of a journey into the heart of an alien world"—Lorca does his best to identify himself with the lyrical "I." Minimizing the distance between life and art, hoping to make difficult poems easier to understand, he creates a fictitious narrative of how he wrote them and interprets his own book, rather too narrowly, as an attack on the United States, a country bereft of spiritual greatness. The title *Poet in New York* was meant to sound paradoxical: How *could* a poet survive there? Lorca's statements to the Spanish-language press in the years following his return from the United States share the anti-American tone of the lecture (an anti-Americanism quite common in the Spain of the early 1930s):

New York is something awful, something monstrous. I like to walk the streets, lost, but I recognize that New York is the world's great lie. New York is Senegal with machines. The English have taken there a civilization with no roots. They have raised more and more houses, but they haven't dug into the earth. They live upwards, upwards . . .

The U.S. influence on the rest of the world is limited to skyscrapers, jazz, and cocktails. That is all. And in Cuba, in *our* America, they make much better cocktails than the Yankees. In Cuba. Precisely where the American spirit thinks it has the most power.

Besides black art, there is only automation and mechanization.[13]

It would be wrong to doubt the sincerity of these remarks, but the scope of *Poet in New York* is wider than Lorca led his first listeners to believe. The

12. Lorca's reference to a capitalist economic system "whose neck must soon be cut" and his emphasis, in the lecture, on socially oriented poems rather than on the more hermetic ones were consistent with sponsorship of the lecture, in 1932, by the Comité de Cooperación Intelectual, a cultural organization founded to further the liberal ideals of the Second Republic.
13. From interviews in 1931, 1933, and 1936, reprinted in García Lorca, *Obras completas*, Vol. II (Barcelona: Galaxia Gutenberg, 1997), pp. 377, 401, 632. This book is referred to in the notes that follow as *OC*.

"poet" does indeed condemn white urban American civilization, but that civilization is merely the most immediate, clearest possible image of the spiritual poverty of twentieth-century man. The "sleepless city" of the poems is late-night Manhattan, going down with all its lights ablaze, but it is also the vigil of modern man in quest of the cosmic *meaning* of so much suffering. The wrathful poet-priest presides over the destruction of city streets: "Cobras shall hiss on the top floors. / Nettles shall shake courtyards and terraces" and social injustice will meet its just reward. But he does more. He looks beyond circumstance to the edge of the unknown, in order to understand the pain around him; and much of that suffering does not seem to have any "social" or "moral" explanation.

> Everyone understands the pain that accompanies death,
> but genuine pain doesn't live in the spirit,
> nor in the air, nor in our lives,
> nor on these terraces of billowing smoke.
> The genuine pain that keeps everything awake
> is a tiny, infinite burn
> on the innocent eyes of other systems.

The poet's awareness and consolidarity with these "other systems"—birds and insects, idiot children, tree trunks, water and sand, the moon and planets—lies a measure of the greatness of *Poet in New York* and of all Lorca's poetry. No Spanish poet ever made his readers more conscious of the sinister, alien qualities of things and of the inadequacy of reason:

> We forget that the mind has boroughs
> where Chinese and caterpillars devour the philosopher.

Several years later, in a new lecture on artistic inspiration, he would return to the same thought: artistic inspiration is more precious than intelligence. The latter "is often the enemy of poetry, because it limits too much, and it elevates the poet to a sharp-edged throne, making him forget that ants could eat him or that a great arsenic lobster could fall on his head" ("Play and Theory of the *Duende*"). The sharp edges, the *aristas*, of that throne—"throne of rational thought"—are analogous to those of Manhattan. If there *is* a moral explanation for the suffering Lorca sees in New York, it lies in this: man's ignorance of, or indifference to, "the other." The redemptive role of the poet is to remind the reader in memorable, mysterious speech of the limits of human thought: to remind him of the "living earth" under the patterns and pavements of the metropolis and of the otherness that lies *beyond* human speech.

> There is a world of broken rivers and distances just beyond our
>   grasp
> in the cat's paw smashed by a car.

In an essay on Lorca's apocalyptic vision, Dennis Costa writes of Lorca's sympathy for those whom "the culture at large has named as marginal and therefore expendable: the blacks, suffering children, impoverished immigrants," "the hieratic figure of Walt Whitman." *Poet in New York* "would at one and the same time parry the adversary—the monster-mechanical city of illicit commerce—and celebrate those individuals and communities whose attitude marks them as being different."[14] The stubborn hermeticism—and sometimes the aphoristic clarity—of *Poet in New York* may be seen as a refusal to ignore that "otherness," that "difference," whose most visible symbol, in all Lorca's work, is the earth—dumb, terrifying image of two inseparable mysteries: life and death.

A certain critical account of *Poet in New York* identifies its three major themes as "social injustice, dark love, and lost faith."[15] Their common element is the alienation, or otherness, just mentioned. The social aspect of the book is easiest to grasp; *Poet in New York* condemns capitalist society and all that it seems to entail: an anthropocentric world view; a culture of consumption ("New York: Office and Denunciation"); the degradation of

---

14. Dennis Costa, "¿Cuanto falta para Jerusalén?: Lorca's Apocalyptic and the Paradigms of Peace in *Poeta en Nueva York* and *El público*," *Literature and Theology* 22:1 (2008), p. 67.
15. Richard L. Predmore, *Lorca's New York Poetry: Social Injustice, Dark Love, Lost Faith* (Durham: Duke University Press, 1980).

nature; indifference to suffering; the materialistic corruption of love and religion; the alienation of social groups, particularly the blacks.

The poems about the blacks were the first Lorca wrote in the New World. Little more than a month after his arrival in New York, he went to explore Harlem with the black novelist Nella Larsen, and dreamed of writing a book that would "sound an entirely new note" about the black experience. He had arrived in New York in the last days of what is now known as the Harlem Renaissance.[16] "Standards and Paradise of the Blacks" is an attempt to define the blacks through their aesthetic and vital norms, above all through their longing for the "deserted blue": the blue of infinity and the timeless blue of ancestral African skies, "blue of a night without fear of day," night of the blues, coal-black blues of the blackest members of the race. The object of their longing, the "paradise" named in the title, is a sort of celestial graveyard, where torsos lie dreaming, returning to the void.

The vision entitled "The King of Harlem" is both protest and warning: protest (as Lorca states in his lecture) that "the blacks do not want to be black"; warning that the blood raging under their skin ". . . will flow / on rooftops everywhere, / and burn the blond women's chlorophyll, / and groan at the foot of the beds near the washstands' insomnia, / and burst into an aurora of tobacco and low yellow" as the black race overwhelms the white. What Lorca saw of racial discrimination in New York troubled him for the rest of his life. In 1933 he told an interviewer in Buenos Aires that he wanted to write a tragedy about the blacks, but could not do so until he had fully understood "a world shameless and cruel enough to divide people by color when in fact color is the sign of God's artistic genius."

The blacks' loss of cultural identity—their supposed nostalgia for their ancestral roots—is analogous to the poet's own. *Poet in New York* owes some of its uniqueness to the way that the "social" domain reflects the private, and poems of protest mingle with elegy. The poem entitled "1910

---

16. On Lorca's view of black culture, see Christopher Maurer, ed., *Federico García Lorca escribe a su familia desde Nueva York y La Habana (1929–1930)*, in *Poesía* (Madrid) 23–24 (1986), pp. 143–50.

(Intermezzo)" is an elegy for the poet's own lost childhood, a time when he was less preoccupied with suffering, sexual problems, and death, and was able to stare wonderingly at the simple, immediate realities of rural life: the horror of "the bull's muzzle, the poisonous mushroom," a religious engraving of St. Rose of Lima, the family garden, "where cats devour frogs," the "pony's neck," and "an incomprehensible moon." By now, he has lost his sense of self. Only once, far from the city, in rural surroundings that evoke the world of his childhood, does he speak of having regained his "old voice":

Ay, my love's voice from before,
ay, voice of my truth,
ay, voice of my open side,
when all the roses spilled from my tongue . . .

That voice has now turned to "tin and talc" ("Double Poem of Lake Eden," written, perhaps, near the Vermont asbestos mine he may have visited with Cummings. Embedded in almost all the poems are faintly identifiable fragments of American reality).

Other retrospective poems—"Your Childhood in Menton," "Fable of Three Friends to Be Sung in Rounds"—seem to have grown from the emotional crisis and the feelings of abandonment and betrayal that preceded the trip to New York. Critics have tried in vain to identify the person to whom "Your Childhood . . ." is addressed. Some argue that the poet is addressing himself. But the bitterness of lines 9–12 seem directed to a lover who has spurned the poet's norms of homoerotic love:

What I gave you, Apollonian man, was a standard of love,
bursts of tears with an estranged nightingale.
But ruin fed upon you, you whittled yourself to nothing for the
    sake of
fleeting, aimless dreams.

In the "Fable of Three Friends . . . ," which alludes, perhaps, to the affair with Aladrén, and in eight other passages in the book, the poet speaks of his assassination ("I knew they had murdered me").[17] The many images of mutilation, murder, and disintegration of the self—whether this is seen as annihilation or as communion with the other—point to the questioning of "identity" alluded to earlier.

Lorca divided *Poet in New York* into ten chapters, the headings of which provide a narrative framework and allow the book to be read as the story of a psychological voyage. By section IV the poet has moved from the city to the rural scenario of Vermont. But he is as haunted by death in the "rural" poems of sections IV, V, and VI as he is in the "urban" ones. The transmutations we read of in "Death"—the longing of the horse to be a dog and of the swallow to be a bee—reflect the desire for otherness that governs all creation; a desire that culminates, as it always does in Lorca, in death. The poet himself, who would be a "burning angel," must pass, like the rest of creation, through the "plaster arch," the narrows of death, the void or divestment of self that some readers have seen as leading to peace and to redemption.[18] Life is seen in this book as metamorphosis: Ovid read in a deathly light. *Son mentira las formas* ("Shapes [or forms] are a lie"), the poet exclaims in another poem. In life and in death, everything flows. Behind the broken windowpanes of an abandoned country house, about to be overpowered by grass and weeds, the poet senses "sand struggling with water" ("Ruin"):

17. "The effect of this . . . is to lend a weird pathos to the squalid occasion in 1936 when Lorca was taken out to a road near his native Granada, and literally assassinated . . . [But] Lorca's poems were not his epitaphs. They were poems, and the result of reading them into Lorca's death is to prettify a very unpretty business and to make the poems look rather slight into the bargain." Michael Wood, "The Lorca Murder Case," *The New York Review of Books*, November 24, 1977, p. 38.
18. For Dennis Costa, death in *Poet in New York* forms part of a violent but also "irenic" or peaceful apocalypse enacted by a Johannine-like revelator. Referring to Lorca's "particular, and especially linguistic, solitude in the United States," Costa writes: "Lost in his Manhattan, like John the Divine in his Patmos, Lorca entered into more intimate communion with those beings who bear the brunt of reality" ("¿Cuanto falta para Jerusalén?," p. 69). For another view on *Poet in New York* and the book of *Revelation*, see Martha Nandorfy, *The Poetics of Apocalypse: Federico García Lorca's "Poet in New York"* (Lewisburg: Bucknell University Press, 2003).

Soon it was clear that the moon
was a horse's skull,
and the air, a dark apple.

The "timeless doors" of the earth lead back to the "blush of the fruit," and even the deceased have no rest: thus the uneasy slumber of Christians in "Jewish Cemetery" or the conversation between two dead men in a Vermont graveyard, who sit up to hear the howling of a dog: "Cancer's three nymphs" have been dancing, and someone else is about to join them. Even here there is an echo of childhood. One of the dead men says he has "loved a child / who had a tiny feather on his tongue, / and we lived inside a knife for a hundred years." In his lecture "On Lullabies" (1928), Lorca speaks of a cradle song from southern Spain:

Lullaby, little boy,
in the country we'll build
a tiny hut
and live inside.

"Danger is near," Lorca says, explaining the lullaby. "We must make ourselves smaller, tiny . . . Outside, they are waiting to hurt us. We must live in a tiny place. If we can, we will live in an orange, you and me. Even better, in a grape!" In the desolation of New York, the orange (or grape) becomes a knife. No immediate religious consolation is apparent, here or anywhere else in the book; formal religion has failed the poet ("Cry Toward Rome"), and man is as alienated from God as he is from his childhood, or from the rest of creation. "The world [is] alone in the lonely sky" ("Christmas on the Hudson").

Lorca's vision of the impermanence or emptiness of forms—forms abandoned in the senseless flux of life: the "husks of insects," lost gloves, cast-off suits of clothes—gives rise to one of the most frequent and most untranslatable images in the book: the *hueco*: void or hollow, space or emptied space. The atmosphere of New York is riddled with *huecos*: "There are spaces (or voids) that ache in the uninhabited air." In *Poet in New York*, as in all of Lorca's writing, abstract concepts and perceptions turn into astonishingly *tangible* poetic figures. Master of the elegy, able to compare what *is* and what is *not*, the object and its "void," Lorca gives color and weight to the notion of annihilation itself, an example of the "sharp profiles and visible mystery" noted in the lecture on imagination mentioned earlier.

In the void that is at the center of his swirling images, in the eye of the storm, in the resonant hollow of the well, is an absent child. No psychological explanation can account for the verbal adventure of *Poet in New York*, but figures like "Little Stanton," the "Little Girl Drowned in the Well," and the dead son in "Abandoned Church" serve as ghastly images of the "unengendered" or incomplete. It is as though the pent-up aching water of the well— water that "never reaches the sea" or, more literally, has no outlet or never disgorges—were unspent life. The child who cannot leave the well—or the womb—is present in one of Lorca's earliest books of poetry, *Suites* (1920–23):

LITTLE SONG OF THE UNBORN CHILD

You have left me on a flower
of the water's dark sobs!
The weeping I learned
will grow old,
trailing its bustle
of sighs and tears.
Without arms, how can I push open
the door of the Light?
Some other child has used them
to row his little boat . . .[19]

The anguish of *Suites*, which was not published during Lorca's lifetime, suffuses much of the New York poetry. Lorca quotes from the book in *Once*

19. See Federico García Lorca, *Selected Verse* (New York: Farrar, Straus and Giroux, 1994), pp. 114–17.

Five Years Pass, a play whose gay protagonist dreams of the son he will never engender.[20] For both the "Young Man" of the play and the subject of *Poet in New York*, the unengendered child becomes the child *within*, the child borne into adulthood; and, in a way typical of surrealist art, the child within is also an image of the Orphic imagination that can understand "celestial words / that sleep in tree trunks, clouds, and turtles" ("Little Stanton"), and of the poetic voice that the writer has lost and must struggle to recover.

The theme of homosexuality is of fundamental importance in *Poet in New York*—gay men too are marginalized here—and the "Ode to Walt Whitman," first published in a limited, private edition, is Lorca's most extensive, and most ambitious, treatment of that subject. Here the thought of death lends urgency to love and seems to grant man the freedom to love as he chooses:

Tomorrow, loves will become stones, and Time
a breeze that drowses in the branches.

And thus man can guide his desire "through a vein of coral" or through a "nude as blue as the sky." One of the unresolved tensions in the book, as perhaps in Lorca's life, is this: on the one hand, grief for the "unengendered child," for unrealized possibility, for "what might have been"; on the other, the calm certainty, expressed in the "Ode," that not all men are destined for procreation:

. . . it's fitting if a man doesn't look for his delight
in tomorrow morning's jungle of blood.
The sky has shores where life can be avoided
and there are bodies that shouldn't repeat themselves in the dawn.

Despite the force and clarity of lines like these, the "Ode" is a strangely ambiguous poem, drawing a confusing distinction between the "classical"

---

20. For an excellent discussion of the "unengendered child" in this play and in the rest of Lorca's work, see José Ángel Valente, "Pez luna," in *Trece de nieve* (Madrid) 1–2 (1976), pp. 191–201.

homosexual (the Whitmanesque "camerado") and those whom the poet would exclude from the symposium: "urban faggots," "slaves of women," pederasts: "all the greedy and neurotic riff-raff who form [part] of what is often called the 'gay scene,'"[21] a group that has no right to claim kinship with Whitman. The "classical" element is rather more difficult to characterize. Social concerns blend here with sexual ones in a way that is characteristic of Lorca: American capitalism has somehow corrupted Whitman's vision of love and thwarted the coming of "the kingdom of wheat." Paul Binding has explained the analogy implicit in the "Ode": "the failure of homosexual life to live up to the Whitmanesque image of it is inextricable from the failure of American society to live up to Whitman's social pastorals for it."[22] Like *The Audience*, Lorca's drama about homoerotic love, the "Ode" was written in Havana, where he seems to have accepted, with a new degree of openness, his own sexuality.

Poet in New York comes to an end with three dance poems that imply a healing of the psychic wounds described earlier in the book. The "Two Waltzes Toward Civilization" bring to poetic fulfillment an aesthetic ideal that animates much of Lorca's poetry and drama, from the earliest works on: the oneness of literature and music. In his adolescent writings of 1917–18, shortly after he had abandoned the study of the piano, the poet had tried to realize this unity through the use of suggestively "musical" titles and subtitles, metaphors and images. The underlying structural principle of some of the *Suites* had been the theme and variation. By the time he wrote *Poeta en Nueva York*, a book that he regarded as *"symphonic*, like the noise and complexity" of the city itself, musical ideas had become *formative*, rather than merely decorative, elements in his writing. *Blood Wedding* (1932) is an extreme example: the contrapuntal structure of an entire scene was inspired by, and directly modeled on, the technique of "imitative entry"

21. Paul Binding, *Lorca: The Gay Imagination* (London: GMP, 1985), p. 139. The same ambiguity may be found in *El público*. See Carlos Jérez Farrán, "El Sadomasoquismo homoerótico como expresión de homofobia en el cuadro 2 de *El público* de GL," in *Modern Philology* 93, 4 (1996), pp. 468–97.
22. Binding, *Lorca*, p. 141.

used by Bach in one of his cantatas.[23] Parts of the two waltzes are written in a lilting three-quarter time impossible to imitate, without loss of sense, in English: this must be one of the most stunning experiments in "musical" literature in all of modern poetry. In "Little Viennese Waltz," the poet's darkest, most secret yearning is expressed in the lightest, most playful cadences imaginable. It is a love poem, the most explicitly homoerotic one Lorca had yet written. The strains of the waltz lead the poet to a declaration of love, the flaunting of his own beauty—"See how the hyacinths line my banks!"—and the imagining, in the final five lines, of the consummation of the sexual act. The ribbons of the waltz will be broken and buried in the dark movements of the beloved.[24]

Lorca never returned to New York, and his book was not read here until 1939–40, when the translations of Stephen Spender and J. L. Gili were published in Britain and those of Rolfe Humphries in the United States. The poet's death in Granada (1936) was still recent, and that tragedy, and the defeat of the Republican cause, colored the first English readings of the poems.[25] The element of social criticism in *Poet in New York* was all but ignored by American reviewers. Only Conrad Aiken, who later wrote a moving "Homage to Lorca,"[26] seems to have responded to it:

> There has been no more terribly acute critic of America than this steel-conscious and death-conscious Spaniard, with his curious

23. See Christopher Maurer, "García Lorca y las formas de la música," in *Lecciones sobre Federico García Lorca*, ed. Andrés Soria Olmedo (Granada: Ediciones del Cincuentenario, 1986), pp. 235–50.

24. For a discussion, see John K. Walsh, " 'Las cintas del vals': Three dance-poems from Lorca's *Poeta en Nueva York*," *Romantic Review* 79, 3 (1988), pp. 502–16.

25. The Gili/Spender and Humphries translations of Lorca's poetry were reviewed in the 1940s by Louise Bogan, Muriel Rukeyser, and Conrad Aiken, among others. An excellent review of the Gili/Spender anthology is V. S. Pritchett's "Lorca," *The New Statesman and Nation*, July 29, 1939, p. 192. For a discussion of Lorca's reception in English, see Howard Young, "La primera recepción . . . ," in Andrew A. Anderson, *América en un poeta* . . . (Sevilla: Universidad Internacional de Andalucía / Fundación Focus-Abengoa, 1999), pp. 109 ff.

26. He titles it "The Poet in Granada." *Collected Poems* (New York: Oxford University Press, 1953), pp. 650–58.

passion for the modernities of nickel and tinfoil and nitre, and for the eternities of the desert and the moon. He hated us, and rightly, for the right reasons.

V. S. Pritchett wrote: "What we call civilization, he called slime and wire." Hardly a word was said of the poet's religious and sexual concerns, or of his disconsolate vision of solitude and death. One reviewer referred to Lorca's "flamboyant impressions of New York." The "myth" of his gypsiness had outlived him: he was admired in the United States as a "troubadour" and "folk poet," and more than one writer was unwilling to pardon him for having posed as a *surréaliste*. *Poet in New York* had not revealed "another" Lorca; it seemed a "jungle of disembodied surrealistic countersigns" or a book of "finger-exercises in automatic writing."[27] Even Rolfe Humphries, who translated *Poet in New York* into English for the first time, found the book "rather hysterical": in the New World, the poet "bit off more than he could chew."[28] A decade later, Roy Campbell would concur: in New York, Lorca had "lost his depth . . . His metaphors and images fall out of focus; his verse becomes loose, plaintive and slightly mephitic. It took him a long time to recover his poetical eyesight and insight . . ."[29] Those negative judgments began to crumble after the American poet Ben Belitt retranslated the book in 1955, celebrating Lorca's sense of "the savagery of the psychic occasion."[30]

Many decades after the first publication of *Poet in New York*, a far different opinion prevails. No one would argue now that the book is a stylistic "exercise." Lorca's strange poetic idiom is now seen to answer to a dark, and deadly serious, vision of human life, one whose mystery will trouble a

27. From reviews by James A. Magner in *Commonweal*, November 3, 1940, and R. W. Short in *Yale Review* XXX (1940), pp. 214–16.
28. Daniel Eisenberg, *Poeta en Nueva York: Historia y problemas de un texto de Lorca* (Barcelona: Ariel, 1976), p. 58. I have translated from the Spanish text.
29. Roy Campbell, *Lorca: An Appreciation of His Poetry* (New Haven: Yale University Press, 1952), pp. 94–95.
30. For an excellent study of Lorca's reception among American poets from Robert Duncan to Jerome Rothenberg, see Jonathan Mayhew, *Apocryphal Lorca: Translation, Parody, Kitsch* (Chicago: University of Chicago Press, 2009).

new generation of readers. The years have broadened the meaning of the poems. The title has all but lost its paradox and the evils of the city seem no more characteristic of Manhattan than of Madrid or, for that matter, of Granada. The "gypsy poet" has disappeared, but Lorca's cry of anguish, his vision of human solitude, and his hope for solidarity and redemption seem destined to endure.

Christopher Maurer

Lorca, passport, 1929. In a letter to Carlos Morla Lynch, dated June 6, 1929, the poet writes: "I can't resist sending you this most spiritualistic of portraits—the one they took for my passport. It borders on the light of murder; borders on the nocturnal street corner where the delicate pickpocket stashes his wad of money. The whimsical lens has captured, over my shoulder, a sort of harp, soft as a jellyfish, and the whole atmosphere has a certain finite tic, like the ash of a cigarette . . ."

POET IN NEW YORK /
POETA EN NUEVA YORK

Los poemas de este libro están escritos en la ciudad de Nueva York, el año 1929–30, en que el poeta vivió como estudiante en Columbia University.

Dedicado a Bebé y Carlos Morla

[F.G.L.]

The poems in this book were written in New York City in 1929–30, while the poet was living as a student at Columbia University.

Dedicated to Bebé and Carlos Morla

[F.G.L.]

I
POEMAS DE LA SOLEDAD EN COLUMBIA UNIVERSITY

Furia color de amor,
amor color de olvido.
—LUIS CERNUDA

I
POEMS OF SOLITUDE IN COLUMBIA UNIVERSITY

Fury, color of love.
love, color of oblivion.
—LUIS CERNUDA

Lorca, *Self-Portrait Embracing a
Fabulous Beast,* 1929

Vuelta de paseo

Asesinado por el cielo.
Entre las formas que van hacia la sierpe
y las formas que buscan el cristal
dejaré crecer mis cabellos.

Con el árbol de muñones que no canta
y el niño con el blanco rostro de huevo.

Con los animalitos de cabeza rota
y el agua harapienta de los pies secos.

Con todo lo que tiene cansancio sordomudo
y mariposa ahogada en el tintero.

Tropezando con mi rostro distinto de cada día.
¡Asesinado por el cielo!

After a Walk

Cut down by the sky.
Between shapes moving toward the serpent
and crystal-craving shapes,
I'll let my hair grow long.

With the amputated tree that doesn't sing
and the child with the blank face of an egg.

With the little animals whose skulls are cracked
and the water, dressed in rags, but with dry feet.

With all the bone-tired, deaf-and-dumb things
and a butterfly drowned in the inkwell.

Bumping into my own face, different each day.
Cut down by the sky!

1910
(Intermedio)

Aquellos ojos míos de mil novecientos diez
no vieron enterrar a los muertos,
ni la feria de ceniza del que llora por la madrugada,
ni el corazón que tiembla arrinconado como un caballito de mar.

Aquellos ojos míos de mil novecientos diez
vieron la blanca pared donde orinaban las niñas,
el hocico del toro, la seta venenosa
y una luna incomprensible que iluminaba por los rincones
los pedazos de limón seco bajo el negro duro de las botellas.

Aquellos ojos míos en el cuello de la jaca,
en el seno traspasado de Santa Rosa dormida,
en los tejados del amor, con gemidos y frescas manos,
en un jardín donde los gatos se comían a las ranas.

Desván donde el polvo viejo congrega estatuas y musgos.
Cajas que guardan silencio de cangrejos devorados.
En el sitio donde el sueño tropezaba con su realidad.
Allí mis pequeños ojos.

No preguntarme nada. He visto que las cosas
cuando buscan su curso encuentran su vacío.
Hay un dolor de huecos por el aire sin gente
y en mis ojos criaturas vestidas ¡sin desnudo!

Nueva York, agosto 1929

1910
(Intermezzo)

Those eyes of mine in nineteen-ten
saw no one dead and buried,
no village fair of ash from the one who weeps at dawn,
no trembling heart cornered like a sea horse.

Those eyes of mine in nineteen-ten
saw the white wall where little girls pissed,
the bull's muzzle, the poisonous mushroom,
and an incomprehensible moon illuminating dried lemon rinds
in corners, under the hard black of bottles.

Those eyes of mine on the pony's neck,
on the pierced breast of Santa Rosa as she sleeps,
on the rooftops of love, with moans and cool hands,
on a garden where cats devour frogs.

Attic where the ancient dust assembles statues and moss.
Boxes that keep the silence of devoured crabs.
In the place where the dream was colliding with its reality.
My little eyes were there.

Don't ask me any questions. I've seen how things
that seek their way find their void instead.
There are emptied spaces that ache in the uninhabited air
and in my eyes, completely dressed creatures—no one naked there!

New York, August 1929

Fábula y rueda de los tres amigos

Enrique,
Emilio,
Lorenzo.
Estaban los tres helados:
Enrique por el mundo de las camas,
Emilio por el mundo de los ojos y las heridas de las manos,
Lorenzo por el mundo de las universidades sin tejados.

Lorenzo,
Emilio,
Enrique.
Estaban los tres quemados:
Lorenzo por el mundo de las hojas y las bolas de billar,
Emilio por el mundo de la sangre y los alfileres blancos,
Enrique por el mundo de los muertos y los periódicos abandonados.

Lorenzo,
Emilio,
Enrique.
Estaban los tres enterrados:
Lorenzo en un seno de Flora,
Emilio en la yerta ginebra que se olvida en el vaso,
Enrique en la hormiga, en el mar y en los ojos vacíos de los pájaros.

Lorenzo,
Emilio,
Enrique.
Fueron los tres en mis manos
tres montañas chinas,
tres sombras de caballo,

Fable of Three Friends to Be Sung in Rounds

Enrique,
Emilio,
Lorenzo.
The three of them were frozen:
Enrique in the world of beds,
Emilio in the world of eyes and wounded hands,
Lorenzo in the world of roofless universities.

Lorenzo,
Emilio,
Enrique.
The three of them were burned:
Lorenzo in the world of leaves and billiard balls,
Emilio in the world of blood and white pins,
Enrique in the world of the dead and discarded newspapers.

Lorenzo,
Emilio,
Enrique.
The three of them were buried:
Lorenzo in Flora's breast,
Emilio in the forgotten shot of gin,
Enrique in the ant, the sea, the empty eyes of the birds.

Lorenzo,
Emilio,
Enrique.
In my hands the three of them were
three Chinese mountains,
three shadows of horses,

tres paisajes de nieve y una cabaña de azucenas
por los palomares donde la luna se pone plana bajo el gallo.

Uno
y uno
y uno.
Estaban los tres momificados,
con las moscas del invierno,
con los tinteros que orina el perro y desprecia el vilano,
con la brisa que hiela el corazón de todas las madres,
por los blancos derribos de Júpiter donde meriendan muerte los borrachos.

Tres
y dos
y uno.
Los vi perderse llorando y cantando
por un huevo de gallina,
por la noche que enseñaba su esqueleto de tabaco,
por mi dolor lleno de rostros y punzantes esquirlas de luna,
por mi alegría de ruedas dentadas y látigos,
por mi pecho turbado por las palomas,
por mi muerte desierta con un solo paseante equivocado.

Yo había matado la quinta luna
y bebían agua por las fuentes los abanicos y los aplausos.
Tibia leche encerrada de las recién paridas
agitaba las rosas con un largo dolor blanco.
Enrique,
Emilio,
Lorenzo.
Diana es dura,
pero a veces tiene los pechos nublados.
Puede la piedra blanca latir en la sangre del ciervo
y el ciervo puede soñar por los ojos de un caballo.

three snowy landscapes and a little house of lilies
by the dovecotes where the moon lies flat beneath the rooster.

One
and one
and one.
The three of them were mummified
with winter flies,
with the inkwells that dogs piss and thistledown despises,
with the breeze that chills every mother's heart,
by Jupiter's white wreckage, where the drunks lunch on death.

Three
and two
and one.
I saw them lose themselves, weeping and singing,
in a hen's egg,
in the night that showed its tobacco skeleton,
in my sorrow, full of faces and piercing lunar shrapnel,
in my joy of serrated wheels and whips,
in my breast that is clouded with doves,
in my deserted death with a lone mistaken passerby.

I had killed the fifth moon,
and the fans and applause were drinking water from the fountains.
Warm milk trapped inside the new mothers
was stirring the roses with a long white sorrow.
Enrique,
Emilio,
Lorenzo.
Diana is hard,
but sometimes her breasts are banked with clouds.
The white stone can throb in deer blood
and the deer can dream through the eyes of a horse.

Cuando se hundieron las formas puras
bajo el cri cri de las margaritas,
comprendí que me habían asesinado.
Recorrieron los cafés y los cementerios y las iglesias.
Abrieron los toneles y los armarios.
Destrozaron tres esqueletos para arrancar sus dientes de oro.
Ya no me encontraron.
¿No me encontraron?
No. No me encontraron.
Pero se supo que la sexta luna huyó torrente arriba,
y que el mar recordó ¡de pronto!
los nombres de todos sus ahogados.

When the pure shapes sank
under the chirping of daisies,
I knew they had murdered me.
They combed the cafés, graveyards, and churches for me,
pried open casks and cabinets,
destroyed three skeletons in order to rip out their gold teeth.
But they couldn't find me anymore.
They couldn't?
No, they couldn't find me.
But they discovered the sixth moon had fled upstream,
and the sea—suddenly!—remembered
the names of all its drowned.

Tu infancia en Menton

Sí, tu niñez: ya fábula de fuentes.
—JORGE GUILLÉN

Sí, tu niñez: ya fábula de fuentes.
El tren y la mujer que llena el cielo.
Tu soledad esquiva en los hoteles
y tu máscara pura de otro signo.
Es la niñez del mar y tu silencio
donde los sabios vidrios se quebraban.
Es tu yerta ignorancia donde estuvo
mi torso limitado por el fuego.
Norma de amor te di, hombre de Apolo,
llanto con ruiseñor enajenado,
pero, pasto de ruina, te afilabas
para los breves sueños indecisos.
Pensamiento de enfrente, luz de ayer,
índices y señales del acaso.
Tu cintura de arena sin sosiego
atiende sólo rastros que no escalan.
Pero yo he de buscar por los rincones
tu alma tibia sin ti que no te entiende,
con el dolor de Apolo detenido
con que he roto la máscara que llevas.
Allí, león, allí, furia de cielo,
te dejaré pacer en mis mejillas;
allí, caballo azul de mi locura,
pulso de nebulosa y minutero.
He de buscar las piedras de alacranes
y los vestidos de tu madre niña,
llanto de media noche y paño roto
que quitó luna de la sien del muerto.

Your Childhood in Menton

Yes, your childhood: now a fable of fountains.
—JORGE GUILLÉN

Yes, your childhood: now a fable of fountains.
The train and the woman who fills the sky.
Your shy loneliness in hotels
and your pure mask of another sign.
The sea's childhood and your silence
where the crystals of wisdom shattered.
Your rigid ignorance where
my torso was circumscribed by fire.
What I gave you, Apollonian man, was a standard of love,
bursts of tears with an estranged nightingale.
But you were food for ruin and whittled yourself to nothing
for the sake of fleeting, aimless dreams.
Thoughts before you, yesterday's light,
traces and signs of what might be.
Your waist of restless sand
follows only trails that do not climb.
But in every corner I must look for your warm soul
that is without you and doesn't understand you,
with the sorrow of Apollo stopped in his tracks,
the sorrow with which I shattered your mask.
It's there, lion, there, sky's fury,
where I'll let you graze on my cheeks;
there, blue horse of my insanity,
pulse of the nebula and hand that counts the minutes.
There I'll look for the scorpions' stones
and the clothes of the girl who was your mother,
midnight wailing and torn cloth
that wiped moonlight from the temple of the dead man.

Sí, tu niñez: ya fábula de fuentes.
Alma extraña de mi hueco de venas,
te he de buscar pequeña y sin raíces.
¡Amor de siempre, amor, amor de nunca!
¡Oh, sí! Yo quiero. ¡Amor, amor! Dejadme.
No me tapen la boca los que buscan
espigas de Saturno por la nieve
o castran animales por un cielo,
clínica y selva de la anatomía.
Amor, amor, amor. Niñez del mar.
Tu alma tibia sin ti que no te entiende.
Amor, amor, un vuelo de la corza
por el pecho sin fin de la blancura.
Y tu niñez, amor, y tu niñez.
El tren y la mujer que llena el cielo.
Ni tú, ni yo, ni el aire, ni las hojas.
Sí, tu niñez: ya fábula de fuentes.

Yes, your childhood: now a fable of fountains.
Strange soul, tiny and adrift, ripped
from the emptied space of my veins—I must look until I find you.
The same love as ever, love; love of never.
Yes, I do love! Love! Leave me alone, all of you.
And don't try to cover my mouth, you who seek
the wheat of Saturn in snowfields,
or castrate animals in a sky,
anatomy's clinic and jungle.
Love, love, love. The sea's childhood.
Your warm soul that is without you and doesn't understand you.
Love, love, the flight of the doe
over the endless breast of whiteness.
And your childhood, love, your childhood.
The train and the woman who fills the sky.
Not you, not me, not the air, not the leaves.
Yes, your childhood: now a fable of fountains.

II
LOS NEGROS

Para Ángel del Río

II
THE BLACKS

For Ángel del Río

Lorca, *Vase on a Tile Roof*, 1929

Norma y paraíso de los negros

Odian la sombra del pájaro
sobre el pleamar de la blanca mejilla
y el conflicto de luz y viento
en el salón de la nieve fría.

Odian la flecha sin cuerpo,
el pañuelo exacto de la despedida,
la aguja que mantiene presión y rosa
en el gramíneo rubor de la sonrisa.

Aman el azul desierto,
las vacilantes expresiones bovinas,
la mentirosa luna de los polos,
la danza curva del agua en la orilla.

Con la ciencia del tronco y el rastro
llenan de nervios luminosos la arcilla
y patinan lúbricos por aguas y arenas
gustando la amarga frescura de su milenaria saliva.

Es por el azul crujiente,
azul sin un gusano ni una huella dormida,
donde los huevos de avestruz quedan eternos
y deambulan intactas las lluvias bailarinas.

Es por el azul sin historia,
azul de una noche sin temor de día,
azul donde el desnudo del viento va quebrando
los camellos sonámbulos de las nubes vacías.

Standards and Paradise of the Blacks

They hate the bird's shadow
on the white cheek's high tide
and the conflict of light and wind
in the great cold hall of snow.

They hate the unbodied arrow,
the punctual handkerchief of farewell,
the needle that sustains a rosy tension
in the grassy blush of their smiles.

They love the deserted blue,
the swaying bovine faces,
the deceitful moon of both poles,
and water's bent dance on the shoreline.

They use the science of tree trunk and tracking
to cover the clay with luminous nerves,
and as they glide with easy desire over water and sand,
they taste the bitter freshness of their millenary spit.

It's in the crackling blue,
blue without a single worm or sleeping footprint,
where the ostrich eggs stay forever
and the untouched rains dance and stroll.

It's in the blue that has no history,
blue of a night without fear of day,
blue where the nude of the wind breaks up
camels of empty clouds moving in their sleep.

Es allí donde sueñan los torsos bajo la gula de la hierba.
Allí los corales empapan la desesperación de la tinta,
los durmientes borran sus perfiles bajo la madeja de los caracoles
y queda el hueco de la danza sobre las últimas cenizas.

It's there the torsos dream beneath the hungry grass,
there the coral absorbs the ink's desperation,
the sleepers erase their profiles under the skein of snails,
and the emptied space of the dance stays above the last of the ashes.

El rey de Harlem

Con una cuchara
le arrancaba los ojos a los cocodrilos
y golpeaba el trasero de los monos.
Con una cuchara.

Fuego de siempre dormía en los pedernales
y los escarabajos borrachos de anís
olvidaban el musgo de las aldeas.

Aquel viejo cubierto de setas
iba al sitio donde lloraban los negros
mientras crujía la cuchara del rey
y llegaban los tanques de agua podrida.

Las rosas huían por los filos
de las últimas curvas del aire
y en los montones de azafrán
los niños machacaban pequeñas ardillas
con un rubor de frenesí manchado.

Es preciso cruzar los puentes
y llegar al rumor negro
para que el perfume de pulmón
nos golpee las sienes con su vestido
de caliente piña.

Es preciso matar al rubio vendedor de aguardiente,
a todos los amigos de la manzana y de la arena;
y es necesario dar con los puños cerrados
a las pequeñas judías que tiemblan llenas de burbujas,
para que el rey de Harlem cante con su muchedumbre,

The King of Harlem

With a spoon
he plucked out the crocodiles' eyes,
and swatted the monkeys on their asses.
With a spoon.

Age-old fire slept in the flints
and the beetles drunk on anisette
forgot about the moss of the villages.

The old man covered with mushrooms
was on his way to the place where the blacks wept
while the king's spoon cracked
and the vats of putrid water arrived.

The roses fled along the blades
of the air's last curves,
and on the piles of saffron
the children flattened tiny squirrels
with the flush of stained frenzy.

It's necessary to cross the bridges
and reach the black murmur
so the perfume of lungs
can buffet our temples with its covering
of hot pineapple.

It's necessary to kill the blond vendor of firewater
and every friend of apple and sand,
and it's necessary to use the fists
against the little Jewish women who tremble, filled with bubbles,
so the king of Harlem sings with his multitude,

para que los cocodrilos duerman en largas filas
bajo el amianto de la luna,
y para que nadie dude la infinita belleza
de los plumeros, los ralladores, los cobres y las cacerolas de las cocinas.

¡Ay, Harlem! ¡Ay, Harlem! ¡Ay, Harlem!
No hay angustia comparable a tus rojos oprimidos,
a tu sangre estremecida dentro del eclipse oscuro,
a tu violencia granate, sordomuda en la penumbra,
a tu gran rey prisionero, con un traje de conserje.

• • •

Tenía la noche una hendidura y quietas salamandras de marfil.
Las muchachas americanas
llevaban niños y monedas en el vientre
y los muchachos se desmayaban en la cruz del desperezo.

Ellos son.
Ellos son los que beben el whisky de plata junto a los volcanes
y tragan pedacitos de corazón por las heladas montañas del oso.

• • •

Aquella noche el rey de Harlem, con una durísima cuchara,
le arrancaba los ojos a los cocodrilos
y golpeaba el trasero de los monos.
Con una durísima cuchara.

Los negros lloraban confundidos
entre paraguas y soles de oro,
los mulatos estiraban gomas, ansiosos de llegar al torso blanco,
y el viento empañaba espejos
y quebraba las venas de los bailarines.

so crocodiles sleep in long rows
beneath the moon's asbestos,
and so no one doubts the infinite beauty
of feather dusters, graters, copper pans, and kitchen casseroles.

Ay, Harlem! *Ay*, Harlem! *Ay*, Harlem!
There is no anguish like that of your oppressed reds,
or your blood shuddering with rage inside the dark eclipse,
or your garnet violence, deaf and dumb in the penumbra,
or your grand king, a prisoner in the uniform of a doorman.

• • •

The night was cracked, and there were motionless ivory salamanders.
American girls
were carrying babies and coins in their wombs,
and the boys stretched their arms and fainted on the cross.

They are the ones.
The ones who drink silver whisky near the volcanoes
and swallow pieces of heart by the bear's frozen mountains.

• • •

That night the king of Harlem, with an unbreakable spoon,
plucked out the crocodiles' eyes
and swatted the monkeys on their asses.
With a spoon.

The blacks cried in confusion
among umbrellas and gold suns,
the mulattoes stretched rubber, longing to reach the white torso,
and the wind clouded mirrors
and shattered the veins of the dancers.

Negros. Negros. Negros. Negros.
La sangre no tiene puertas en vuestra noche boca arriba.
No hay rubor. Sangre furiosa por debajo de las pieles.
Viva en la espina del puñal y en el pecho de los paisajes,
bajo las pinzas y las retamas de la celeste luna de Cáncer.

Sangre que busca por mil caminos muertes enharinadas y ceniza de
       nardo,
cielos yertos en declive donde las colonias de planetas
rueden por las playas con los objetos abandonados.

Sangre que mira lenta con el rabo del ojo,
hecha de espartos exprimidos, néctares de subterráneos.
Sangre que oxida al alisio descuidado en una huella
y disuelve a las mariposas en los cristales de la ventana.

Es la sangre que viene, que vendrá
por los tejados y azoteas, por todas partes,
para quemar la clorofila de las mujeres rubias,
para gemir al pie de las camas, ante el insomnio de los lavabos,
y estrellarse en una aurora de tabaco y bajo amarillo.

¡Hay que huir!,
huir por las esquinas y encerrarse en los últimos pisos,
porque el tuétano del bosque penetrará por las rendijas
para dejar en vuestra carne una leve huella de eclipse
y una falsa tristeza de guante desteñido y rosa química.

· · ·

Es por el silencio sapientísimo
cuando los camareros y los cocineros y los que limpian con la lengua
las heridas de los millonarios
buscan al rey por las calles o en los ángulos del salitre.

Blacks. Blacks. Blacks. Blacks.
The blood has no doors in your recumbent night.
No blush in your face. Blood rages beneath skin.
Alive in the dagger's spine and the landscapes' breast,
under the pincers and Scotch broom of Cancer's celestial moon.

Blood that searches a thousand roads for deaths dusted with flour and
        ashes of spikenards,
lifeless, descending skies where colonies of planets
can wheel with the litter on the beaches.

Blood that looks slowly from the corner of an eye,
blood wrung from hemp and subway nectars.
Blood that rusts the careless trade wind in a footprint
and dissolves butterflies in windowpanes.

This is the blood that flows and will flow
on rooftops everywhere,
and burn the blond women's chlorophyll,
and groan at the foot of the beds near the washstands' insomnia,
and burst into an aurora of tobacco and low yellow.

There must be some way out of here,
some street to flee down, some locked room on the top floor to hide in,
because the forest's marrow will slip through the cracks
to leave on your skin a faint trace of an eclipse
and a false sorrow of faded glove and chemical rose.

•   •   •

Through the all-knowing silence,
waiters, cooks, and those whose tongues lick clean
the wounds of millionaires
seek the king in the streets or on the sharp angles of saltpeter.

Un viento sur de madera, oblicuo en el negro fango,
escupe a las barcas rotas y se clava puntillas en los hombros.
Un viento sur que lleva
colmillos, girasoles, alfabetos
y una pila de Volta con avispas ahogadas.

El olvido estaba expresado por tres gotas de tinta sobre el monóculo.
El amor, por un solo rostro invisible a flor de piedra.
Médulas y corolas componían sobre las nubes
un desierto de tallos, sin una sola rosa.

A la izquierda, a la derecha, por el Sur y por el Norte,
se levanta el muro impasible
para el topo y la aguja del agua.
No busquéis, negros, su grieta
para hallar la máscara infinita.

Buscar el gran sol del centro
hechos una piña zumbadora.
El sol que se desliza por los bosques
seguro de no encontrar una ninfa.
El sol que destruye números y no ha cruzado nunca un sueño,
el tatuado sol que baja por el río
y muge seguido de caimanes.

Negros. Negros. Negros. Negros.

Jamás sierpe, ni cebra, ni mula
palidecieron al morir.
El leñador no sabe cuándo expiran
los clamorosos árboles que corta.
Aguardad bajo la sombra vegetal de vuestro rey
a que cicutas y cardos y ortigas turben postreras azoteas.

A wooden wind from the south, slanting through the black mire,
spits on the broken boats and drives tacks into its shoulders.
A south wind that carries
tusks, sunflowers, alphabets,
and a battery with drowned wasps.

Oblivion was expressed by three drops of ink on the monocle.
Love, by a single, invisible, stone-deep face.
And above the clouds, marrow and corollas
composed a desert of stems without a single rose.

To the left and right, south and north,
the wall rises, impassable
for the mole and the needle of water.
Blacks, don't look for some kind of crack
to find the infinite mask.

Look for the great central sun.
Turn into a swarm of buzzing pineapple.
The sun that slides through the forests,
sure that a nymph will not be there.
The sun that destroys numbers, and has never crossed a dream,
the tattooed sun that descends the river
and bellows just ahead of the crocodiles.

Blacks. Blacks. Blacks. Blacks.

No serpent, no zebra or mule
ever turned pale when they died.
The woodcutter doesn't know when the clamorous trees
that he cuts down expire.
Wait in your king's plant shade
until hemlock, thistles, and nettles disturb the last rooftops.

Entonces, negros, entonces, entonces,
podréis besar con frenesí las ruedas de las bicicletas,
poner parejas de microscopios en las cuevas de las ardillas
y danzar al fin sin duda, mientras las flores erizadas
asesinan a nuestro Moisés casi en los juncos del cielo.

¡Ay, Harlem disfrazada!
¡Ay, Harlem, amenazada por un gentío de trajes sin cabeza!
Me llega tu rumor,
me llega tu rumor atravesando troncos y ascensores,
a través de láminas grises,
donde flotan tus automóviles cubiertos de dientes,
a través de los caballos muertos y los crímenes diminutos,
a través de tu gran rey desesperado,
cuyas barbas llegan al mar.

Then, blacks, and only then
will you be able to frantically kiss bicycle wheels,
place pairs of microscopes in squirrel lairs,
and dance fearlessly at last while the bristling flowers
cut down our Moses in the bulrushes that border heaven.

Ay, Harlem in disguise!
Ay, Harlem, threatened by a throng of headless suits!
I hear your murmur,
I hear it moving through tree trunks and elevator shafts,
through gray sheets
where your cars float covered with teeth,
through dead horses and petty crimes,
through your grand, despairing king
whose beard reaches the sea.

Iglesia abandonada
(Balada de la Gran Guerra)

Yo tenía un hijo que se llamaba Juan.
Yo tenía un hijo.
Se perdió por los arcos un viernes de todos los muertos.
Lo vi jugar en las últimas escaleras de la misa
y echaba un cubito de hojalata en el corazón del sacerdote.
He golpeado los ataúdes. ¡Mi hijo! ¡Mi hijo! ¡Mi hijo!
Saqué una pata de gallina por detrás de la luna, y luego
comprendí que mi niña era un pez
por donde se alejan las carretas.
Yo tenía una niña.
Yo tenía un pez muerto bajo la ceniza de los incensarios.
Yo tenía un mar. ¿De qué? Dios mío. ¡Un mar!
Subí a tocar las campanas, pero las frutas tenían gusanos
y las cerillas apagadas
se comían los trigos de la primavera.
Yo vi la transparente cigüeña de alcohol
mondar las negras cabezas de los soldados agonizantes
y vi las cabañas de goma
donde giraban las copas llenas de lágrimas.
En las anémonas del ofertorio te encontraré, ¡corazón mío!,
cuando el sacerdote levante la mula y el buey con sus fuertes brazos,
para espantar los sapos nocturnos que rondan los helados paisajes del cáliz.
Yo tenía un hijo que era un gigante,
pero los muertos son más fuertes y saben devorar pedazos de cielo.
Si mi niño hubiera sido un oso,
yo no temería el sigilo de los caimanes,
ni hubiese visto al mar amarrado a los árboles
para ser fornicado y herido por el tropel de los regimientos.
¡Si mi niño hubiera sido un oso!

Abandoned Church
(Ballad of the Great War)

Once I had a son named John.
Once I had a son.
He was lost in the arches, one Friday, Day of the Dead.
I saw him playing on the last raised steps of the Mass
and he lowered a little tin bucket into the priest's heart.
I pounded on the coffins. My son! My son! My son!
I pulled a chicken leg from behind the moon and suddenly
realized that my girl had become a fish
where carts recede in the distance.
Once I had a little girl.
Once I had a dead fish beneath the ashes of the censers.
Once I had a sea. Of what? My God. A sea!
I climbed up to ring the bells, but the fruit was wormy
and the snuffed-out matches
had eaten the spring wheat.
I saw the transparent stork of alcohol
picking clean the black heads of dying soldiers
and I saw the little rubber houses
where spinning goblets brimmed with tears.
I'll find you, my dear son, in anemones of the offertory
when the priest lifts the mule and the ox with his powerful arms,
to frighten nocturnal toads that roam the chalice's frozen landscape.
Once I had a son who was a giant,
but the dead are more powerful and can devour pieces of the sky.
If my boy had been a bear,
I wouldn't fear the crocodiles lying in ambush,
or have seen the sea lashed to the trees
for the brutal pleasure of the regiments.
If only my boy had been a bear!

Me envolveré sobre esta lona dura para no sentir el frío de los musgos.
Sé muy bien que me darán una manga o la corbata;
pero en el centro de la misa yo romperé el timón y entonces
vendrá a la piedra la locura de pingüinos y gaviotas
que harán decir a los que duermen y a los que cantan por las esquinas:
Él tenía un hijo.
Un hijo. Un hijo. Un hijo
que no era más que suyo, porque era su hijo.
Su hijo. Su hijo. Su hijo.

I'll lie down and wrap myself in this rough canvas so I won't feel the cold
        moss.
I know very well that I'll be given shirt sleeves or a tie;
but in the middle of Mass I'll break the rudder and then
the insanity of penguins and gulls will come to the stone
and make those who sleep and sing on street corners say:
Once he had a son.
A son. A son. A son
who was his alone, because he was his son.
His son. His son. His son.

III
CALLES Y SUEÑOS

A Rafael R. Rapún

> *Un pájaro de papel en el pecho*
> *dice que el tiempo de los besos no ha llegado.*
> —VICENTE ALEIXANDRE

III
STREETS AND DREAMS

To Rafael R. Rapún

A paper bird inside the breast
says the time for kisses is still not here.
—VICENTE ALEIXANDRE

Lorca, *Young Man and Pyramids*, 1929,
included in the first edition of *Poeta en
Nueva York*, Mexico, 1940

Danza de la muerte

El mascarón. Mirad el mascarón
cómo viene del África a New York.

Se fueron los árboles de la pimienta,
los pequeños botones de fósforo.
Se fueron los camellos de carne desgarrada
y los valles de luz que el cisne levantaba con el pico.

Era el momento de las cosas secas:
de la espiga en el ojo y el gato laminado;
del óxido de hierro de los grandes puentes
y el definitivo silencio del corcho.

Era la gran reunión de los animales muertos
traspasados por las espadas de la luz.
La alegría eterna del hipopótamo con las pezuñas de ceniza
y de la gacela con una siempreviva en la garganta.

En la marchita soledad sin onda
el abollado mascarón danzaba.
Medio lado del mundo era de arena,
mercurio y sol dormido el otro medio.

El mascarón. ¡Mirad el mascarón!
Arena, caimán y miedo sobre Nueva York.

Desfiladeros de cal aprisionaban un cielo vacío
donde sonaban las voces de los que mueren bajo el guano.
Un cielo mondado y puro, idéntico a sí mismo,
con el bozo y lirio agudo de sus montañas invisibles.

Dance of Death

The mask. Look how the mask
comes from Africa to New York.

They are gone, the pepper trees,
the tiny buds of phosphorus.
They are gone, the camels with torn flesh,
and the valleys of light the swan lifted in its beak.

It was the time of parched things,
the wheat spear in the eye, the laminated cat,
the time of great rusting bridges
and the deathly silence of cork.

It was the great gathering of dead animals
pierced by the swords of light.
The endless joy of the hippopotamus with cloven feet of ash
and of the gazelle with an immortelle in its throat.

In the withered, waveless solitude,
the dented mask was dancing.
Half of the world was sand,
the other half mercury and dormant sunlight.

The mask. Look at the mask!
Sand, crocodile, and fear above New York.

Canyons of lime imprisoned an empty sky,
where the voices of those who die under the guano were heard.
A pure, naked sky, identical with itself,
with the down and the keen-edged iris of its invisible mountains.

Acabó con los más leves tallitos del canto
y se fue al diluvio empaquetado de la savia,
a través del descanso de los últimos desfiles
levantando con el rabo pedazos de espejo.

Cuando el chino lloraba en el tejado
sin encontrar el desnudo de su mujer,
y el director del banco observaba el manómetro
que mide el cruel silencio de la moneda,
el mascarón llegaba a Wall Street.

No es extraño para la danza
este columbario que pone los ojos amarillos.
De la esfinge a la caja de caudales hay un hilo tenso
que atraviesa el corazón de todos los niños pobres.
El ímpetu primitivo baila con el ímpetu mecánico,
ignorantes en su frenesí de la luz original.
Porque si la rueda olvida su fórmula,
ya puede cantar desnuda con las manadas de caballos;
y si una llama quema los helados proyectos
el cielo tendrá que huir ante el tumulto de las ventanas.

No es extraño este sitio para la danza. Yo lo digo.
El mascarón bailará entre columnas de sangre y de números,
entre huracanes de oro y gemidos de obreros parados
que aullarán, noche oscura, por tu tiempo sin luces.
¡Oh salvaje Norteamérica!, ¡oh impúdica!, ¡oh salvaje!
Tendida en la frontera de la nieve.

El mascarón. ¡Mirad el mascarón!
¡Qué ola de fango y luciérnagas sobre Nueva York!

•   •   •

It finished off the slenderest stems of song
and was swept away toward channels of sap,
through the stillness of the last parades,
lifting pieces of mirror with its tail.

While the Chinaman wept on the roof,
not finding the nude of his wife,
and the bank director was watching the gauge
that measures the cruel silence of money,
the mask arrived on Wall Street.

It isn't a strange place for the dance,
these cemetery niches that turn the eyes yellow.
Between the sphinx and the bank vault, there is a taut thread
that pierces the heart of all poor children.
The primitive impetus dances with the mechanical one,
unaware, in their frenzy, of the original light.
Because if the wheel forgets its formula,
it will sing nude with herds of horses;
and if a flame burns the frozen blueprints,
the sky will have to flee before the tumult of windows.

This isn't a strange place for the dance, I tell you.
The mask will dance among columns of blood and numbers,
among hurricanes of gold and groans of the unemployed,
who will howl, in the dead of night, for your dark time.
Oh, savage, shameless North America!
Stretched out on the frontier of snow.

The mask. Look at the mask!
Such a wave of mire and fireflies above New York!

•   •   •

Yo estaba en la terraza luchando con la luna.
Enjambres de ventanas acribillaban un muslo de la noche.
En mis ojos bebían las dulces vacas de los cielos
y las brisas de largos remos
golpeaban los cenicientos cristales del Broadway.

La gota de sangre buscaba la luz de la yema del astro
para fingir una muerta semilla de manzana.
El aire de la llanura, empujado por los pastores,
temblaba con un miedo de molusco sin concha.

Pero no son los muertos los que bailan.
Estoy seguro.
Los muertos están embebidos devorando sus propias manos.
Son los otros los que bailan con el mascarón y su vihuela.
Son los otros, los borrachos de plata, los hombres fríos,
los que duermen en el cruce de los muslos y llamas duras,
los que buscan la lombriz en el paisaje de las escaleras,
los que beben en el banco lágrimas de niña muerta
o los que comen por las esquinas diminutas pirámides del alba.

¡Que no baile el Papa!
¡No,
que no baile el Papa!
Ni el Rey,
ni el millonario de dientes azules,
ni las bailarinas secas de las catedrales,
ni constructores, ni esmeraldas, ni locos, ni sodomitas.
Sólo este mascarón.
Este mascarón de vieja escarlatina.
¡Sólo este mascarón!

Que ya las cobras silbarán por los últimos pisos.
Que ya las ortigas estremecerán patios y terrazas.

I was on the terrace, wrestling with the moon.
Swarms of windows riddled one of the night's thighs.
The sweet sky-cattle drank from my eyes
and breezes on long oars
struck the ashen store windows on Broadway.

The drop of blood looked for light in the star's yolk
so as to seem a dead apple seed.
The prairie air, driven by the shepherds,
trembled in fear like a mollusk without its shell.

But I'm sure there are no dancers
among the dead.
The dead are absorbed in devouring their own hands.
It's the others who dance with the mask and its *vihuela*.
Others, drunk on silver, cold men,
who sleep where thighs and hard flames intersect,
who seek the earthworm in the landscape of fire escapes,
who drink a dead girl's tears at the bank
or eat tiny pyramids of dawn on the street corners.

But don't let the Pope dance!
No,
don't let the Pope dance!
Nor the King,
nor the millionaires with blue teeth,
nor the barren dancers of the cathedrals,
nor builders, nor emeralds, nor madmen, nor sodomites.
Only this mask.
This mask of ancient scarlet fever.
Only this mask!

Cobras shall hiss on the top floors.
Nettles shall shake courtyards and terraces.

Que ya la Bolsa será una pirámide de musgo.
Que ya vendrán lianas después de los fusiles
y muy pronto, muy pronto, muy pronto.
¡Ay, Wall Street!

El mascarón. ¡Mirad el mascarón!
¡Cómo escupe veneno de bosque
por la angustia imperfecta de Nueva York!

Diciembre 1929

The Stock Exchange shall become a pyramid of moss.
Jungle vines shall come in behind the rifles
and all so quickly, so very, very quickly.
Ay, Wall Street!

The mask. Look at the mask!
And how it spits its forest poison
through New York's imperfect anguish!

December 1929

Paisaje de la multitud que vomita
(Anochecer de Coney Island)

La mujer gorda venía delante
arrancando las raíces y mojando el pergamino de los tambores.
La mujer gorda,
que vuelve del revés los pulpos agonizantes.
La mujer gorda, enemiga de la luna,
corría por las calles y los pisos deshabitados
y dejaba por los rincones pequeñas calaveras de paloma
y levantaba las furias de los banquetes de los siglos últimos
y llamaba al demonio del pan por las colinas del cielo barrido
y filtraba un ansia de luz en las circulaciones subterráneas.
Son los cementerios. Lo sé. Son los cementerios
y el dolor de las cocinas enterradas bajo la arena.
Son los muertos, los faisanes y las manzanas de otra hora
los que nos empujan en la garganta.

Llegaban los rumores de la selva del vómito
con las mujeres vacías, con niños de cera caliente,
con árboles fermentados y camareros incansables
que sirven platos de sal bajo las arpas de la saliva.
Sin remedio, hijo mío. ¡Vomita! No hay remedio.
No es el vómito de los húsares sobre los pechos de la prostituta,
ni el vómito del gato que se tragó una rana por descuido.
Son los muertos que arañan con sus manos de tierra
las puertas de pedernal donde se pudren nublos y postres.
La mujer gorda venía delante
con las gentes de los barcos, de las tabernas y de los jardines.
El vómito agitaba delicadamente sus tambores
entre algunas niñas de sangre
que pedían protección a la luna.

Landscape of a Vomiting Multitude
(Dusk at Coney Island)

The fat lady came first,
tearing out roots and moistening drumskins.
The fat lady
who turns dying octopuses inside out.
The fat lady, the moon's antagonist,
was running through the streets and deserted buildings
and leaving tiny skulls of pigeons in the corners
and stirring up the furies of the last centuries' feasts
and summoning the demon of bread through the sky's clean-swept hills
and filtering a longing for light into subterranean tunnels.
The graveyards, yes, the graveyards
and the sorrow of the kitchens buried in sand,
the dead, pheasants and apples of another era,
pushing into our throat.

There were murmurings from the jungle of vomit
with the empty women, with hot wax children,
with fermented trees and tireless waiters
who serve platters of salt beneath harps of saliva.
There's no other way, my son, vomit! There's no other way.
It's not the vomit of hussars on the breasts of their whores,
nor the vomit of a cat choking down a frog,
but the dead who scratch with clay hands
on flint gates where clouds and desserts decay.
The fat lady came first
with the crowds from the ships, taverns, and parks.
Vomit was delicately shaking its drums
among a few little girls of blood
who were begging the moon for protection.

¡Ay de mí! ¡Ay de mí! ¡Ay de mí!
Esta mirada mía fue mía, pero ya no es mía.
Esta mirada que tiembla desnuda por el alcohol
y despide barcos increíbles
por las anémonas de los muelles.
Me defiendo con esta mirada
que mana de las ondas por donde el alba no se atreve.
Yo, poeta sin brazos, perdido
entre la multitud que vomita,
sin caballo efusivo que corte
los espesos musgos de mis sienes.
Pero la mujer gorda seguía delante
y la gente buscaba las farmacias
donde el amargo trópico se fija.
Sólo cuando izaron la bandera y llegaron los primeros canes
la ciudad entera se agolpó en las barandillas del embarcadero.

Nueva York, 29 de diciembre de 1929

Who could imagine my sadness?
The look on my face was mine, but now isn't me.
The naked look on my face, trembling in alcohol
and launching incredible ships
through the anemones of the piers.
I protect myself with this look
that flows from waves where the dawn would never go,
I, poet without arms, lost
in the vomiting multitude,
with no effusive horse to shear
the thick moss from my temples.
But the fat lady went first
and the crowds kept looking for the pharmacies
where the bitter tropics could be found.
Only when a flag went up and the first dogs arrived
did the entire city rush to the railings of the boardwalk.

New York, December 29, 1929

Paisaje de la multitud que orina
(Nocturno de Battery Place)

Se quedaron solos.
Aguardaban la velocidad de las últimas bicicletas.
Se quedaron solas.
Esperaban la muerte de un niño en el velero japonés.
Se quedaron solos y solas.
Soñando con los picos abiertos de los pájaros agonizantes,
con el agudo quitasol que pincha
al sapo recién aplastado,
bajo un silencio con mil orejas
y diminutas bocas de agua
en los desfiladeros que resisten
el ataque violento de la luna.
Lloraba el niño del velero y se quebraban los corazones
angustiados por el testigo y la vigilia de todas las cosas
y porque todavía en el suelo celeste de negras huellas
gritaban nombres oscuros, salivas y radios de níquel.
No importa que el niño calle cuando le claven el último alfiler.
Ni importa la derrota de la brisa en la corola del algodón.
Porque hay un mundo de la muerte con marineros definitivos
que se asomarán a los arcos y os helarán por detrás de los árboles.
Es inútil buscar el recodo
donde la noche olvida su viaje
y acechar un silencio que no tenga
trajes rotos y cáscaras y llanto,
porque tan sólo el diminuto banquete de la araña
basta para romper el equilibrio de todo el cielo.
No hay remedio para el gemido del velero japonés,
ni para estas gentes ocultas que tropiezan con las esquinas.
El campo se muerde la cola para unir las raíces en un punto

Landscape of a Pissing Multitude
(Battery Place Nocturne)

The men kept to themselves.
They were waiting for the swiftness of the last cyclists.
The women kept to themselves.
They were expecting the death of a boy on a Japanese schooner.
They all kept to themselves—
dreaming of the open beaks of dying birds,
the sharp parasol that punctures
a recently flattened toad,
beneath silence with a thousand ears
and tiny mouths of water
in the canyons that resist
the violent attack of the moon.
The boy on the schooner was crying and hearts were breaking
in anguish over everything's witness and vigil,
and because on the sky-blue ground of black footprints,
obscure names, saliva, and chrome radios were crying.
It doesn't matter if the boy grows silent when stuck with the last pin,
or if the breeze is defeated in cupped cotton flowers,
because there is a world of death whose perpetual sailors
will appear in the arches and freeze you from behind the trees.
It's useless to look for the bend
where night loses its way
and to wait in ambush for a silence that has no
torn clothes, no shells, and no tears,
because even the tiny banquet of a spider
is enough to throw off the whole equilibrium of the sky.
There is no cure for the moaning from a Japanese schooner,
nor for those shadowy people who stumble on street corners.
The countryside bites its own tail in order to join its roots

y el ovillo busca por la grama su ansia de longitud insatisfecha.
¡La luna! Los policías. ¡Las sirenas de los transatlánticos!
Fachadas de orín, de humo, anémonas, guantes de goma.
Todo está roto por la noche,
abierta de piernas sobre las terrazas.
Todo está roto por los tibios caños
de una terrible fuente silenciosa.
¡Oh gentes! Oh mujercillas. ¡Oh soldados!
Será preciso viajar por los ojos de los idiotas,
campos libres donde silban mansas cobras deslumbradas,
paisajes llenos de sepulcros que producen fresquísimas manzanas,
para que venga la luz desmedida
que temen los ricos detrás de sus lupas,
el olor de un solo cuerpo con la doble vertiente de lis y rata
y para que se quemen estas gentes que pueden orinar alrededor de un
        gemido
o en los cristales donde se comprenden las olas nunca repetidas.

and a ball of yarn looks anxiously in the grass for unrealized longitude.
The moon! The police. The foghorns of the ocean liners!
Facades of rust, of smoke, anemones, rubber gloves.
Everything is shattered in the night
that spreads its legs on the terraces.
Everything is shattered in the tepid faucets
of a terrible silent fountain.
Oh, crowds! Loose women! Soldiers!
We will have to journey through the eyes of idiots,
open country where the tame cobras hiss in a daze,
landscapes full of graves that yield the freshest apples,
so that overwhelming light will arrive
to frighten the rich behind their magnifying glasses—
the odor of a single corpse from the double dimension of lily and rat—
and so that fire will consume those crowds still able to piss around a
        moan
or on the crystals in which each inimitable wave is understood.

Asesinato

(Dos voces de madrugada en Riverside Drive)

—*¿Cómo fue?*
—Una grieta en la mejilla.
¡Eso es todo!
Una uña que aprieta el tallo.
Un alfiler que bucea
hasta encontrar las raicillas del grito.
Y el mar deja de moverse.
—*¿Cómo, cómo fue?*
—Así.
—*¡Déjame! ¿De esa manera?*
—Sí.
El corazón salió solo.
—*¡Ay, ay de mí!*

Murder
(Two Early Morning Voices on Riverside Drive)

"How did it happen?"
"A gash on the cheek.
That's all!
A fingernail that pinches the stem.
A pin that dives
until it finds the roots of a scream.
And the sea stops still."
"How, how did it happen?"
"Like this."
"Really! Like that?"
"Yes.
The heart came out on its own."
"I'm done for!"

Navidad en el Hudson

¡Esa esponja gris!
Ese marinero recién degollado.
Ese río grande.
Esa brisa de límites oscuros.
Ese filo, amor, ese filo.
Estaban los cuatro marineros luchando con el mundo.
Con el mundo de aristas que ven todos los ojos.
Con el mundo que no se puede recorrer sin caballos.
Estaban uno, cien, mil marineros
luchando con el mundo de las agudas velocidades,
sin enterarse de que el mundo
estaba solo por el cielo.

El mundo solo por el cielo solo.
Son las colinas de martillos y el triunfo de la hierba espesa.
Son los vivísimos hormigueros y las monedas en el fango.
El mundo solo por el cielo solo
y el aire a la salida de todas las aldeas.

Cantaba la lombriz el terror de la rueda
y el marinero degollado
cantaba al oso de agua que lo había de estrechar;
y todos cantaban aleluya,
aleluya. Cielo desierto.
Es lo mismo, ¡lo mismo!, aleluya.

He pasado toda la noche en los andamios de los arrabales
dejándome la sangre por la escayola de los proyectos,
ayudando a los marineros a recoger las velas desgarradas
y estoy con las manos vacías en el rumor de la desembocadura.
No importa que cada minuto

Christmas on the Hudson

That gray sponge!
That sailor whose throat was just cut.
That great river.
Those dark boundaries of the breeze.
That keen blade, my love, that keen blade.
The four sailors wrestled with the world.
With that sharp-edged world that all eyes see.
With the world no one can know without horses.
One, a hundred, a thousand sailors
wrestling with the world of keen-edged velocities,
unaware that the world
was alone in the sky.

The world alone in the lonely sky.
Hills of hammers and the thick grass's triumph.
Teeming anthills and coins in the mire.
The world alone in the lonely sky,
and the air where all the villages end.

The earthworm sang its terror of the wheel,
and the sailor whose throat was slashed
sang to the water-bear that held him close;
and they were all singing alleluia,
alleluia. Deserted sky.
It's all the same—the same!—alleluia.

I stood all night on scaffolding in the boroughs,
leaving my blood on the plastered walls of the projects,
helping the sailors lower their ripped sails,
and I stand with empty hands in the murmur of the river's mouth.
It doesn't matter if every minute

un niño nuevo agite sus ramitos de venas,
ni que el parto de la víbora, desatado bajo las ramas,
calme la sed de sangre de los que miran el desnudo.
Lo que importa es esto: hueco. Mundo solo. Desembocadura.
Alba no. Fábula inerte.
Sólo esto: desembocadura.
Oh esponja mía gris.
Oh cuello mio recién degollado.
Oh río grande mío.
Oh brisa mía de límites que no son míos.
Oh filo de mi amor, oh hiriente filo.

Nueva York, 27 de diciembre de 1929

a newborn child waves the little branches of its veins,
or if a newborn viper, set free beneath the branches,
calms the blood lust of those who look at the nude.
What matters is this: emptied space. Lonely world. River's mouth.
Not dawn. Idle fable.
This alone: river's mouth.
Oh, my gray sponge!
Oh, my throat just cut open!
Oh, my great river!
Oh, my breeze's boundaries that are not mine!
Oh, the keen blade of my love, oh, the cutting blade!

New York, December 27, 1929

Ciudad sin sueño
(Nocturno del Brooklyn Bridge)

No duerme nadie por el cielo. Nadie, nadie.
No duerme nadie.
Las criaturas de la luna huelen y rondan las cabañas.
Vendrán las iguanas vivas a morder a los hombres que no sueñan
y el que huye con el corazón roto encontrará por las esquinas
al increíble cocodrilo quieto bajo la tierna protesta de los astros.

No duerme nadie por el mundo. Nadie, nadie.
No duerme nadie.
Hay un muerto en el cementerio más lejano
que se queja tres años
porque tiene un paisaje seco en la rodilla;
y el niño que enterraron esta mañana lloraba tanto
que hubo necesidad de llamar a los perros para que callase.

No es sueño la vida. ¡Alerta! ¡Alerta! ¡Alerta!
Nos caemos por las escaleras para comer la tierra húmeda
o subimos al filo de la nieve con el coro de las dalias muertas.
Pero no hay olvido ni sueño:
carne viva. Los besos atan las bocas
en una maraña de venas recientes
y al que le duele su dolor le dolerá sin descanso
y el que teme la muerte la llevará sobre los hombros.

Un día
los caballos vivirán en las tabernas
y las hormigas furiosas
atacarán los cielos amarillos que se refugian en los ojos de las vacas.
Otro día

Sleepless City
(Brooklyn Bridge Nocturne)

Out in the sky, no one sleeps. No one, no one.
No one sleeps.
Lunar creatures sniff and circle the dwellings.
Live iguanas will come to bite the men who don't dream,
and the brokenhearted fugitive will meet on street corners
an incredible crocodile resting beneath the tender protest of the stars.

Out in the world, no one sleeps. No one, no one.
No one sleeps.
There is a corpse in the farthest graveyard
complaining for three years
because of an arid landscape in his knee;
and a boy who was buried this morning cried so much
they had to call the dogs to quiet him.

Life is no dream. Watch out! Watch out! Watch out!
We fall down stairs and eat the humid earth,
or we climb to the snow's edge with the choir of dead dahlias.
But there is no oblivion, no dream:
raw flesh. Kisses tie mouths
in a tangle of new veins
and those in pain will bear it with no respite
and those who are frightened by death will carry it on their shoulders.

One day
horses will live in the taverns
and furious ants
will attack the yellow skies that take refuge in the eyes of cattle.
Another day

veremos la resurrección de las mariposas disecadas
y aun andando por un paisaje de esponjas grises y barcos mudos
veremos brillar nuestro anillo y manar rosas de nuestra lengua.
¡Alerta! ¡Alerta! ¡Alerta!
A los que guardan todavía huellas de zarpa y aguacero,
a aquel muchacho que llora porque no sabe la invención del puente
o a aquel muerto que ya no tiene más que la cabeza y un zapato,
hay que llevarlos al muro donde iguanas y sierpes esperan,
donde espera la dentadura del oso,
donde espera la mano momificada del niño
y la piel del camello se eriza con un violento escalofrió azul.

No duerme nadie por el cielo. Nadie, nadie.
No duerme nadie.
Pero si alguien cierra los ojos,
¡azotadlo, hijos míos, azotadlo!
Haya un panorama de ojos abiertos
y amargas llagas encendidas.
No duerme nadie por el mundo. Nadie, nadie.
Ya lo he dicho.
No duerme nadie.
Pero si alguien tiene por la noche exceso de musgo en las sienes,
abrid los escotillones para que vea bajo la luna
las copas falsas, el veneno y la calavera de los teatros.

we'll witness the resurrection of dried butterflies,
and still walking in a landscape of gray sponges and silent ships,
we'll see our ring shine and roses spill from our tongues.
Watch out! Watch out! Watch out!
Those still marked by claws and cloudburst,
that boy who cries because he doesn't know bridges exist,
or that corpse that has nothing more than its head and one shoe—
they all must be led to the wall where iguanas and serpents wait,
where the bear's teeth wait,
where the mummified hand of a child waits
and the camel's fur bristles with a violent blue shiver.

Out in the sky, no one sleeps. No one, no one.
No one sleeps.
But if someone closes his eyes,
whip him, my children, whip him!
Let there be a panorama of open eyes
and bitter inflamed wounds.
Out in the world, no one sleeps. No one. No one.
I've said it before.
No one sleeps.
But at night, if someone has too much moss on his temples,
open the trap doors so he can see in moonlight
the fake goblets, the venom, and the skull of the theaters.

Panorama ciego de Nueva York

Si no son los pájaros
cubiertos de ceniza,
si no son los gemidos que golpean las ventanas de la boda,
serán las delicadas criaturas del aire
que manan la sangre nueva por la oscuridad inextinguible.
Pero no, no son los pájaros.
Porque los pájaros están a punto de ser bueyes.
Pueden ser rocas blancas con la ayuda de la luna
y son siempre muchachos heridos
antes de que los jueces levanten la tela.

Todos comprenden el dolor que se relaciona con la muerte,
pero el verdadero dolor no está presente en el espíritu.
No está en el aire, ni en nuestra vida,
ni en estas terrazas llenas de humo.
El verdadero dolor que mantiene despiertas las cosas
es una pequeña quemadura infinita
en los ojos inocentes de los otros sistemas.

Un traje abandonado pesa tanto en los hombros
que muchas veces el cielo los agrupa en ásperas manadas;
y las que mueren de parto saben en la última hora
que todo rumor será piedra y toda huella latido.
Nosotros ignoramos que el pensamiento tiene arrabales
donde el filósofo es devorado por los chinos y las orugas
y algunos niños idiotas han encontrado por las cocinas
pequeñas golondrinas con muletas
que sabían pronunciar la palabra amor.

No, no son los pájaros.
No es un pájaro el que expresa la turbia fiebre de laguna,

Blind Panorama of New York

If it isn't the birds
covered with ash,
if it isn't the sobbing that strikes the windows of the wedding,
it is the delicate creatures of the air
that spill fresh blood in the inextinguishable darkness.
But no, it isn't the birds,
because the birds will soon become oxen.
They could become white rocks with the moon's help
and they are always wounded boys
before the judges lift the shroud.

Everyone understands the pain that accompanies death,
but genuine pain doesn't live in the spirit,
nor in the air, nor in our lives,
nor on these terraces of billowing smoke.
The genuine pain that keeps everything awake
is a tiny, infinite burn
on the innocent eyes of other systems.

An abandoned suit weighs so heavily on the shoulders
that the sky often shrugs them into rugged herds.
And those who die in childbirth learn in their last hour
that every murmur will be stone and every footprint will throb.
We forget that the mind has boroughs
where Chinese and caterpillars devour the philosopher.
And some feebleminded children in the kitchens have discovered
tiny swallows on crutches
that could pronounce the word love.

No, it isn't the birds.
A bird can't express the cloudy fever of a lagoon

ni el ansia de asesinato que nos oprime cada momento,
ni el metálico rumor de suicidio que nos anima cada madrugada.
Es una cápsula de aire donde nos duele todo el mundo,
es un pequeño espacio vivo al loco unisón de la luz,
es una escala indefinible donde las nubes y rosas olvidan
el griterío chino que bulle por el desembarcadero de la sangre.
Yo muchas veces me he perdido
para buscar la quemadura que mantiene despiertas las cosas
y sólo he encontrado marineros echados sobre las barandillas
y pequeñas criaturas del cielo enterradas bajo la nieve.
Pero el verdadero dolor estaba en otras plazas
donde los peces cristalizados agonizaban dentro de los troncos;
plazas del cielo extraño para las antiguas estatuas ilesas
y para la tierna intimidad de los volcanes.

No hay dolor en la voz. Sólo existen los dientes,
pero dientes que callarán aislados por el raso negro.
No hay dolor en la voz. Aquí sólo existe la tierra.
La tierra con sus puertas de siempre
que llevan al rubor de los frutos.

or the urge to murder someone that oppresses us every moment,
or the metallic hum of suicide that revives us every morning.
It's a capsule of air where we suffer the whole world,
a tiny space alive in the crazy unison of light,
an indefinable ladder on which clouds and roses forget
the Chinese howl that boils over on the waterfront of the blood.
I've often lost myself
in order to find the burn that keeps everything awake
and all I've found are sailors leaning over the railings
and tiny sky creatures buried under the snow.
There was genuine pain on other plazas
where crystallized fish were dying inside tree trunks;
plazas of blue sky alien to the unscathed statues of antiquity
and to the intimate tenderness of volcanoes.

There is no pain in the voice. Only the teeth exist,
but isolated teeth that will be silenced by black satin.
There is no pain in the voice. Only the earth exists here.
The earth and its timeless doors
which lead to the blush of the fruit.

Nacimiento de Cristo

Un pastor pide teta por la nieve que ondula
blancos perros tendidos entre linternas sordas.
El Cristito de barro se ha partido los dedos
en los filos eternos de la madera rota.

¡Ya vienen las hormigas y los pies ateridos!
Dos hilillos de sangre quiebran el cielo duro.
Los vientres del demonio resuenan por los valles
golpes y resonancias de carne de molusco.

Lobos y sapos cantan en las hogueras verdes
coronadas por vivos hormigueros del alba.
La mula tiene un sueño de grandes abanicos
y el toro sueña un toro de agujeros y de agua.

El niño llora y mira con un tres en la frente.
San José ve en el heno tres espinas de bronce.
Los pañales exhalan un rumor de desierto
con cítaras sin cuerdas y degolladas voces.

La nieve de Manhattan empuja los anuncios
y lleva gracia pura por las falsas ojivas.
Sacerdotes idiotas y querubes de pluma
van detrás de Lutero por las altas esquinas.

The Birth of Christ

A shepherd begs to be suckled in snow that ripples
white dogs stretched out among flashlights.
The little clay Christ has split its fingers
on the eternally keen edges of the splintered wood.

Here come the ants and the feet stiff with cold!
Two small threads of blood break up the hard sky.
The demon's intestines fill the valleys
with the blows and resonances of mollusk flesh.

Wolves and toads sing in green bonfires
crowned by the flaming anthills of dawn.
The mule has a dream of enormous fans
and the bull dreams a pierced bull and water.

The child with a three on its forehead cries and stares.
St. Joseph sees three bronze thorns in the hay.
And the swaddling clothes exhale a desert's rumbling
with stringless zithers and beheaded voices.

The snow of Manhattan blows against billboards
and carries pure grace through the fake Gothic arches.
Idiot clergymen and cherubim in feathers
follow Luther in a line around the high corners.

La aurora

La aurora de Nueva York tiene
cuatro columnas de cieno
y un huracán de negras palomas
que chapotean las aguas podridas.
La aurora de Nueva York gime
por las inmensas escaleras
buscando entre las aristas
nardos de angustia dibujada.
La aurora llega y nadie la recibe en su boca
porque allí no hay mañana ni esperanza posible.
A veces las monedas en enjambres furiosos
taladran y devoran abandonados niños.
Los primeros que salen comprenden con sus huesos
que no habrá paraíso ni amores deshojados:
saben que van al cieno de números y leyes,
a los juegos sin arte, a sudores sin fruto.
La luz es sepultada por cadenas y ruidos
en impúdico reto de ciencia sin raíces.
Por los barrios hay gentes que vacilan insomnes
como recién salidas de un naufragio de sangre.

Dawn

Dawn in New York has
four columns of mire
and a hurricane of black pigeons
splashing in the putrid waters.
Dawn in New York groans
on enormous fire escapes
searching between the angles
for spikenards of drafted anguish.
Dawn arrives and no one receives it in his mouth
because tomorrow and hope are impossible there.
Sometimes the furious swarming coins
penetrate like drills and devour abandoned children.
Those who go out early know in their bones
there will be no paradise or loves that bloom and die:
they know they will be mired in numbers and laws,
in mindless games, in fruitless labors.
The light is buried under chains and noises
in a shameless challenge of rootless science.
And crowds stagger sleeplessly through the boroughs
as if they had just escaped a shipwreck of blood.

IV
POEMAS DEL LAGO EDEN MILLS

A Eduardo Ugarte

IV
POEMS OF LAKE EDEN MILLS

To Eduardo Ugarte

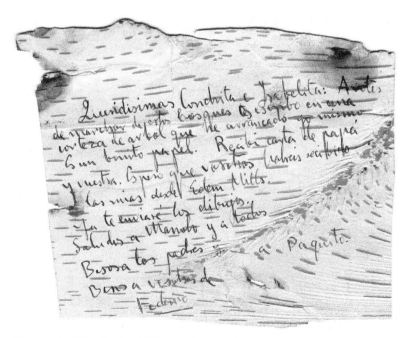

"Autumn in New England," Lorca's letter to his sisters from Eden Mills, Vermont, on a piece of birch bark, August 1929

Poema doble del Lago Eden

Nuestro ganado pace, el viento espira.
—GARCILASO

Era mi voz antigua
ignorante de los densos jugos amargos,
la que vino lamiendo mis pies
bajo los frágiles helechos mojados.

¡Ay, voz antigua de mi amor!
Ay, voz de mi verdad.
Ay, voz de mi abierto costado,
cuando todas las rosas manaban de mi lengua
y el césped no conocía la impasible dentadura del caballo.

Estás aquí bebiendo mi sangre,
bebiendo mi humor de niño pesado,
mientras mis ojos se quiebran en el viento
con el aluminio y las voces de los borrachos.

Dejarme pasar la puerta
donde Eva come hormigas
y Adán fecunda peces deslumbrados.
Dejarme pasar, hombrecillos de los cuernos,
al bosque de los desperezos
y los alegrísimos saltos.

Yo sé el uso más secreto
que tiene un viejo alfiler oxidado
y sé del horror de unos ojos despiertos
sobre la superficie concreta del plato.

Double Poem of Lake Eden

Our cattle graze, the wind sends forth its breath.
—GARCILASO

It was the voice I had before,
ignorant of the dense and bitter sap,
the one that came lapping at my feet
beneath the moist and fragile ferns.

Ay, my love's voice from before
ay, voice of my truth,
ay, voice of my open side,
when all the roses spilled from my tongue
and the grass hadn't felt the horse's impassable teeth!

Here you are drinking my blood,
drinking the humor of the heavy child I was,
while my eyes are shattered by aluminum
and drunken voices in the wind.

Let me pass through the arch
where Eve devours ants
and Adam impregnates the dazzling fish.
Little men with horns, let me return
to the grove of easy living
and the somersaults of pure joy.

I know the most secret way
to use an old rusty pin,
and I know the horror of eyes wide-awake
on the concrete surface of a plate.

Pero no quiero mundo ni sueño, voz divina,
quiero mi libertad, mi amor humano
en el rincón más oscuro de la brisa que nadie quiera.
¡Mi amor humano!

Esos perros marinos se persiguen
y el viento acecha troncos descuidados.
¡Oh voz antigua, quema con tu lengua
esta voz de hojalata y de talco!

Quiero llorar porque me da la gana,
como lloran los niños del último banco,
porque yo no soy un hombre, ni un poeta, ni una hoja,
pero sí un pulso herido que sonda las cosas del otro lado.

Quiero llorar diciendo mi nombre,
rosa, niño y abeto a la orilla de este lago,
para decir mi verdad de hombre de sangre
matando en mí la burla y la sugestión del vocablo.

No, no. Yo no pregunto, yo deseo,
voz mía libertada que me lames las manos.
En el laberinto de biombos es mi desnudo el que recibe
la luna de castigo y el reloj encenizado.

Así hablaba yo.
Así hablaba yo cuando Saturno detuvo los trenes
y la bruma y el Sueño y la Muerte me estaban buscando.
Me estaban buscando
allí donde mugen las vacas que tienen patitas de paje
y allí donde flota mi cuerpo entre los equilibrios contrarios.

But I want neither world nor dream, divine voice,
I want my liberty, my human love
in the darkest corner of the breeze no one wants.
My human love!

Those sea-dogs chase each other
and the wind lies in ambush for careless tree trunks.
Oh, voice of before, let your tongue burn
this voice of tin and talc!

I want to cry because I feel like it—
the way children cry in the last row of seats—
because I'm not a man, not a poet, not a leaf,
only a wounded pulse that probes the things of the other side.

I want to cry saying my name,
rose, child, and fir on the shore of this lake,
to speak truly as a man of blood
killing in myself the mockery and suggestive power of the word.

No, no, I'm not asking, I desire,
my liberated voice lapping at my hands.
In the labyrinth of folding screens my nakedness receives
the punishing moon and the clock covered with ash.

I was speaking that way.
I was speaking that way when Saturn stopped the trains
and the fog and the Dream and Death were looking for me.
Looking for me
where cattle with the little feet of a page bellow
and my body floats between contrary equilibriums.

Cielo vivo

Yo no podré quejarme
si no encontré lo que buscaba.
Cerca de las piedras sin jugo y los insectos vacíos
no veré el duelo del sol con las criaturas en carne viva.

Pero me iré al primer paisaje
de choques, líquidos y rumores
que trasmina a niño recién nacido
y donde toda superficie es evitada,
para entender que lo que busco tendrá su blanco de alegría
cuando yo vuele mezclado con el amor y las arenas.

Allí no llega la escarcha de los ojos apagados
ni el mugido del árbol asesinado por la oruga.
Allí todas las formas guardan entrelazadas
una sola expresión frenética de avance.

No puedes avanzar por los enjambres de corolas
porque el aire disuelve tus dientes de azúcar,
ni puedes acariciar la fugaz hoja del helecho
sin sentir el asombro definitivo del marfil.

Allí bajo las raíces y en la médula del aire,
se comprende la verdad de las cosas equivocadas.
El nadador de níquel que acecha la onda más fina
y el rebaño de vacas nocturnas con rojas patitas de mujer.

Yo no podré quejarme
si no encontré lo que buscaba,
pero me iré al primer paisaje de humedades y latidos
para entender que lo que busco tendrá su blanco de alegría
cuando yo vuele mezclado con el amor y las arenas.

Living Sky

I won't be able to complain
though I never found what I was looking for.
Near the dried-up stones and the husks of insects,
I won't see the sun's duel with the creatures of flesh and blood.

But I'll go to the first landscape
of shocks, fluids, and murmurs
that seeps into a newborn child,
and where all surfaces are avoided,
so I'll know that my search has a joyful target
when I'm flying, jumbled with love and sands.

There, the frost of snuffed-out eyes won't reach,
nor the bellowing of a tree, murdered by the caterpillar.
There, all the shapes intertwine and have
the same frenetic, forward expression.

You can't pass through the swarming corollas—
the air dissolves your teeth of sugar.
And you can't caress the elusive fern
without feeling the utter astonishment of ivory.

There, under roots and in the marrow of the air,
you can grasp the truth of mistaken things.
The finest wave about to pounce on the chrome swimmer
and the flock of nocturnal cattle with a woman's little red feet . . .

I won't be able to complain
though I never found what I was looking for;
but I'll go to the first humid landscape of heartbeats
so I'll know that my search has a joyful target
when I'm flying, jumbled with love and sands.

Vuelo fresco de siempre sobre lechos vacíos.
Sobre grupos de brisas y barcos encallados.
Tropiezo vacilante por la dura eternidad fija
y amor al fin sin alba. Amor. ¡Amor visible!

Eden Mills, Vermont, 24 de agosto de 1929

I'm used to the cool air when I fly over empty beds.
Over squalls and ships run aground.
I stumble sleepily through eternity's fixed hardness
and love at last without dawn. Love. Visible love!

Eden Mills, Vermont, August 24, 1929

V
EN LA CABAÑA DEL FARMER
(Campo de Newburgh)

A Concha Méndez y Manuel Altolaguirre

V
IN THE FARMER'S CABIN
(In the Newburgh Countryside)

To Concha Méndez and Manuel Altolaguirre

Lorca, *Sexual Forest*, 1933, included in
the first edition of *Poeta en Nueva York*,
Mexico, 1940

El niño Stanton

—*Do you like me?*
—*Yes, and you?*
—*Yes, yes.*

Cuando me quedo solo
me quedan todavía tus diez años,
los tres caballos ciegos,
tus quince rostros con el rostro de la pedrada
y las fiebres pequeñas heladas sobre las hojas del maíz.
Stanton. Hijo mío. Stanton.
A las doce de la noche el cáncer salía por los pasillos
y hablaba con los caracoles vacíos de los documentos.
El vivísimo cáncer lleno de nubes y termómetros
con su casto afán de manzana para que lo piquen los ruiseñores.
En la casa donde hay un cáncer
se quiebran las blancas paredes en el delirio de la astronomía
y por los establos más pequeños y en las cruces de los bosques
brilla por muchos años el fulgor de la quemadura.
Mi dolor sangraba por las tardes
cuando tus ojos eran dos muros.
Cuando tus manos eran dos países
y mi cuerpo rumor de hierba.
Mi agonía buscaba su traje,
polvorienta, mordida por los perros,
y tú la acompañaste sin temblar
hasta la puerta del agua oscura.
¡Oh mi Stanton, idiota y bello entre los pequeños animalitos!
Con tu madre fracturada por los herreros de las aldeas,
con un hermano bajo los arcos,
otro comido por los hormigueros,
¡y el cáncer sin alambradas latiendo por las habitaciones!

Little Stanton

"Do you like me?"
"Yes, and you?"
"Yes, yes."

When I'm by myself
your ten years stay with me.
So do the three blind horses,
your fifteen faces with the face after the stoning
and tiny frozen fevers on leaves of corn.
Stanton, my son, Stanton.
At twelve midnight, cancer wandered through the corridors
and spoke with the documents' empty snails,
cancer springing to life, full of clouds and thermometers,
with an apple's chaste longing to be pecked by nightingales.
In the house where there is cancer,
the white walls shatter in the delirium of astronomy
and the burn glows brightly for many years
in the smallest stables, in forests where paths intersect.
My sorrow bled in the afternoons
when your eyes became two walls,
when your hands became two countries
and my body murmured like grass.
My agony went looking for its clothes,
dusty, bitten by dogs,
and you went with it, without trembling,
to the threshold of dark water.
Oh, Stanton, idiotic and beautiful among the little animals,
your mother hammered to pieces by the village blacksmiths,
one brother under the arches
and the other one eaten by the anthills,
and cancer, free of barbed wire, beating in the rooms like a heart!

Hay nodrizas que dan a los niños
ríos de musgo y amargura de pie
y algunas negras suben a los pisos para repartir filtro de rata.
Porque es verdad que la gente
quiere echar las palomas a las alcantarillas
y yo sé lo que esperan los que por la calle
nos oprimen de pronto las yemas de los dedos.

Tu ignorancia es un monte de leones, Stanton.
El día que el cáncer te dió una paliza
y te escupió en el dormitorio donde murieron los huéspedes en la epidemia
y abrió su quebrada rosa de vidrios secos y manos blandas
para salpicar de lodo las pupilas de los que navegan,
tú buscaste en la hierba mi agonía,
mi agonía con flores de terror,
mientras que el agrio cáncer mudo que quiere acostarse contigo
pulverizaba rojos paisajes por las sábanas de amargura
y ponía sobre los ataúdes
helados arbolitos de ácido bórico.
Stanton, vete al bosque con tus arpas judías,
vete para aprender celestiales palabras
que duermen en los troncos, en nubes, en tortugas,
en los perros dormidos, en el plomo, en el viento,
en lirios que no duermen, en aguas que no copian,
para que aprendas, hijo, lo que tu pueblo olvida.
Cuando empiece el tumulto de la guerra
dejaré un pedazo de queso para tu perro en la oficina.
Tus diez años serán las hojas
que vuelan en los trajes de los muertos,
diez rosas de azufre débil
en el hombro de mi madrugada.
Y yo, Stanton, yo solo, en olvido,
con tus caras marchitas sobre mi boca,
iré penetrando a voces las verdes estatuas de la Malaria.

There are wet nurses who give children
rivers of moss and bitter feet,
and black women who go upstairs to spread rat potion.
Because it's true, there are people
who want to dump doves in the sewers
and I know what else they want—the people
hanging out in the street who suddenly squeeze our fingertips.

Your ignorance is a mountain of lions, Stanton.
The day cancer gave you a beating,
and spit on you in the bedroom where the guests died in the epidemic,
and opened its broken rose of dry glass and soft hands
to spatter mud in the eyes of sailors—
you looked for my agony in the grass,
my agony and its flowers of pure fear,
while the speechless, sour cancer that wants to go to bed with you
pulverized red landscapes on the bedsheets of bitterness
and placed on the coffins
little frozen trees of boric acid.
Stanton, go to the woods with your jew's harp,
go to learn celestial words
that sleep in tree trunks, clouds, and turtles,
in sleeping dogs, in lead and wind,
in irises that don't sleep and waters that copy nothing.
Go to learn, my son, what your people forget.
When the tumult of war begins,
I'll leave a piece of cheese for your dog in the office.
Your ten years will be the leaves
flying in the clothes of the dead,
ten roses of powerless sulfur
on the shoulder of my dawn.
And I, Stanton, by myself, forgotten,
your withered faces on my mouth—
I'll go shouting my way through the green statues of Malaria.

Vaca

A Luis Lacasa

Se tendió la vaca herida.
Árboles y arroyos trepaban por sus cuernos.
Su hocico sangraba en el cielo.

Su hocico de abejas
bajo el bigote lento de la baba.
Un alarido blanco puso en pie la mañana.

Las vacas muertas y las vivas,
rubor de luz o miel de establo,
balaban con los ojos entornados.

Que se enteren las raíces
y aquel niño que afila su navaja
de que ya se pueden comer la vaca.

Arriba palidecen
luces y yugulares.
Cuatro pezuñas tiemblan en el aire.

Que se entere la luna
y esa noche de rocas amarillas
que ya se fue la vaca de ceniza.

Que ya se fue balando
por el derribo de los cielos yertos,
donde meriendan muerte los borrachos.

Cow

To Luis Lacasa

The wounded cow lay down,
trees and streams climbing over its horns.
Its muzzle bled in the sky.

Its muzzle of bees
under the slow mustache of slobber.
A white cry brought the morning to its feet.

Cows, dead and alive,
blushing light or honey from the stables,
bellowed with half-closed eyes.

Tell the roots
and that child sharpening his knife:
now they can eat the cow.

Above them, lights
and jugulars turn pale.
Four cloven hoofs tremble in the air.

Tell the moon
and that night of yellow rocks:
now the cow of ash has gone.

Now it has gone bellowing
through the wreckage of the rigid skies
where the drunks lunch on death.

Niña ahogada en el pozo
(Granada y Newburgh)

Las estatuas sufren con los ojos por la oscuridad de los ataúdes,
pero sufren mucho más por el agua que no desemboca . . .
que no desemboca.

El pueblo corría por las almenas rompiendo las cañas de los pescadores.
¡Pronto! ¡Los bordes! ¡De prisa! Y croaban las estrellas tiernas.
. . . que no desemboca.

Tranquila en mi recuerdo, astro, círculo, meta,
lloras por las orillas de un ojo de caballo.
. . . que no desemboca.

Pero nadie en lo oscuro podrá darte distancias,
sino afilado límite: porvenir de diamante.
. . . que no desemboca.

Mientras la gente busca silencios de almohada,
tú lates para siempre definida en tu anillo.
. . . que no desemboca.

Eterna en los finales de unas ondas que aceptan
combate de raíces y soledad prevista.
. . . que no desemboca.

¡Ya vienen por las rampas! ¡Levántate del agua!
¡Cada punto de luz te dará una cadena!
. . . que no desemboca.

Little Girl Drowned in the Well
(Granada and Newburgh)

Statues suffer the darkness of coffins with their eyes,
but they suffer even more from water that never reaches the sea . . .
that never reaches the sea.

The townspeople ran along the battlements, breaking the fishermen's poles.
Quickly! To the edge! Hurry! And the tender stars sounded like bullfrogs.
. . . that never reaches the sea.

At peace in my memory, heavenly body, circumference, boundary,
you cry on the shores of a horse's eye.
. . . that never reaches the sea.

But no one in the darkness will be able to give you distances,
only sharpened limits: diamond future.
. . . that never reaches the sea.

While the people look for pillowed silences,
you will pulse forever, defined by your ring.
. . . that never reaches the sea.

You'll always be undying at the end of waves that accept
the combat of roots and anticipated solitude.
. . . that never reaches the sea.

They're coming down the ramps! Arise from the water!
Every point of light will toss you a chain!
. . . that never reaches the sea.

Pero el pozo te alarga manecitas de musgo,
insospechada ondina de su casta ignorancia.
. . . que no desemboca.

No, que no desemboca. Agua fija en un punto.
Respirando con todos sus violines sin cuerdas.
En la escala de las heridas y los edificios deshabitados.
¡Agua que no desemboca!

But the well pulls you back with small mossy hands,
you, unforeseen nymph of its chaste ignorance.
. . . that never reaches the sea.

No, that never reaches the sea. Water fixed in one place,
breathing with all its unstrung violins
on the musical scale of wounds and deserted buildings.
Water that never reaches the sea!

VI
INTRODUCCIÓN A LA MUERTE
(Poemas de la soledad en Vermont)

Para Rafael Sánchez Ventura

VI
INTRODUCTION TO DEATH
(Poems of Solitude in Vermont)

For Rafael Sánchez Ventura

Lorca, *Dead Man*, 1932, included in
the first edition of *Poeta en Nueva
York*, Mexico, 1940

Muerte

A Isidoro de Blas

Qué esfuerzo,
qué esfuerzo del caballo
por ser perro,
qué esfuerzo del perro por ser golondrina,
qué esfuerzo de la golondrina por ser abeja,
qué esfuerzo de la abeja por ser caballo.
Y el caballo,
¡qué flecha aguda exprime de la rosa!,
¡qué rosa gris levanta de su belfo!
Y la rosa,
qué rebaño de luces y alaridos
ata en el vivo azúcar de su tronco;
y el azúcar,
¡qué puñalitos sueña en su vigilia!
Y los puñales diminutos,
¡qué luna sin establos!, ¡qué desnudos!,
piel eterna y rubor, andan buscando.
Y yo, por los aleros,
qué serafín de llamas busco y soy.
Pero el arco de yeso,
¡qué grande, qué invisible, qué diminuto!,
sin esfuerzo.

Death

To Isidoro de Blas

How hard they try!
How hard the horse tries
to become a dog.
How hard the dog tries to become a swallow.
How hard the swallow tries to become a bee.
How hard the bee tries to become a horse.
And the horse,
what a sharp arrow it squeezes from the rose,
what an ashen rose rising from its lips!
And the rose,
what a flock of lights and cries
knotted in the living sugar of its trunk.
And the sugar,
what daggers it dreams in its vigils!
And these miniature daggers,
what a moon without stables, what naked flesh,
what undying and rosy skin they seek out!
And I, on the roof's edge,
what a burning angel I look for and am.
But the plaster arch,
how vast, how invisible, how minute,
without even trying!

Nocturno del hueco

I

Para ver que todo se ha ido,
para ver los huecos y los vestidos,
¡dame tu guante de luna,
tu otro guante de hierba,
amor mío!

Puede el aire arrancar los caracoles
muertos sobre el pulmón del elefante
y soplar los gusanos ateridos
de las yemas de luz o de las manzanas.

Los rostros bogan impasibles
bajo el diminuto griterío de las hierbas
y en el rincón está el pechito de la rana,
turbio de corazón y mandolina.

En la gran plaza desierta
mugía la bovina cabeza recién cortada
y eran duro cristal definitivo
las formas que buscaban el giro de la sierpe.

Para ver que todo se ha ido
dame tu mudo hueco, ¡amor mío!
Nostalgia de academia y cielo triste.
¡Para ver que todo se ha ido!

Dentro de ti, amor mío, por tu carne,
¡qué silencio de trenes boca arriba!
¡cuánto brazo de momia florecido!
¡qué cielo sin salida, amor, qué cielo!

Nocturne of Emptied Space

I

If you want to see that nothing is left,
see the emptied spaces and the clothes,
give me your lunar glove,
you other glove of grass,
my love!

The air can tear dead snails
from the elephant's lung
and blow on the stiff, cold worms
from budding light or apples.

Faces erased of all emotion sail
beneath the faint uproar of the grass
and the frog's little breast is in the corner
with a clouded heart and mandolin.

On the great deserted plaza,
the cow's freshly severed head kept bellowing
and shapes that looked for the serpent's coiling
crystallized completely.

If you want to see that nothing is left,
give me your speechless, emptied space, my love,
nostalgia for the academy and sad sky!
If you want to see that nothing is left!

Inside you, my love, in your flesh,
the silence of derailed trains!
So many mummies' arms in bloom!
What a dead-end sky, my love, what a sky!

Es la piedra en el agua y es la voz en la brisa
bordes de amor que escapan de su tronco sangrante.
Basta tocar el pulso de nuestro amor presente
para que broten flores sobre los otros niños.

Para ver que todo se ha ido.
Para ver los huecos de nubes y ríos.
Dame tus ramos de laurel, amor.
¡Para ver que todo se ha ido!

Ruedan los huecos puros, por mí, por ti, en el alba
conservando las huellas de las ramas de sangre
y algún perfil de yeso tranquilo que dibuja
instantáneo dolor de luna apuntillada.

Mira formas concretas que buscan su vacío.
Perros equivocados y manzanas mordidas.
Mira el ansia, la angustia de un triste mundo fósil
que no encuentra el acento de su primer sollozo.

Cuando busco en la cama los rumores del hilo
has venido, amor mío, a cubrir mi tejado.
El hueco de una hormiga puede llenar el aire,
pero tú vas gimiendo sin norte por mis ojos.

No, por mis ojos no, que ahora me enseñas
cuatro ríos ceñidos en tu brazo.
En la dura barraca donde la luna prisionera
devora a un marinero delante de los niños.

Para ver que todo se ha ido,
¡amor inexpugnable, amor huido!
No, no me des tu hueco,
¡que ya va por el aire el mío!

Stone in water, voice on the breeze—
love's limits burst free from their bleeding trunk.
Feeling the pulse of our love today is enough
to make flowers spring from other children.

If you want to see that nothing is left,
see the emptied spaces of clouds and rivers,
give me your laurel boughs, my love.
If you want to see that nothing is left!

The pure spaces spin through me, through you, at dawn,
preserving the tracks of the bloody branches
and some profile of tranquil plaster that depicts
the sudden pain of the moon, finished off with the dagger.

Look at the concrete shapes in search of their void.
Mistaken dogs and half-eaten apples.
Look at this sad fossil world, with its anxiety and anguish,
a world that can't find the accent of its very first sob.

When I search the bed for murmuring thread,
I know you've come, my love, to cover my roof.
The emptied space of an ant can fill the air,
but you moan with nothing to guide you through my eyes.

No, not through my eyes, because now you show me
four rivers wrapped tightly around your arm,
in the rough lean-to where the imprisoned moon
devours a sailor in front of the children.

If you want to see that nothing is left,
my impenetrable love, now that you have gone,
don't give me your emptied space. No.
Mine is already traveling through the air!

¡Ay de ti, ay de mí, de la brisa!
Para ver que todo se ha ido.

II

Yo.
Con el hueco blanquísimo de un caballo,
crines de ceniza. Plaza pura y doblada.

Yo.
Mi hueco traspasado con las axilas rotas.
Piel seca de uva neutra y amianto de madrugada.

Toda la luz del mundo cabe dentro de un ojo.
Canta el gallo y su canto dura más que sus alas.

Yo.
Con el hueco blanquísimo de un caballo.
Rodeado de espectadores que tienen hormigas en las palabras.

En el circo del frío sin perfil mutilado.
Por los capiteles rotos de las mejillas desangradas.

Yo.
Mi hueco sin ti, ciudad, sin tus muertos que comen.
Ecuestre por mi vida definitivamente anclada.

Yo.

No hay siglo nuevo ni luz reciente.
Sólo un caballo azul y una madrugada.

Who will pity you, or me, or the breeze?
If you want to see that nothing is left.

II

Me.
With the white emptied space of a horse,
ashen-maned. Pure and folded plaza.

Me.
My emptied space pierced with what remains of my armpits.
Like a neutered grape's shriveled skin and asbestos of dawn.

All the world's light fits inside an eye.
The rooster crows and his song lasts longer than his wings.

Me.
With the white emptied space of a horse.
Ringed by onlookers with their ant-teeming words.

In the circus of cold weather with no mutilated profile.
Among the chipped capitals of cheeks bled white.

Me.
My emptied space without you, city, without your voracious dead.
Rider through my life finally at anchor.

Me.

No new age. No enlightenment.
Only a blue horse and dawn.

Paisaje con dos tumbas y un perro asirio

Amigo:
levántate para que oigas aullar
al perro asirio.
Las tres ninfas del cáncer han estado bailando,
hijo mío.
Trajeron unas montañas de lacre rojo
y unas sábanas duras donde estaba el cáncer dormido.
El caballo tenía un ojo en el cuello
y la luna estaba en un cielo tan frío
que tuvo que desgarrarse su monte de Venus
y ahogar en sangre y ceniza los cementerios antiguos.

Amigo,
despierta, que los montes todavía no respiran
y las hierbas de mi corazón están en otro sitio.
No importa que estés lleno de agua de mar.
Yo amé mucho tiempo a un niño
que tenía una plumilla en la lengua
y vivimos cien años dentro de un cuchillo.
Despierta. Calla. Escucha. Incorpórate un poco.
El aullido
es una larga lengua morada que deja
hormigas de espanto y licor de lirios.
Ya viene hacia la roca. ¡No alargues tus raíces!
Se acerca. Gime. No solloces en sueños, amigo.

¡Amigo!
Levántate para que oigas aullar
al perro asirio.

Landscape with Two Graves and an Assyrian Dog

Friend,
get up and listen
to the Assyrian dog howl.
Cancer's three nymphs have been dancing,
my son.
They carried mountains of red sealing wax
and stiff bed sheets to the place where cancer slept.
The horse had an eye in its neck
and the moon was in a sky so cold
that she had to tear open her mound of Venus
and drown the ancient graveyards in blood and ashes.

Friend,
wake up, the mountains still aren't breathing
and the grass of my heart is somewhere else.
It doesn't matter if you're full of seawater.
For a long time I loved a child
who had a tiny feather on his tongue,
and we lived inside a knife for a hundred years.
Wake up. Be still. Listen. Sit up in your bed.
The howling
is a long purple tongue that releases
terrifying ants and the liquor of irises.
Here it comes toward the rock. Don't spread out your roots!
It approaches. Moans. Friend, don't sob in your dreams.

Friend!
Get up and listen
to the Assyrian dog howl.

Ruina

A Regino Sáinz de la Maza

Sin encontrarse.
Viajero por su propio torso blanco.
¡Así iba el aire!

Pronto se vió que la luna
era una calavera de caballo
y el aire una manzana oscura.

Detrás de la ventana,
con látigos y luces, se sentía
la lucha de la arena con el agua.

Yo ví llegar las hierbas
y les eché un cordero que balaba
bajo sus dientecillos y lancetas.

Volaba dentro de una gota
la cáscara de pluma y celuloide
de la primer paloma.

Vienen las hierbas, hijo.
Ya suenan sus espadas de saliva
por el cielo vacío.

Mi mano, amor. ¡Las hierbas!
Por los cristales rotos de la casa
la sangre desató sus cabelleras.

Ruin

To Regino Sáinz de la Maza

Never finding itself,
traveling through its own white torso,
the air made its way!

Soon it was clear that the moon
was a horse's skull,
and the air, a dark apple.

Behind the window,
with whips and lights, I felt
sand struggling with water.

I saw all the blades of grass arrive
and I threw a bleating lamb
to their little teeth and lancets.

The first dove, encased
in feathers and plastic,
flew inside a single drop.

Here comes the grass, son.
Its spit-swords ring
through the empty sky.

Hold my hand, my love. The grass!
Through the house's broken windows,
the blood unleashed its waves of hair.

Tú sólo y yo quedamos.
Prepara tu esqueleto para el aire.
Yo sólo y tú quedamos.

Prepara tu esqueleto.
Hay que buscar de prisa, amor, de prisa,
nuestro perfil sin sueño.

Only you and I are left.
Prepare your skeleton for the air.
We're the only ones who remain.

Prepare your skeleton.
Hurry, love, hurry, we've got to look
for our sleepless profile.

Amantes asesinados por una perdiz

—Los dos lo han querido,—me dijo su madre—. Los dos . . .

—No es posible, señora,—dije yo—. Usted tiene demasiado temperamento y a su edad ya se sabe por qué caen los alfileres del rocío.

—Calle usted, Luciano, calle usted . . . No, no, Luciano, no.

—Para resistir este nombre necesito contener el dolor de mis recuerdos. ¿Y usted cree que aquella pequeña dentadura y esa mano de niño que se han dejado olvidadas dentro de la ola me pueden consolar de esta tristeza?

—Los dos lo han querido—me dijo su prima—. Los dos.

Me puse a mirar el mar y lo comprendí todo.

¿Será posible que del pico de esa paloma cruelísima que tiene corazón de elefante salga la palidez lunar de aquel transatlántico que se aleja?

—Recuerdo que tuve que hacer varias veces uso de mi cuchara para defenderme de los lobos. Yo no tenía culpa ninguna, usted lo sabe. ¡Dios mío! Estoy llorando.

—Los dos lo han querido —dije yo—. Los dos. Una manzana será siempre un amante, pero un amante no podrá ser jamás una manzana.

Por eso se han muerto, por eso. Con veinte ríos y un solo invierno desgarrado.

—Fue muy sencillo. Se amaban por encima de todos los museos.

Mano derecha,
con mano izquierda.

Mano izquierda,
con mano derecha.

Pie derecho,
con pie derecho.

Pie izquierdo,
con nube.

Cabello,
con planta de pie.

Two Lovers Murdered by a Partridge

"They both wanted it," his mother told me. "Both of them."

"My dear woman," I said, "that's impossible. You're too emotional, and at your age you should know why the dewdrops settle on the ground like pins."

"Be quiet, Luciano, be quiet. No, no, Luciano, no."

"In order to make that name bearable, I need to restrain my painful memories. And you think I could be consoled for my sadness by that tiny set of teeth, and that child's hand, forgotten inside the wave?"

"They both wanted it," his cousin told me. "Both of them."

I contemplated the sea and suddenly I understood everything.

"Could it be that the moonlit pallor of that departing ocean liner comes from the beak of that cruel dove with an elephant's heart?"

"I remember I had to use my spoon several times to ward off the wolves. I wasn't to blame for anything. You know that. My God, I'm crying!"

"They both wanted it," I said. "Both of them. An apple will always be a lover, but a lover can't ever be an apple."

"That's why they died. That's why. At the age of twenty rivers and a single shredded winter."

"It was very simple. They made love above and beyond the museums."

Right hand
with left hand.

Left hand
with right hand.

Right foot
with right foot.

Left foot
with cloud.

Hair
with sole of the foot.

Planta de pie,
con mejilla izquierda.

¡Oh mejilla izquierda! ¡Oh noroeste de barquitos y hormigas de
mercurio . . . ! Dame el pañuelo, Genoveva; voy a llorar . . . Voy a llorar
hasta que de mis ojos salga una muchedumbre de siemprevivas . . . Se
acostaban.

No había otro espectáculo más tierno.

¿Me ha oído usted?

¡Se acostaban!

Muslo izquierdo,
con antebrazo izquierdo.

Ojos cerrados,
con uñas abiertas.

Cintura, con nuca
y con playa.

Y las cuatro orejitas eran cuatro ángeles en la choza de la nieve. Se
querían. Se amaban. A pesar de la Ley de la gravedad. La diferencia que
existe entre una espina de rosa y una Star es sencillísima.

Cuando descubrieron esto, se fueron al campo.

Se amaban.

¡Dios mío! Se amaban ante los ojos de los químicos.

Espalda, con tierra,
tierra, con anís.

Luna, con hombro dormido.

Y las cinturas se entrecruzaban con un rumor de vidrios.

Yo vi temblar sus mejillas cuando los profesores de la Universidad les
traían hiel y vinagre en una esponja diminuta. Muchas veces tenían que
espantar a los perros que gemían por las yedras blanquísimas del lecho.
Pero ellos se amaban.

Eran un hombre y una mujer,
o sea,
un hombre
y un pedacito de tierra,
un elefante

Sole of the foot
with left cheek.

Oh, left cheek! Oh, northwest of little boats and ants of mercury! Give me the handkerchief, Genoveva; I'm going to cry . . . I'm going to cry until a bunch of immortelles emerges from my eyes . . . They were going to bed.

There was no other spectacle so tender . . .

Did you hear me?

They were going to bed!

Left thigh
with left forearm.

Closed eyes
with open fingernails.

Waist with nape,
and with shoreline.

And the four little ears were four angels in a snowy cabin. They yearned for each other. They made love. Defying the law of gravity. The difference between a rose thorn and a Star is very simple.

When they figured this out, they left for the countryside.

They made love.

My God! They made love while the chemists watched.

Their backs with the earth,
earth with anise.

Moon with a sleeping shoulder.

And their waists entwined, whispering like glass.

I saw their cheeks tremble when the professors brought them honey and vinegar in a tiny sponge. Many times they had to scare away the dogs that howled in the pure white ivy of the bed. But they made love.

They were man and woman,
in other words,
a man
and a little piece of earth,
an elephant

y un niño,
un niño y un junco.

Eran dos mancebos desmayados
y una pierna de níquel.

¡Eran los barqueros!

Sí.

Eran los terribles barqueros del Guadiana que machacan con sus remos todas las rosas del mundo.

El viejo marinero escupió el tabaco de su boca y dio grandes voces para espantar a las gaviotas. Pero ya era demasiado tarde.

Cuando las mujeres enlutadas llegaron a casa del Gobernador, éste comía tranquilamente almendras verdes y pescados fríos en un exquisito plato de oro. Era preferible no haber hablado con él.

En las islas Azores.

Casi no puedo llorar.

Yo puse dos telegramas, pero desgraciadamente ya era tarde.

Muy tarde.

Sólo sé deciros que dos niños que pasaban por la orilla del bosque vieron una perdiz que echaba un hilito de sangre por el pico.

Esta es la causa, querido capitán, de mi extraña melancolía.

and a child,

a child and a bulrush.

They were two young men who had fainted

and a chrome-plated leg.

They were the boatmen!

Yes.

They were the terrible boatmen of the Guadiana, who crush all the world's roses with their oars.

The old sailor spit tobacco from his mouth, and yelled to frighten away the gulls. But it was too late.

When the women in mourning arrived at the governor's mansion, he was quietly eating green almonds and cold fish from an exquisite gold plate. It would have been better not to have spoken with him.

In the Azores.

I'm nearly unable to cry.

I sent two telegrams, but unfortunately it was too late.

Very late.

I can only tell you that two children, passing by the edge of the forest, saw a partridge that trailed a little thread of blood from its beak.

That's the reason, my dear captain, for my strange melancholia.

Luna y panorama de los insectos
(Poema de amor)

Mi corazón tendría la forma de un zapato
si cada aldea tuviera una sirena.
Pero la noche es interminable cuando se apoya en los enfermos
y hay barcos que buscan ser mirados para poder hundirse tranquilos.

Si el aire sopla blandamente
mi corazón tiene la forma de una niña.
Si el aire se niega a salir de los cañaverales
mi corazón tiene la forma de una milenaria boñiga de toro.

Bogar, bogar, bogar, bogar,
hacia el batallón de puntas desiguales,
hacia un paisaje de acechos pulverizados.
Noche igual de la nieve, de los sistemas suspendidos.
Y la luna.
¡La luna!
Pero no la luna.
La raposa de las tabernas.
El gallo japonés que se comió los ojos.
Las hierbas masticadas.

No nos salvan las solitarias en los vidrios,
ni los herbolarios donde el metafísico
encuentra las otras vertientes del cielo.

Moon and Panorama of the Insects
(Love Poem)

The moon shimmers on the sea,
the wind moans in the sail
and raises gently swelling
blue and silver waves.
—ESPRONCEDA

My heart would take the shape of a shoe
if a siren lived in every village.
But the night never ends when it leans on the sick,
and there are ships that want to be seen in order to sink in peace.

If the wind blows softly,
my heart takes the shape of a girl.
If the wind won't leave the cane fields,
my heart takes the shape of a millenary cow pie.

Row, row, row, row,
toward the army of jagged points,
toward a landscape of pulverized ambushes.
Equal night of the snow, the discontinued systems.
And the moon.
The moon!
But not the moon.
The taverns' vixen.
The Japanese rooster that ate its own eyes.
The cud.

The tapeworms behind glass won't save us,
nor herbariums where the metaphysician
meets the other slopes of the sky.

Son mentira las formas. Sólo existe
el círculo de bocas del oxígeno.
Y la luna.
Pero no la luna.
Los insectos.
Los muertos diminutos por las riberas.
Dolor en longitud.
Yodo en un punto.
Las muchedumbres en el alfiler.
El desnudo que amasa la sangre de todos,
y mi amor que no es un caballo ni una quemadura.
Criatura de pecho devorado.
¡Mi amor!

Ya cantan, gritan, gimen: *Rostro. ¡Tu rostro! Rostro.*
Las manzanas son unas.
Las dalias son idénticas.
La luz tiene un sabor de metal acabado
y el campo de todo un lustro cabrá en la mejilla de la moneda.
Pero tu rostro cubre los cielos del banquete.
¡Ya cantan!, ¡gritan!, ¡gimen!,
¡cubren!, ¡trepan!, ¡espantan!

Es necesario caminar, ¡de prisa!, por las ondas, por las ramas,
por las calles deshabitadas de la Edad Media que bajan al río,
por las tiendas de las pieles donde suena un cuerno de vaca herida,
por las escalas, ¡sin miedo!, por las escalas.
Hay un hombre descolorido que se está bañando en el mar;
es tan tierno que los reflectores le comieron jugando el corazón,
y en el Perú viven mil mujeres, ¡oh insectos!, que noche y día
hacen nocturnos y desfiles entrecruzando sus propias venas.

Un diminuto guante corrosivo me detiene. ¡Basta!
En mi pañuelo he sentido el tris
de la primera vena que se rompe.

Shapes are a lie. What is there?
The circle of mouths of the oxygen.
And the moon.
But not the moon.
The insects,
little dead things lining the shores,
sorrow on longitude,
iodine on stitched flesh,
the crowd on the head of a pin,
the naked man who kneads everyone's blood,
and my love who is neither horse nor burn,
creature whose breast was consumed.
My love!

Now they sing, scream, moan: *A face. Your face! A face.*
The apples are one,
the dahlias identical,
the light tastes like worn-out metal
and the countryside of half a decade will fit on the cheek of a coin.
But your face covers the skies of the feast.
Now they sing, scream, moan,
cover everything, climb, terrify!

We've got to move—Hurry up!—through the waves, the branches,
the deserted streets of the Middle Ages going down to the river,
the stores of hides where a wounded cow's horn bellows,
up the ladders—Don't be scared!—up the ladders.
A discolored man is bathing in the sea;
he's so tender that searchlights ate him as he gambled away his heart,
and a thousand women live in Peru—Oh, insects!—night and day
they weave nocturnes and parades among their own veins.

One tiny corrosive glove stops me. That's enough!
I feel the crackle of the first
broken vein on my handkerchief.

Cuida tus pies, ¡amor mío!, ¡tus manos!,
ya que yo tengo que entregar mi rostro.
¡Mi rostro, mi rostro, ¡ay, mi comido rostro!

Este fuego casto para mi deseo,
esta confusión por anhelo de equilibrio,
este inocente dolor de pólvora en mis ojos,
aliviará la angustia de otro corazón
devorado por las nebulosas.

No nos salva la gente de las zapaterías
ni los paisajes que se hacen música al encontrar las llaves oxidadas.
Son mentira los aires. Sólo existe
una cunita en el desván
que recuerda todas las cosas.
Y la luna.
Pero no la luna.
Los insectos.
Los insectos solos,
crepitantes, mordientes, estremecidos, agrupados,
y la luna
con un guante de humo sentada en la puerta de sus derribos.
¡¡La luna!!

Nueva York, 4 de enero de 1930

Watch out for your hands and feet, my love,
since I must give up my face,
my face, my face, yes, my half-eaten face!

This chaste, burning desire of mine,
this confusion from longing for equilibrium,
this innocent sorrow of gunpowder in my eyes,
will lighten the anguish of another heart
consumed by the nebulae.

The people in shoe stores won't save us,
nor the landscapes becoming music when they find the rusted keys.
Breezes are a lie. Only a small cradle
exists, in the attic,
that remembers everything.
And the moon.
But not the moon.
The insects.
Just the insects,
crackling, biting, quivering, swarming,
and the moon
with a glove of smoke in the doorway of its wreckage.
The moon!!

New York, January 4, 1930

VII
VUELTA A LA CIUDAD

Para Antonio Hernández Soriano

VII
RETURN TO THE CITY

For Antonio Hernández Soriano

Lorca, *Self-Portrait in New York,*
1929–30

New York
(Oficina y denuncia)

A Fernando Vela

Debajo de las multiplicaciones
hay una gota de sangre de pato;
debajo de las divisiones
hay una gota de sangre de marinero;
debajo de las sumas, un río de sangre tierna.
Un río que viene cantando
por los dormitorios de los arrabales,
y es plata, cemento o brisa
en el alba mentida de New York.
Existen las montañas. Lo sé.
Y los anteojos para la sabiduría.
Lo sé. Pero yo no he venido a ver el cielo.
He venido para ver la turbia sangre,
la sangre que lleva las máquinas a las cataratas
y el espíritu a la lengua de la cobra.
Todos los días se matan en New York
cuatro millones de patos,
cinco millones de cerdos,
dos mil palomas para el gusto de los agonizantes,
un millón de vacas,
un millón de corderos
y dos millones de gallos,
que dejan los cielos hechos añicos.
Más vale sollozar afilando la navaja
o asesinar a los perros en las alucinantes cacerías,
que resistir en la madrugada
los interminables trenes de leche,
los interminables trenes de sangre

New York
(Office and Denunciation)

Under the multiplications,
a drop of duck's blood;
under the divisions,
a drop of sailor's blood;
under the additions, a river of tender blood.
A river that sings and flows
past bedrooms in the boroughs—
and it's money, cement, or wind
in New York's counterfeit dawn.
I know the mountains exist.
And wisdom's eyeglasses,
too. But I didn't come to see the sky.
I'm here to see the clouded blood,
the blood that sweeps machines over waterfalls
and the soul toward the cobra's tongue.
Every day in New York, they slaughter
four million ducks,
five million hogs,
two thousand pigeons to accommodate the tastes of the dying,
one million cows,
one million lambs,
and two million roosters
that smash the skies to pieces.
It's better to sob while honing the blade
or kill dogs on the delirious hunts
than to resist at dawn
the endless milk trains,
the endless blood trains

y los trenes de rosas maniatadas
por los comerciantes de perfumes.
Los patos y las palomas,
y los cerdos y los corderos
ponen sus gotas de sangre
debajo de las multiplicaciones,
y los terribles alaridos de las vacas estrujadas
llenan de dolor el valle
donde el Hudson se emborracha con aceite.
Yo denuncio a toda la gente
que ignora la otra mitad,
la mitad irredimible
que levanta sus montes de cemento
donde laten los corazones
de los animalitos que se olvidan
y donde caeremos todos
en la última fiesta de los taladros.
Os escupo en la cara.
La otra mitad me escucha
devorando, orinando, volando en su pureza,
como los niños de las porterías
que llevan frágiles palitos
a los huecos donde se oxidan
las antenas de los insectos.
No es el infierno, es la calle.
No es la muerte. Es la tienda de frutas.
Hay un mundo de ríos quebrados y distancias inasibles
en la patita de ese gato quebrada por un automóvil,
y yo oigo el canto de la lombriz
en el corazón de muchas niñas.
Óxido, fermento, tierra estremecida.
Tierra tú mismo que nadas por los números de la oficina.
¿Qué voy a hacer, ordenar los paisajes?
¿Ordenar los amores que luego son fotografías?

and the trains of roses, manacled
by the dealers in perfume.
The ducks and the pigeons,
and the hogs and the lambs
lay their drops of blood
under the multiplications,
and the terrified bellowing of the cows wrung dry
fills the valley with sorrow
where the Hudson gets drunk on oil.
I denounce everyone
who ignores the other half,
the half that can't be redeemed,
who lift their mountains of cement
where the hearts beat
inside forgotten little animals
and where all of us will fall
in the last feast of pneumatic drills.
I spit in all your faces.
The other half hears me,
devouring, pissing, flying in their purity,
like the supers' children in lobbies
who carry fragile twigs
to the emptied spaces where
the insect antennae are rusting.
This is not hell, but the street.
Not death, but the fruit stand.
There is a world of broken rivers and distances just beyond our grasp
in the cat's paw smashed by a car,
and I hear the earthworm's song
in the hearts of many girls.
Rust, fermentation, quaking earth.
You yourself are the earth as you drift in office numbers.
What shall I do now? Set the landscapes in order?
Order the loves that soon become photographs,

Que luego son pedazos de madera y bocanadas de sangre.
No, no; yo denuncio.
Yo denuncio la conjura
de estas desiertas oficinas
que no radian las agonías,
que borran los programas de la selva,
y me ofrezco a ser comido por las vacas estrujadas
cuando sus gritos llenan el valle
donde el Hudson se emborracha con aceite.

that soon become pieces of wood and mouthfuls of blood?
No, no: I denounce it all.
I denounce the conspiracy
of these deserted offices
that radiate no agony,
that erase the forest's plans,
and I offer myself as food for the cows wrung dry
when their bellowing fills the valley
where the Hudson gets drunk on oil.

Cementerio judío

Las alegres fiebres huyeron a las maromas de los barcos
y el judío empujó la verja con el pudor helado del interior de la
      lechuga.

Los niños de Cristo dormían,
y el agua era una paloma,
y la madera era una garza,
y el plomo era un colibrí,
y aun las vivas prisiones de fuego
estaban consoladas por el salto de la langosta.

Los niños de Cristo bogaban y los judíos llenaban los muros
con un solo corazón de paloma
por el que todos querían escapar.
Las niñas de Cristo cantaban y las judías miraban la muerte
con un solo ojo de faisán,
vidriado por la angustia de un millón de paisajes.

Los médicos ponen en el níquel sus tijeras y guantes de goma
cuando los cadáveres sienten en los pies
la terrible claridad de otra luna enterrada.
Pequeños dolores ilesos se acercan a los hospitales
y los muertos se van quitando un traje de sangre cada día.

Las arquitecturas de escarcha,
las liras y gemidos que se escapan de las hojas diminutas
al otoño, mojando las últimas vertientes,
se apagaban en el negro de los sombreros de copa.

Jewish Cemetery

The fevers fled with great joy to the hawsers of moored ships
and the Jew pushed against the gate chastely the way lettuce grows coldly
      from its center.

Christ's children slept,
and the water was a dove,
and the wood was a heron,
and the lead was a hummingbird,
and even the living prisons of fire
were consoled by the locust's leap.

Christ's children rowed and the Jews packed the walls
with a single dove's heart
through which all of them wished to escape.
Christ's little girls sang and the Jewish women looked at death
with a pheasant's solitary eye,
glazed by the anguish of a million landscapes.

The doctors put their scissors and surgical gloves on the chrome table
when the feet of the corpses feel
the terrible brightness of another buried moon.
Tiny unscathed pains approach the hospitals
and the dead take off a suit of blood every day.

The architecture of frost,
the lyres and moans that escape from the small leaves
in autumn, drenching the farthest slopes,
were extinguished in the blackness of their top hats.

La hierba celeste y sola de la que huye con miedo el rocío
y las blancas entradas de mármol que conducen al aire duro
mostraban su silencio roto por las huellas dormidas de los zapatos.

El judío empujó la verja;
pero el judío no era un puerto
y las barcas de nieve se agolparon
por las escalerillas de su corazón:
las barcas de nieve que acechan
un hombre de agua que las ahogue.
Las barcas de los cementerios
que a veces dejan ciegos a los visitantes.

Los niños de Cristo dormían
y el judío ocupó su litera.
Tres mil judíos lloraban en el espanto de las galerías
porque reunían entre todos con esfuerzo media paloma,
porque uno tenía la rueda de un reloj
y otro un botín con orugas parlantes
y otro una lluvia nocturna cargada de cadenas
y otro la uña de un ruiseñor que estaba vivo;
y porque la media paloma gemía
derramando una sangre que no era la suya.

Las alegres fiebres bailaban por las cúpulas humedecidas
y la luna copiaba en su mármol
nombres viejos y cintas ajadas.
Llegó la gente que come por detrás de las yertas columnas
y los asnos de blancos dientes
con los especialistas de las articulaciones.
Verdes girasoles temblaban
por los páramos del crepúsculo
y todo el cementerio era una queja
de bocas de cartón y trapo seco.

The dew retreats in fear from blue, forsaken grass,
and the white marble entrances that lead to hard air
were showing their silence broken by sleeping footprints.

The Jew pushed against the gate;
but the Jew was not a port
and the boats of snow piled up
on the gangways of his heart:
the boats ready to ambush
a man of water who can drown them.
The boats of the cemeteries
that sometimes blind the visitors.

Christ's children slept
and the Jew lay down in his berth.
Three thousand Jews wept in the galleries of terror
because it was all they could do to gather half a dove among themselves,
because one of them had the wheel from a clock
and another a boot laced with talking caterpillars
and another a nocturnal rain burdened with chains
and another the claw of a nightingale that was still alive;
and because the half-dove moaned,
spilling blood that was not its own.

The fevers danced with great joy on the humid domes,
and the moon inscribed in its marble
ancient names and worn ribbons.
Those who dine behind the rigid columns arrived,
so did the donkeys with their white teeth
and the specialists in the body's joints.
Green sunflowers trembled
in the highlands of dusk
and the whole cemetery began to complain
with cardboard mouths and dry rags.

Ya los niños de Cristo se dormían
cuando el judío, apretando los ojos,
se cortó las manos en silencio
al escuchar los primeros gemidos.

Nueva York, 18 de enero de 1930

Christ's children were going to sleep
when the Jew, squeezing his eyes shut,
silently cut off his hands
as he heard the wailing begin.

New York, January 18, 1930

Crucifixión

La luna pudo detenerse fin por la curva blanquísima de los caballos.
Un rayo de luz violenta que se escapaba de la herida
proyectó en el cielo el instante de la circuncisión de un niño muerto.

La sangre bajaba por el monte y los ángeles la buscaban,
pero los cálices eran de viento y al fin llenaba los zapatos.
Cojos perros fumaban sus pipas y un olor de cuero caliente
ponía grises los labios redondos de los que vomitaban en las esquinas.
Y llegaban largos alaridos por el sur de la noche seca.
Era que la luna quemaba con sus bujías el falo de los caballos.

Un sastre especialista en púrpura
había encerrado a las tres santas mujeres
y les enseñaba una calavera por los vidrios de la ventana.
Los niños en el arrabal rodeaban a un camello blanco
que lloraba asustado porque al alba
tenía que pasar sin remedio por el ojo de una aguja.
¡Oh cruz! ¡Oh clavos! ¡Oh espina!
¡Oh espina clavada en el hueso hasta que se oxiden los planetas!
Como nadie volvía la cabeza, el cielo pudo desnudarse.
Entonces se oyó la gran voz y los fariseos dijeron:
"Esa maldita vaca tiene las tetas llenas de leche."

La muchedumbre cerraba las puertas
y la lluvia bajaba por las calles decidida a mojar el corazón
mientras la tarde se puso turbia de latidos y leñadores
y la oscura ciudad agonizaba bajo el martillo de los carpinteros.
"Esa maldita vaca
tiene las tetas llenas de perdigones,"
dijeron los fariseos.
Pero la sangre mojó sus pies y los espíritus inmundos

Crucifixion

The moon could rest in the end along the pure white curve of the horses.
A violent beam of light that escaped from the wound
projected the instant of a dead child's circumcision on the sky.

Blood flowed down the mountain and angels looked for it,
but the chalices became wind and finally filled the shoes.
Crippled dogs puffed on their pipes and the odor of hot leather
grayed the round lips of those who vomited on street corners.
And long southern howls arrived with the arid night.
It was the moon burning the horses' phallus with its candles.
A tailor, who specialized in purple,
had locked up three saintly women
and was showing them a skull through the window glass.
In the borough, boys circled a white camel
that wept because at daybreak
it would have to go through the needle's eye.
Oh, cross! Oh, nails! Oh, thorn!
Oh, thorn driven to the bone until the planets rust to pieces!
Since no one turned to look, the sky could undress.
Then the great voice was heard, and the Pharisees said:
"That wicked cow has teats full of milk."

The multitude closed their doors
and rain flowed down the streets, determined to drench the heart
and the afternoon clouded over with heartbeats and woodcutters,
and the darkened city agonized under the carpenters' hammer.
"That wicked cow
has teats full of bird shot,"
said the Pharisees.
But blood drenched their feet and unclean spirits
splattered vials of pondwater on the temple walls.

estrellaban ampollas de laguna sobre las paredes del templo.
Se supo el momento preciso de la salvación de nuestra vida,
porque la luna lavó con agua
las quemaduras de los caballos
y no la primera vida que callaron en la arena.
Entonces salieron los fríos cantando sus canciones
y las ranas encendieron sus lumbres en la doble orilla del río.
"Esa maldita vaca, maldita, maldita, maldita,
no nos dejará dormir," dijeron los fariseos,
y se alejaron a sus casas por el tumulto de la calle
dando empujones a los borrachos y escupiendo la sal de los sacrificios
mientras la sangre los seguía con un balido de cordero.

Fue entonces
y la tierra despertó arrojando temblorosos ríos de polilla.

Nueva York, 18 de octubre de 1929

Someone discovered the precise moment of our salvation
because the moon washed the burns
of the horses with water
but not the living girl whom they silenced in the sand.
Then the chills went out singing their songs
and frogs ignited their fires on the river's double shore.
"That wicked cow, wicked, wicked, wicked,
won't let us sleep," said the Pharisees,
and they withdrew to their houses through the riotous street,
pushing drunks aside and spitting sacrificial salt
while the blood followed them like a bleating lamb.

That's how it was.
And the awakened earth cast off trembling rivers of moths.

New York, October 18, 1929

VIII
DOS ODAS

A mi editor, Armando Guibert

VIII
TWO ODES

To my publisher, Armando Guibert

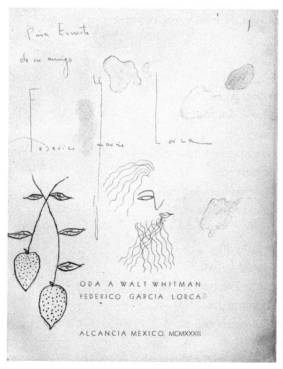

Lorca, *Head of a Bearded Young Man*, 1934, on the cover of *Oda a Walt Whitman*, dedicated to Ernesto da Cal

Grito hacia Roma
(Desde la torre del Chrysler Building)

Manzanas levemente heridas
por finos espadines de plata,
nubes rasgadas por una mano de coral
que lleva en el dorso una almendra de fuego,
peces de arsénico como tiburones,
tiburones como gotas de llanto para cegar una multitud,
rosas que hieren
y agujas instaladas en los caños de la sangre,
mundos enemigos y amores cubiertos de gusanos
caerán sobre ti. Caerán sobre la gran cúpula
que unta de aceite las lenguas militares,
donde un hombre se orina en una deslumbrante paloma
y escupe carbón machacado
rodeado de miles de campanillas.

Porque ya no hay quien reparta el pan y el vino,
ni quien cultive hierbas en la boca del muerto,
ni quien abra los linos del reposo,
ni quien llore por las heridas de los elefantes.
No hay más que un millón de herreros
forjando cadenas para los niños que han de venir.
No hay más que un millón de carpinteros
que hacen ataúdes sin cruz.
No hay más que un gentío de lamentos
que se abren las ropas en espera de la bala.
El hombre que desprecia la paloma debía hablar,
debía gritar desnudo entre las columnas
y ponerse una inyección para adquirir la lepra
y llorar un llanto tan terrible

Cry to Rome
(From the Tower of the Chrysler Building)

Apples barely grazed
by slender, silver rapiers,
clouds torn apart by a coral hand
that carries a fiery almond on its back,
arsenic fish like sharks,
sharks like wailing drops that blind the masses,
roses that wound
and needles that lace the blood's plumbing,
enemy worlds and loves covered with worms
will fall on you. Will fall on the great dome
that anoints the military tongues with oil,
where a man pisses on a dazzling dove
and spits pulverized coal
surrounded by thousands of hand bells.

Because there is no one to bestow the bread or the wine,
or make grass grow in the mouths of the dead,
or spread the linen of rest and peace,
or weep for the wounded elephants.
There are only a million blacksmiths
who forge chains for tomorrow's children.
Only a million carpenters
who make coffins with no cross.
Only a crowd of laments
unbuttoning their clothes, waiting for the bullet.
The man who scorns the dove should speak,
scream naked between the columns,
inject himself with leprosy
and shed tears terrible enough

que disolviera sus anillos y sus teléfonos de diamante.
Pero el hombre vestido de blanco
ignora el misterio de la espiga,
ignora el gemido de la parturienta,
ignora que Cristo puede dar agua todavía,
ignora que la moneda quema el beso de prodigio
y da la sangre del cordero al pico idiota del faisán.

Los maestros enseñan a los niños
una luz maravillosa que viene del monte;
pero lo que llega es una reunión de cloacas
donde gritan las oscuras ninfas del cólera.
Los maestros señalan con devoción las enormes cúpulas
          sahumadas;
pero debajo de las estatuas no hay amor,
no hay amor bajo los ojos de cristal definitivo.
El amor está en las carnes desgarradas por la sed,
en la choza diminuta que lucha con la inundación;
el amor está en los fosos donde luchan las sierpes del hambre,
en el triste mar que mece los cadáveres de las gaviotas
y en el oscurísimo beso punzante debajo de las almohadas.

Pero el viejo de las manos traslúcidas
dirá: amor, amor, amor,
aclamado por millones de moribundos;
dirá: amor, amor, amor,
entre el tisú estremecido de ternura;
dirá: paz, paz, paz,
entre el tirite de cuchillos y melones de dinamita;
dirá: amor, amor, amor,
hasta que se le pongan de plata los labios.

Mientras tanto, mientras tanto, ¡ay!, mientras tanto,
los negros que sacan las escupideras,

to dissolve his rings and diamond telephones.
But the man dressed in white
knows nothing of the mystery of the wheat ear,
or the moans of a woman giving birth,
or the fact that Christ can still give water,
or the coin that burns the kiss of prodigy
and gives the blood of the lamb to the pheasant's idiot beak.

The schoolteachers show the children
a marvelous light coming from the mountain;
but what arrives is a junction of sewers
where cholera's nymphs scream in the shadows.
The teachers point devoutly to the enormous domes filled with burning
        incense;
but beneath the statues there is no love,
no love beneath the final crystal eyes.
Love is in the flesh shredded by thirst,
in the tiny thatched hut struggling against the flood;
love is in the pits where the serpents of famine writhe,
in the sad sea that cradles the dead gulls
and in the obscurest kiss bristling beneath the pillows.

But the old man with translucent hands
will say: Love, love, love,
acclaimed by millions of the dying;
he will say: Love, love, love,
amidst the gold lamé that trembles with tenderness;
he will say: Peace, peace, peace,
among the shivering of knives and melons of dynamite;
he will say: Love, love, love,
until his lips have turned to silver.

Meanwhile, meanwhile, *ay!*, meanwhile
the blacks who empty the spittoons,

los muchachos que tiemblan bajo el terror pálido de los directores,
las mujeres ahogadas en aceites minerales,
la muchedumbre de martillo, de violín o de nube,
ha de gritar aunque le estrellen los sesos en el muro,
ha de gritar frente a las cúpulas,
ha de gritar loca de fuego,
ha de gritar loca de nieve,
ha de gritar con la cabeza llena de excremento,
ha de gritar como todas las noches juntas,
ha de gritar con voz tan desgarrada
hasta que las ciudades tiemblen como niñas
y rompan las prisiones del aceite y la música.
Porque queremos el pan nuestro de cada día,
flor de aliso y perenne ternura desgranada;
porque queremos que se cumpla la voluntad de la Tierra,
que da sus frutos para todos.

the boys who tremble beneath the pallid terror of executives,
the women who drown in mineral oil,
the multitudes with their hammers, violins, or clouds—
they'll scream even if they bash their brains against the wall,
scream in front of the domes,
scream driven crazy by fire,
scream driven crazy by snow,
scream with their heads full of excrement,
scream as if all the nights converged,
scream with such a heartrending voice
until the cities tremble like little girls
and knock down the prisons of oil and music.
Because we demand our daily bread,
alder in bloom and perennially harvested tenderness,
because we demand that Earth's will be done,
that its fruits be offered to everyone.

Oda a Walt Whitman

Por el East River y el Bronx
los muchachos cantaban enseñando sus cinturas,
con la rueda, el aceite, el cuero y el martillo.
Noventa mil mineros sacaban la plata de las rocas
y los niños dibujaban escaleras y perspectivas.

Pero ninguno se dormía,
ninguno quería ser el río,
ninguno amaba las hojas grandes,
ninguno la lengua azul de la playa.

Por el East River y el Queensborough
los muchachos luchaban con la industria,
y los judíos vendían al fauno del río
la rosa de la circuncisión,
y el cielo desembocaba por los puentes y los tejados
manadas de bisontes empujadas por el viento.

Pero ninguno se detenía,
ninguno quería ser nube,
ninguno buscaba los helechos
ni la rueda amarilla del tamboril.

Cuando la luna salga
las poleas rodarán para turbar al cielo;
un límite de agujas cercará la memoria
y los ataúdes se llevarán a los que no trabajan.

Nueva York de cieno,
Nueva York de alambres y de muerte.
¿Qué ángel llevas oculto en la mejilla?

Ode to Walt Whitman

By the East River and the Bronx
boys were singing, exposing their waists,
with the wheel, with oil, with rawhide and hammer.
Ninety thousand miners taking silver from the rocks
and children drawing stairs and perspectives.

But none of them could sleep,
none of them wanted to be the river,
none of them loved the huge leaves
or the shoreline's blue tongue.

By the East River and the Queensboro
boys were battling with industry
and the Jews sold to the river faun
the rose of circumcision,
and over bridges and rooftops, the mouth of the sky emptied
herds of bison driven by the wind.

But none of them paused,
none of them wanted to be a cloud,
none of them looked for ferns
or the yellow wheel of the tambourine.

As soon as the moon rises
the pulleys will spin to upset the sky;
a border of needles will besiege memory
and the hearses will bear away those who don't work.

New York, mire,
New York, wires and death.
What angel is hidden in your cheek?

¿Qué voz perfecta dirá las verdades del trigo?
¿Quién el sueño terrible de tus anémonas manchadas?

Ni un solo momento, viejo hermoso Walt Whitman,
he dejado de ver tu barba llena de mariposas,
ni tus hombros de pana gastados por la luna,
ni tus muslos de Apolo virginal,
ni tu voz como una columna de ceniza;
anciano hermoso como la niebla,
que gemías igual que un pájaro
con el sexo atravesado por una aguja.
Enemigo del sátiro,
enemigo de la vid
y amante de los cuerpos bajo la burda tela.

Ni un solo momento, hermosura viril
que en montes de carbón, anuncios y ferrocarriles,
soñabas ser un río y dormir como un río
con aquel camarada que pondría en tu pecho
un pequeño dolor de ignorante leopardo.

Ni un solo momento, Adán de sangre, Macho,
hombre solo en el mar, viejo hermoso Walt Whitman,
porque por las azoteas,
agrupados en los bares,
saliendo en racimos de las alcantarillas,
temblando entre las piernas de los chauffeurs
o girando en las plataformas del ajenjo,
los maricas, Walt Whitman, te señalan.

¡También ese! ¡También! Y se despeñan
sobre tu barba luminosa y casta
rubios del norte, negros de la arena,
muchedumbre de gritos y ademanes

Whose perfect voice will sing the truths of wheat?
Who, the terrible dream of your stained anemones?

Not for a moment, Walt Whitman, lovely old man,
have I failed to see your beard full of butterflies,
nor your corduroy shoulders frayed by the moon,
nor your thighs as pure as Apollo's,
nor your voice like a column of ash;
old man, beautiful as the mist,
you moaned like a bird
with its sex pierced by a needle.
Enemy of the satyr,
enemy of the vine,
and lover of bodies beneath rough cloth . . .

Not for a moment, virile beauty,
who among mountains of coal, billboards, and railroads,
dreamed of becoming a river and sleeping like a river
with that comrade who would place in your breast
the small ache of an ignorant leopard.

Not for a moment, Adam of blood, Macho,
man alone at sea, Walt Whitman, lovely old man,
because on penthouse roofs,
gathered at bars,
emerging in bunches from the sewers,
trembling between the legs of chauffeurs,
or spinning on the platforms of absinthe,
the faggots, Walt Whitman, point you out.

He's one, too! That's right! And they land
on your luminous chaste beard,
blonds from the north, blacks from the sands,
crowds of howls and gestures,

como los gatos y como las serpientes,
los maricas, Walt Whitman, los maricas,
turbios de lágrimas, carne para fusta,
bota o mordisco de los domadores.

¡También ese! ¡También! Dedos teñidos
apuntan a la orilla de tu sueño,
cuando el amigo come tu manzana
con un leve sabor de gasolina
y el sol canta por los ombligos
de los muchachos que juegan bajo los puentes.

Pero tú no buscabas los ojos arañados,
ni el pantano oscurísimo donde sumergen a los niños,
ni la saliva helada,
ni las curvas heridas como panza de sapo
que llevan los maricas en coches y en terrazas
mientras la luna los azota por las esquinas del terror.

Tú buscabas un desnudo que fuera como un río.
Toro y sueño que junte la rueda con el alga,
padre de tu agonía, camelia de tu muerte,
y gimiera en las llamas de tu ecuador oculto.

Porque es justo que el hombre no busque su deleite
en la selva de sangre de la mañana próxima.
El cielo tiene playas donde evitar la vida
y hay cuerpos que no deben repetirse en la aurora.

Agonía, agonía, sueño, fermento y sueño.
Este es el mundo, amigo: agonía, agonía.
Los muertos se descomponen bajo el reloj de las ciudades,
la guerra pasa llorando con un millón de ratas grises,
los ricos dan a sus queridas

like cats or like snakes,
the faggots, Walt Whitman, the faggots,
clouded with tears, flesh for the whip,
the boot, or the teeth of the lion tamers.

He's one, too! That's right! Stained fingers
point to the shore of your dream
when a friend eats your apple
with a slight taste of gasoline
and the sun sings in the navels
of boys who play under bridges.

But you didn't look for scratched eyes,
nor the darkest swamp where someone submerges children,
nor frozen saliva,
nor the curves slit open like a toad's belly
that the faggots wear in cars and on terraces
while the moon lashes them on the street corners of terror.

You looked for a nude like a river.
Bull and dream who would join wheel with seaweed,
father of your agony, camellia of your death,
who would groan in the blaze of your hidden equator.

Because it's fitting if a man doesn't look for his delight
in tomorrow morning's jungle of blood.
The sky has shores where life can be avoided
and there are bodies that shouldn't repeat themselves in the dawn.

Agony, agony, dream, ferment and dream.
This is the world, my friend: agony, agony.
The dead decompose beneath the city clocks,
war passes by in tears, followed by a million gray rats,
the rich give their mistresses

pequeños moribundos iluminados,
y la vida no es noble, ni buena, ni sagrada.

Puede el hombre, si quiere, conducir su deseo
por vena de coral o celeste desnudo.
Mañana los amores serán rocas y el Tiempo
una brisa que viene dormida por las ramas.

Por eso no levanto mi voz, viejo Walt Whitman,
contra el niño que escribe
nombre de niña en su almohada,
ni contra el muchacho que se viste de novia
en la oscuridad del ropero,
ni contra los solitarios de los casinos
que beben con asco el agua de la prostitución,
ni contra los hombres de mirada verde
que aman al hombre y queman sus labios en silencio.

Pero sí contra vosotros, maricas de las ciudades,
de carne tumefacta y pensamiento inmundo.
Madres de lodo. Arpías. Enemigos sin sueño
del Amor que reparte coronas de alegría.

Contra vosotros siempre, que dais a los muchachos
gotas de sucia muerte con amargo veneno.
Contra vosotros siempre,
Fairies de Norteamérica,
Pájaros de La Habana,
Jotos de Méjico,
Sarasas de Cádiz,
Apios de Sevilla,
Cancos de Madrid,
Floras de Alicante,
Adelaidas de Portugal.

small illuminated dying things,
and life is neither noble, nor good, nor sacred.

Man is able, if he wishes, to guide his desire
through a vein of coral or a nude as blue as the sky.
Tomorrow, loves will become stones, and Time
a breeze that drowses in the branches.

That's why I don't raise my voice, old Walt Whitman,
against the little boy who writes
the name of a girl on his pillow,
nor against the boy who dresses as a bride
in the darkness of the wardrobe,
nor against the solitary men in casinos
who drink prostitution's water with revulsion,
nor against the men with that green look in their eyes
who love other men and burn their lips in silence.

But yes against you, urban faggots,
tumescent flesh and unclean thoughts.
Mothers of mud. Harpies. Sleepless enemies
of the love that bestows crowns of joy.

Always against you, who give boys
drops of foul death with bitter poison.
Always against you,
Fairies of North America,
Pájaros of Havana,
Jotos of Mexico,
Sarasas of Cádiz,
Apios of Seville,
Cancos of Madrid,
Floras of Alicante,
Adelaidas of Portugal.

¡Maricas de todo el mundo, asesinos de palomas!
Esclavos de la mujer. Perras de sus tocadores.
Abiertos en las plazas con fiebre de abanico
o emboscados en yertos paisajes de cicuta.

¡No haya cuartel! La muerte
mana de vuestros ojos
y agrupa flores grises en la orilla del cieno.
¡No haya cuartel! ¡¡Alerta!!
Que los confundidos, los puros,
los clásicos, los señalados, los suplicantes
os cierren las puertas de la bacanal.

Y tú, bello Walt Whitman, duerme orillas del Hudson
con la barba hacia el polo y las manos abiertas.
Arcilla blanda o nieve, tu lengua está llamando
camaradas que velen tu gacela sin cuerpo.

Duerme: no queda nada.
Una danza de muros agita las praderas
y América se anega de máquinas y llanto.
Quiero que el aire fuerte de la noche más honda
quite flores y letras del arco donde duermes
y un niño negro anuncie a los blancos del oro
la llegada del reino de la espiga.

Faggots of the world, murderers of doves!
Slaves of women. Their bedroom bitches.
Opening in public squares like feverish fans
or ambushed in rigid hemlock landscapes.

No quarter given! Death
spills from your eyes
and gathers gray flowers at the mire's edge.
No quarter given! Attention!!
Let the confused, the pure,
the classical, the celebrated, the supplicants
close the doors of the bacchanal to you.

And you, lovely Walt Whitman, stay asleep on the Hudson's banks
with your beard toward the pole, openhanded.
Soft clay or snow, your tongue calls for
comrades to keep watch over your unbodied gazelle.

Sleep on, nothing remains.
Dancing walls stir the prairies
and America drowns itself in machinery and lament.
I want the powerful air from the deepest night
to blow away flowers and inscriptions from the arch where you sleep,
and a black child to inform the gold-craving whites
that the kingdom of grain has arrived.

IX
HUIDA DE NUEVA YORK
(Dos valses hacia la civilización)

IX
FLIGHT FROM NEW YORK
(Two Waltzes Toward Civilization)

Lorca, *Self-Portrait with Fabulous
Animal in Black*, 1929–31

Pequeño vals vienés

En Viena hay diez muchachas,
un hombro donde solloza la muerte
y un bosque de palomas disecadas.
Hay un fragmento de la mañana
en el museo de la escarcha.
Hay un salón con mil ventanas.

¡Ay, ay, ay, ay!
Toma este vals con la boca cerrada.

Este vals, este vals, este vals,
de sí, de muerte y de coñac
que moja su cola en el mar.

Te quiero, te quiero, te quiero,
con la butaca y el libro muerto,
por el melancólico pasillo,
en el oscuro desván del lirio,
en nuestra cama de la luna
y en la danza que sueña la tortuga.

¡Ay, ay, ay, ay!
Toma este vals de quebrada cintura.

En Viena hay cuatro espejos
donde juegan tu boca y los ecos.
Hay una muerte para piano
que pinta de azul a los muchachos.
Hay mendigos por los tejados.
Hay frescas guirnaldas de llanto.

Little Viennese Waltz

In Vienna there are ten little girls,
a shoulder for death to cry on,
and a forest of dried pigeons.
There is a fragment of the morning
in the museum of winter frost.
There is a thousand-windowed dance hall.

Ay, ay, ay, ay!
Take this close-mouthed waltz.

Little waltz, little waltz, little waltz,
of itself, of death, and of brandy
that dips its tail in the sea.

I love you, I love you, I love you,
with the armchair and the book of death,
down the melancholy hallway,
in the iris's darkened garret,
in our bed that is the moon's bed,
and in that dance the turtle dreams of.

Ay, ay, ay, ay!
Take this broken-waisted waltz.

In Vienna there are four mirrors
in which your mouth and the echoes play.
There is a death for piano
that paints the little boys blue.
There are beggars on the roof.
There are fresh garlands of tears.

¡Ay, ay, ay, ay!
Toma este vals que se muere en mis brazos.

Porque te quiero, te quiero, amor mío,
en el desván donde juegan los niños,
soñando viejas luces de Hungría
por los rumores de la tarde tibia,
viendo ovejas y lirios de nieve
por el silencio oscuro de tu frente.

¡Ay, ay, ay, ay!
Toma este vals del "te quiero siempre."

En Viena bailaré contigo
con un disfraz que tenga
cabeza de río.
¡Mira qué orillas tengo de jacintos!
Dejaré mi boca entre tus piernas,
mi alma en fotografías y azucenas,
y en las ondas oscuras de tu andar
quiero, amor mío, amor mío, dejar,
violín y sepulcro, las cintas del vals.

Ay, ay, ay, ay!
Take this waltz that dies in my arms.

For I love you, I love you, my love,
in the attic where the children play,
dreaming ancient lights of Hungary
through the noise, the balmy afternoon,
seeing sheep and lilies of snow
through the dark silence of your forehead.

Ay, ay, ay, ay!
Take this "I will always love you" waltz.

In Vienna I will dance with you
in a costume with
a river's head.
See how the hyacinths line my banks!
I will leave my mouth between your legs,
my soul in photographs and lilies,
and in the dark wake of your footsteps,
my love, my love, I want to leave
violin and grave, the ribbons of the waltz.

Vals en las ramas

Homenaje a Vicente Aleixandre por su poema "El vals"

Cayó una hoja
y dos
y tres.
Por la luna nadaba un pez.
El agua duerme una hora
y el mar blanco duerme cien.
La dama
estaba muerta en la rama.
La monja
cantaba dentro de la toronja.
La niña
iba por el pino a la piña.
Y el pino
buscaba la plumilla del trino.
Pero el ruiseñor
lloraba sus heridas alrededor.
Y yo también,
porque cayó una hoja
y dos
y tres.
Y una cabeza de cristal
y un violín de papel.
Y la nieve podría con el mundo
si la nieve durmiera un mes,
y las ramas luchaban con el mundo,
una a una,
dos a dos
y tres a tres.
¡Oh duro marfil de carnes invisibles!

Waltz in the Branches

Homage to Vicente Aleixandre for his poem "The Waltz"

One leaf fell,
a second
and a third.
A fish swam on the moon.
The water sleeps for only an hour,
but the white sea sleeps for a hundred.
There was a dead lady
in the branch of the tree.
The nun in her habit
sang inside the pomegranate.
This girl of mine
reached the pinecone from the pine.
And the pine went along
to look for the tiny feather's song.
But the wounded nightingale cried
throughout the countryside.
And I did too,
because the first leaf fell,
a second
and a third.
And a head of crystal
and a paper fiddle.
And the snow could make its way in the world,
if the snow slept for a month,
and the branches wrestled with the world,
one by one,
two by two
and three by three.
Oh, the hard ivory of invisible flesh!

¡Oh golfo sin hormigas del amanecer!
Con el muuu de las ramas,
con el ay de las damas,
con el croo de las ranas
y el gloo amarillo de la miel.
Llegará un torso de sombra
coronado de laurel.
Será el cielo para el viento
duro como una pared
y las ramas desgajadas
se irán bailando con él.
Una a una
alrededor de la luna,
dos a dos
alrededor del sol,
y tres a tres
para que los marfiles se duerman bien.

Oh, the dawn's abyss with no ants!
With the swoosh of the trees,
with the sighs of the ladies,
with the croaking frogs
and the honey's yellow glug.
A shadow's torso will arrive,
wearing a laurel crown.
For the wind, the sky will
be as hard as a wall
and all the downed branches
will go dancing away.
One by one
around the moon,
two by two
around the sun,
and three by three
so the ivory can sleep.

X
EL POETA LLEGA
A LA HABANA

A don Fernando Ortiz

X
THE POET ARRIVES
IN HAVANA

To Don Fernando Ortiz

Lorca, *Couple: Man and Young Sailor*,
1929, Fundación Camilo José Cela

Son de negros en Cuba

Cuando llegue la luna llena iré a Santiago de Cuba,
iré a Santiago
en un coche de agua negra.
Iré a Santiago.
Cantarán los techos de palmera.
Iré a Santiago.
Cuando la palma quiere ser cigüeña,
iré a Santiago.
Y cuando quiere ser medusa el plátano,
iré a Santiago.
Iré a Santiago
con la rubia cabeza de Fonseca.
Iré a Santiago.
Y con el rosa de Romeo y Julieta
iré a Santiago.
Mar de papel y plata de moneda.
Iré a Santiago.
¡Oh Cuba! ¡Oh ritmo de semillas secas!
Iré a Santiago.
¡Oh cintura caliente y gota de madera!
Iré a Santiago.
Arpa de troncos vivos. Caimán. Flor de tabaco.
Iré a Santiago.
Siempre he dicho que yo iría a Santiago
en un coche de agua negra.
Iré a Santiago.
Brisa y alcohol en las ruedas,
iré a Santiago.
Mi coral en la tiniebla,
iré a Santiago.
El mar ahogado en la arena,

Blacks Dancing to Cuban Rhythms

As soon as the full moon rises, I'm going to Santiago, Cuba,
I'm going to Santiago
in a coach of black water.
I'm going to Santiago.
The thatched roofs will sing.
I'm going to Santiago.
When the palm wants to be a stork,
I'm going to Santiago.
When the banana tree wants to be a sea wasp,
I'm going to Santiago.
I'm going to Santiago
with Fonseca's blond head.
I'm going to Santiago.
And with Romeo and Juliet's rose
I'm going to Santiago.
Paper sea and silver coins.
I'm going to Santiago.
Oh, Cuba, oh, rhythm of dried seeds!
I'm going to Santiago.
Oh, fiery waist, oh, drop of wood!
I'm going to Santiago.
Harp of living tree trunks. Crocodile. Tobacco plant in bloom!
I'm going to Santiago.
I always said I'd go to Santiago
in a coach of black water.
I'm going to Santiago.
Wind and rum on the wheels,
I'm going to Santiago.
My coral in the darkness,
I'm going to Santiago.
The sea drowned in the sand,

iré a Santiago.
Calor blanco, fruta muerta,
iré a Santiago.
¡Oh bovino frescor de cañavera!
¡Oh Cuba! ¡Oh curva de suspiro y barro!
Iré a Santiago.

I'm going to Santiago.
White heat, rotting fruit,
I'm going to Santiago.
Oh, the bovine coolness of sugar cane!
Oh, Cuba! Oh, curve of sigh and clay!
I'm going to Santiago.

Lecture: A Poet in New York

TRANSLATED BY CHRISTOPHER MAURER

The untitled autograph manuscript of this lecture in the archives of the Fundación Federico García Lorca, Madrid, the text followed here, does not appear to be a final draft. This lecture was first given in Madrid (March 1932) and repeated in other cities of Spain, Argentina, and Uruguay. In Spain, the lecture was sponsored by the Comité de Cooperación Intelectual, one of the cultural organizations that flourished under the Second Republic. Lorca had delayed publication of *Poet in New York*, preferring to "make it known in the form of a lecture. I will read poems and explain how they came to be; that is, I will read the book and analyze it at the same time" (from an interview of 1933, *OC*, Vol. III, p. 556). I have followed the transcription of Mario Hernández in Federico García Lorca, *Manuscritos neoyorquinos. Poeta en Nueva York y otras hojas y poemas* (Madrid: Tabapress / Fundación Federico García Lorca), pp. 245–65.

Lorca at Columbia, October 1929

Ladies and gentlemen:

Whenever I speak before a large group I always think I must have opened the wrong door. Some friendly hands have given me a shove, and here I am. Half of us wander around completely lost amid drop curtains, painted trees, and tin fountains, and just when we think we have found our room, or our circle of lukewarm sun, we meet an alligator who swallows us alive, or . . . an audience, as I have. And today the only show I can offer you is some bitter, living poetry. Perhaps I can lash its eyes open for you.

I have said "A Poet in New York" when I ought to have said "New York in a Poet." The poet is me, purely and simply: a poet who has neither talent nor genius, but who can sometimes escape through the murky edge of the looking glass of day more quickly than most children. A poet who comes to this auditorium wanting to imagine that he is back in his room, and that you are my friends; for there can be no written poetry unless eyes are enslaved to the obscure line, and no spoken poetry unless ears are docile and friendly. That way, the word can body forth and carry blood to the speaker's lips and sky to the listener's brow.

In any event, one must speak clearly. I have not come here to entertain you: I do not want to, and simply couldn't care less. I am here to fight. Fight hand to hand against a complacent mass, for I am not about to give a lecture but a poetry reading—my flesh, my joy, and my feelings—and I need to defend myself from the huge dragon out there who could eat me alive with three hundred yawns of his three hundred defrauded heads. And that is what I mean by fighting. Now that I have come, and have broken my long poetic silence for a moment,[1] I badly want to communicate with

---

1. Between 1928, the year the *Gypsy Ballads* was published, and 1932, the year he gave this lecture for the first time, Lorca had published only one book, *Poema del cante jondo*, written many years earlier, in 1921.

you. Not to give you honey (I have none), but sand or hemlock or salt water. Hand-to-hand fighting, and it does not matter if I am defeated.

Let us agree that one of man's most beautiful postures is that of St. Sebastian.[2]

Well then, before reading poems aloud to so many people, the first thing one must do is invoke the *duende*. This is the only way all of you will succeed at the hard task of understanding metaphors as soon as they arise, without depending on intelligence or on a critical apparatus, and be able to capture, as fast as it is read, the rhythmic design of the poem.[3] For the quality of a poem can never be judged on just one reading, especially not poems like these which are full of what I call "poetic events"[4] that respond to a purely poetic logic and follow the constructs of emotion and of poetic architecture. Poems like these are not likely to be understood without the cordial help of the *duende*.

But in any case, I, as a man and as a poet, have a great rain cape, a cape that says "It's *your* fault, not mine," a cape which I hang on the shoulders of anyone who comes to me for an explanation. As for me, I can explain nothing; I can only stammer with the fire that burns inside me and the life that has been bestowed on me.

I will not tell you what New York is like *from the outside*, because New York, like Moscow (two antagonistic cities), is the subject of countless de-

2. To both Lorca and his friend Salvador Dalí, St. Sebastian was a complex and contradictory symbol of homoerotic love, artistic objectivity, and the cool conquest of emotion. See Dalí's prose poem "Sant Sebastià"; Lorca's 1926 letter to Jorge Guillén, where he argues that true poetry is "love, effort and *renunciation* (St. Sebastian)"; and his drawings of the saint (*Sebastian's Arrows*, pp. 139–48, 18–19, and illustration between pp. 96 and 97).

3. Parts of this introductory section are missing in the manuscript, and other parts were crossed out at an unknown date. In the earliest readings of the lecture, Lorca may have explained in detail his concept of *duende*. This material was probably removed from the version read in Buenos Aires and Montevideo (1933–34) because by then it had been incorporated into a new lecture entitled "Play and Theory of the *Duende*" (English translation by C. Maurer in *In Search of Duende* [N.Y.: New Directions, 1997]).

4. See Lorca's lecture "Imagination, Inspiration, Evasion" (1928–30), where he gives as an example of a "poetic event" two lines from *The Gypsy Ballads*: "Green, I want you green, / green wind, green boughs" (*Sebastian's Arrows*, p. 159). On the history of the term (which Dalí borrowed from Le Corbusier), see *Sebastian's Arrows*, p. 214.

scriptive books.[5] Nor will I narrate a voyage. What I will give is my lyrical reaction, with sincerity and simplicity: two qualities that come with difficulty to intellectuals, but easily to the poet. To come here, I have had to overcome my poetic modesty.

The two elements the traveler first captures in the big city are extrahuman architecture and furious rhythm. Geometry and anguish. At first glance, the rhythm may be confused with gaiety, but when you look more closely at the mechanism of social life and the painful slavery of both men and machines, you see that it is nothing but a kind of typical, empty anguish that makes even crime and gangs forgivable means of escape.

The sharp edges rise to the sky with no desire for either clouds or glory. The angles and edges of Gothic architecture surge from the hearts of the dead and buried, but these climb coldly skyward with a beauty that has no roots and reveals no longing, stupidly complacent and utterly unable to transcend or conquer, as does spiritual architecture, the perpetually inferior intentions of the architect. There is nothing more poetic and terrible than the skyscrapers' battle with the heavens that cover them. Snow, rain, and mist highlight, drench, or conceal the vast towers, but those towers, hostile to mystery and blind to any sort of play, shear off the rain's tresses and shine their three thousand swords through the soft swan of the fog.

It only takes a few days to realize that this immense world has no roots, and to understand why the seer Edgar Poe had to hug mystery so close to him and let friendly intoxication boil in his veins.[6]

5. In an interview given upon his return to Spain in 1930, Lorca was careful to distinguish himself from travel writers like Georges Duhamel and Paul Morand: "All [Morand's] eyes seem to catch is the universalist element. Almost always, he mocks New York. In a word, Morand is the person invited to have tea in some high room with a fine view. What *I* am—at least, what I'd like to be—is the man who looks up at the great mechanism of the elevated train, with sparks of burning coal falling into my pupils" (*OC*, III, p. 370). Two popular books about New York were Julio Camba's *La ciudad automática (The Automatic City)* and Concha Espina's *Singladuras: Viaje americano (Sea Routes: A Voyage to America)*. Both authors spent time with Lorca in New York. Two others which Lorca read were John Dos Passos's *Manhattan Transfer* and Juan Ramón Jiménez's *Diario de un poeta recién casado (Diary of a Newlywed Poet)*.
6. Lorca's friend Sofía Megwinoff, who had the unenviable task of tutoring him in English, remembers his fascination with "Annabel Lee" and "The Bells": "He was hypnotized by the rhythm. He understood nothing. But he kept time with his hand . . . and hummed . . . and repeated this or that melodious snatch of the poem . . . He imitated my voice and was absorbed by the sound, and there

A solitary wanderer, I evoked my childhood like this. [He reads the poem "1910 (Intermezzo)."]

In the following little poem, I wandered alone, exhausted by the rhythm of the huge electric billboards in Times Square. I fled from the great army of windows, where not a single person has the time to watch a cloud or converse with one of those delicate breezes stubbornly sent by the unanswered sea. Poem: "Cut Down by the Sky" ["After a Walk"].

But you have to go out and conquer the city, and not surrender to lyrical reactions without having rubbed shoulders with the crowds on the avenues and the medley of people from all over the world.[7]

So I take to the streets, and I encounter the blacks. New York is a meeting place for every race in the world, but the Chinese, Armenians, Russians, and Germans remain foreigners. So does everyone except the blacks. There is no doubt but that the blacks exercise great influence in North America, and, no matter what anyone says, they are the most delicate, most spiritual element in that world.[8] Because they believe, because they hope and they sing, and because they have an exquisite, religious indolence that redeems them of all their dangerous, present-day concerns.

If you travel through the Bronx or Brooklyn, where the blond Americans live, you sense a certain deafness: people who love walls that can shut out the stray glance; a clock in every house; a God glimpsed only by the soles of his feet. But in the black neighborhood there is something like a constant exchange of smiles; a deep earth tremor that rusts the nickel columns; the wounded little boy who, if you stare at him long enough, will offer you his apple pie.

was a look of veneration on his face. He brought me the book every day, so that I could read it to him" (Daniel Eisenberg, "Cuatro pesquisas lorquianas," *Thesaurus* [Bogotá] XXX [1975], p. 15; my translation).

7. Struck from the manuscript: "And I take to the streets. And one night in the deathly Armenian neighborhood, I hear these voices behind the wall, talking about a murder" [text of "Murder"].

8. Lorca is echoing (as he did in an interview) the view expressed by Hermann Keyserling in *Amerika, der Aufgang einer neuen Welt* (1930), translated into Spanish as *Norteamérica libertada* (*North America Liberated*) in 1931.

In the morning I would often walk down from the university where I lived, and I was no longer the frightening "Mister Lorca" of my professors, but the strange "sleepy boy"[9] of the waitresses. And, wanting to find out what the blacks were thinking, I watched them dance, for dance is the unique, poignant way they express their feelings and their pain. I wrote this poem: "Standards and Paradise of the Blacks."

But I still hadn't gotten it right. What I had before my eyes was neither an aesthetic norm nor a blue paradise. What I looked at, strolled through, dreamed about, was the most important black city in the world, Harlem, where obscenity has an accent of innocence that turns it into something disturbing and religious. A neighborhood of reddish houses, full of player pianos and radios and cinemas, but with the *mistrust* that characterizes the race. Doors half closed, black-quartz children afraid of the rich people from Park Avenue, gramophones whose song is suddenly interrupted, the wait for the enemies who could come down the East River and point out exactly where the idols are sleeping. I wanted to write *the* poem of the black race in North America, and to show the pain the blacks feel to be black in a contrary world. They are slaves of all the white man's inventions and machines, perpetually afraid that someday they will forget how to light the gas stove or steer the automobile or fasten the starched collar, afraid of driving a fork through an eye. I mean that these inventions are not theirs. The blacks live on borrowed things, and the black fathers have to maintain strict discipline at home lest their women and children adore the gramophone record or eat the tires of automobiles.

And yet any visitor can easily see that, for all their ebullience, they yearn to be a nation, and even though they occasionally make theater out of themselves, in the depths of their spirit they are incorruptible. In one cabaret—Smalls Paradise[10]—whose dancing audience was as black, wet, and grainy as a tin of caviar, I saw a naked dancer shuddering convulsively under an invisible rain of fire. But while everyone shouted as though

9. "Sleepe boy" in the original. The meaning is not quite clear.
10. A black nightclub owned by Edwin and Charles Smalls, located in 1929 on Fifth Avenue in Harlem, less expensive than Connie's Inn and the Cotton Club.

believing her to be possessed by the rhythm, I stared into her eyes and, just for a second, felt her reserve, her remoteness, her inner certainty that she had nothing to do with that admiring audience of Americans and foreigners. All Harlem was like her.

Another time I saw a little black girl riding a bicycle. Nothing could have been more touching: her smoky legs, the balled-up sheep's hair of her head, her cold teeth in the moribund pink of her lips. I stared at her and she stared right back. But my stare was saying: "Little girl, why are you riding a bicycle? Can a little black girl really ride such a thing? Is it yours? Where did you steal it? Do you think you can steer it?" And sure enough, she did a somersault and fell, all legs and wheels, down a gentle slope.

But every day I protested. I protested to see little black children guillotined by stiff collars, in their suits and violent boots, as they emptied the spittoons of cold men who talked like ducks.

I protested to see so much flesh stolen from paradise and managed by Jews with gelid noses and blotting-paper souls, and I protested against the saddest thing of all, that the blacks do not want to be black, that they invent pomades to take away the delicious curl of their hair, and powders that turn their faces gray, and syrups that fill out their waists and wither the succulent persimmon of their lips.

I protested, and the proof of it is this "Ode to the King of Harlem," the spirit of the black race, a cry of encouragement to those who tremble and search, cautiously and clumsily, for the flesh of the white woman. [Poem.]

And yet the truly savage and frenetic part of New York is not Harlem. In Harlem there is human warmth and the noise of children, and there are homes and grass, and sorrow finds consolation and the wound finds its sweet bandage.

The terrible, cold, cruel part is Wall Street. Rivers of gold flow there from all over the earth, and death comes with it. There, as nowhere else, you feel a total absence of the spirit: herds of men who cannot count past three, herds more who cannot get past six, scorn for pure science and demoniacal respect for the present. And the terrible thing is that the crowd that fills this street believes that the world will always be the same, and that it is their duty to keep that huge machine running, day and night, forever. This is what comes of a Protestant morality that I, as a (thank God) typical Spaniard, found unnerving.

I was lucky enough to see with my own eyes the recent stock-market crash, where they lost several billion dollars, a rabble of dead money that went sliding off into the sea. Never as then, amid suicides, hysteria, and groups of fainting people, have I felt the sensation of real death, death without hope, death that is nothing but rottenness, for the spectacle was terrifying but devoid of greatness. And I, who come from a country where, as the great father Unamuno said, "at night the earth climbs to the sky,"[11] I felt something like a divine urge to bombard that whole canyon of shadow, where ambulances collected suicides whose hands were full of rings.

That is why I situated this "Dance of Death" in Wall Street. The typical African mask, death which is truly dead, without angels or "Resurrexit"; death totally alien to the spirit, barbarous and primitive as the United States, a country which has never fought, and never will fight, for heaven.[12] [Poem.]

And the crowd! No one can imagine just what a New York crowd is like, except perhaps Walt Whitman, who searched it for solitudes, and T. S. Eliot, who squeezes the crowd like a lemon in his poem, extracting wounds, poets, wet hats, and river shades.[13]

But when, in addition, that crowd is drunk, we have one of the most intense spectacles that life can offer.

---

11. From Miguel de Unamuno, "En un cementerio de lugar castellano" ("In a Castilian Country Cemetery"), in *Andanzas y visiones españolas*, 1922: "When the sun has slowly come to earth / and the land climbs to the sky, / at the hour of remembrance, / and bells are tolling for prayers and rest, / the rough-hewn stone cross / atop your mud walls / remains, watching like a sleepless guardian / over the dormant countryside" *(Antología poética* [Madrid: Espasa-Calpe, 1968], p. 69).
12. An allusion to the doctrine of predestination. After the word "Resurrexit" in the manuscript, Lorca deleted: "death of Protestants who think they do not need to fight for heaven, for all is done and will always be the same."
13. Here, and in his remarks on Coney Island, Lorca seems to be remembering the third section ("The Fire Sermon") of *The Waste Land:* "The river bears no empty bottles, sandwich papers, / Silk handkerchiefs, cardboard boxes, cigarette ends / Or other testimony of summer nights . . ." (T. S. Eliot, *The Complete Poems and Plays 1909–1950* [New York: Harcourt, Brace, 1952], p. 42).

Coney Island is a great fair attended on Sundays in the summer by more than a million people. They drink, shout, eat, wallow, and leave the ocean strewn with newspapers and the streets covered with tin cans, cigarette butts, bites of food, and shoes with broken heels. On its way home from the fair, the crowd sings and vomits in groups of a hundred over the railings of the boardwalk. In groups of a thousand it urinates in the corners, on abandoned boats, or on the monument to Garibaldi or to the unknown soldier.

You cannot imagine the loneliness a Spaniard feels there, especially an Andalusian. If you fall they will trample you, and if you slip into the water they will bury you under their lunch wrappers.

The rumble of that terrible multitude fills the whole Sunday of New York, pounding the hollow pavements with the rhythm of a stampede. [He reads "Landscape of a Vomiting Multitude."]

The solitude of the poems I wrote about the crowd rhymes with others of the same style, which I have no time to read, for instance the "Brooklyn Bridge Nocturne" and "Nightfall at Battery Place," where sailors and cheap women, soldiers and policemen dance on the tired sea, a pasture for siren cows, a promenade for bells and bellowing buoys.

The month of August is here. New York is leveled by heat, in the style of Écija,[14] and I must leave for the country.[15]

Green lake, landscape of hemlocks. Suddenly, in the forest, a lost distaff. A little girl, Mary, who eats maple syrup, and a little boy, Stanton, who plays the jew's-harp, keep me company and patiently teach me the list of American Presidents. When we get to the great Lincoln, they give him a military salute. Stanton's father owns four blind horses that he bought in the village of Eden Mills.[16] The mother almost always has a fever. I run, I drink good water, and my mood sweetens among the hemlock trees and my little friends. They introduce me to the Tyler girls, penniless descen-

---

14. A proverbially hot town ("The Frying Pan of Andalusia") in the province of Seville.
15. In the following paragraph Lorca conflates two different summer trips: his visit to Ángel and Amelia del Río in Bushnellsville, New York, and his stay with Philip Cummings in Eden Mills, Vermont.
16. *One* blind horse, according to Stanton Hogan (Eisenberg, "Cuatro pesquisas," p. 12).

dants of an old President, who live in a cabin, take photographs which they title "Exquisite Silence,"[17] and play, on an incredible spinet, songs from the heroic age of Washington. They are old and very tiny and they wear trousers so that the brambles won't scratch them, but they have beautiful white hair and they hold hands and listen to me improvise some songs just for them at the spinet. Sometimes they invite me to dinner and give me nothing but tea and a few pieces of cheese, but they assure me that the teapot is genuine china and that there is jasmine in the tea.[18] At the end of August they take me to their cabin and say, "Haven't you noticed? Autumn is almost here." Sure enough, on the tables and spinet and all around the portrait of Tyler were the yellowest, reddest, most orange maple and grape leaves I had ever seen.

In such surroundings, of course, my poetry took on the tone of the forest. Tired of New York and yearning for the least significant, poorest living things, I wrote an insectary, which I cannot read to you in full, but where I begin by asking help from the Virgin, the Ave Maria Stella of those delightful Catholic folk. I wanted to sing to the insects who spend their lives flying and praising Our Lord with their little instruments.

THE POET PRAYS TO THE VIRGIN FOR HELP

I pray to the Divine Mother of God,
Heavenly Queen of all living things,

---

17. A snapshot of a winter scene, entitled "Exquisite Silence," does indeed form part of an album in the Lorca archive, presented to the poet by the Tyler sisters.

18. Philip Cummings (Federico's host in Eden Mills, Vermont) writes: "The two Miss Tylers [Elizabeth and Dorothea], who were splendid women, depressed school teachers who had ended their careers and were planning to rebuild a derelict farm, may or may not (I suspect not . . .) have been President Tyler's relatives in a diluted way. Both are dead and they lost the farm because it could not be saved by their pitiful efforts . . . In front of their property they rebuilt with great effort the old stone wall which they called the Chinese Wall. Federico and I added many a stone to it and heaved others into line. Then we would sit on the wobbly porch and drink pots of tea and Federico said, 'Vamos a probar otra desesperación de té' [Now we'll have another 'desperation' of tea]" (Letter to C. Maurer, Nov. 12, 1985). See also Cummings's diary, "August in Eden," in García Lorca, *Songs*, tr. Philip Cummings, ed. Daniel Eisenberg (Pittsburgh: Duquesne University Press, 1976), pp. 125–66.

that she grant me the pure light of the little animals
that have a single letter in their vocabulary.
Animals without souls. Simple shapes.
Far from the cat's despicable knowledge.
Far from the owl's fictitious profundity.
Far from the horse's sculptural wisdom.
Creatures that love without eyes,
with a single sense of infinity's waves,
and that gather in great piles
to be eaten by the birds.
Grant me the single dimension
that little flat animals have
so that I can tell of things covered with earth
beneath the hard innocence of the shoe.
No one weeps because he understands
the millions of tiny deaths at the marketplace,
the Chinese multitude of headless onions,
and that great yellow sun of old, flattened fish.
You, Mother, forever to be feared. Whale of all the skies,
You Mother, forever joking. Neighbor of the borrowed parsley.
You know that to speak of the world,
I must understand its slightest flesh.[19]

But one day little Mary fell into a well and drowned. It would not be right
to tell you of the deep sorrow, the true despair I felt that day. I will leave
that to the trees and the walls that saw me.[20] At once I thought of that

19. The text found in Hernández, pp. 224–25, is translated here by Simon and White. For the
Virgin's reply, see Hernández, p. 227. Simon and White translate as follows: "The Holy Virgin
Replies: But I pluck out my eyes of the giraffe. / And I replace them with the crocodile's eyes. /
Because I am the Virgin Mary. / The flies see a black cloud of pepper. / But they are not the
Virgin Mary. / I watch the crimes of the leaves, / the stinging pride of the wasps, / the indifferent
mule driven crazy by the double moon / and the stable where the planet eats all its tiny offspring. /
Because I am the Virgin Mary. // Solitude lives stuck in the mud . . ." A more complete manuscript
of the poem was apparently given by Lorca to the French Hispanist Mathilde Pomès, but has not
been published.
20. The poet is speaking tongue in cheek. According to Ángel del Río, the death of Mary was a

other little girl, from Granada,[21] whom I saw taken out of a cistern, her little hands entwined in the gaffs, her head knocking against the side, and the two girls, Mary and the other one, became the same child, who cried and cried, unable to leave the circle of the well, in the unmoving water that never reaches the sea. ["Little Girl Drowned in the Well (Granada and Newburgh)."]

With the little girl dead, I could stay in the house no longer. Stanton was sadly eating the syrup his sister had left him, and the divine Miss Tylers were madly taking pictures of the autumn woods to give me as presents.

I went down to the lake, and the silent water, the cuckoo, etc., etc., made it impossible for me to sit. Every way that I stood or sat made me feel like a Romantic lithograph below which was written, "Federico lets his thoughts wander."[22] But at last a splendid line of Garcilaso put an end to that statuesque obsession. The line of Garcilaso:

Nuestro ganado pace, el viento espira
Our flocks graze, the wind sends forth its breath[23]

And this "Double Poem of Lake Eden Mills" was born. [He reads.]

Summer vacation is over, for "Saturn stops the trains,"[24] and I have to

product of his "inventive fancy." See del Río, "Fotos de F.G.L. en Norteamérica (1929)," *Papeles de Son Armadans* XLII, no. cxxiv, p. 101; and Eisenberg, "Cuatro pesquisas," pp. 11–12.

21. Lorca may be thinking of the imaginary drowned child mentioned in two poems of his *Diván del Tamarit* (1931–35). See "Ghazal of the Dead Child" and "Qasida of One Wounded by Water" in Federico García Lorca, *Collected Poems*, ed. C. Maurer (Farrar, Straus and Giroux, revised edition, 2002), pp. 776–79 and 786–87. The theme recurs in the "Noiturnio do adoescente morto" in *Seis poemas galegos* (*Collected Poems*, pp. 806–807).

22. Lorca describes his state of mind in a letter to Ángel del Río from Eden Mills: "It never stops raining. This family is very nice, full of gentle charm, but the woods and lake immerse me in an almost unbearable state of poetic desperation. I write all day and at night I feel drained . . . Now night is falling. The oil lamps have been lit and my whole childhood comes back to me, wrapped in a glory of poppies and grainfields. Among the ferns I've found a spinning wheel covered with spiders and in the lake not one frog sings" (*Selected Letters*, tr. David Gershator [New York: New Directions, 1983], p. 150).

23. Garcilaso, Eclogue II, verse 1146.

24. See "Double Poem of Lake Eden," p. 79. The meaning is unclear.

get back to New York. The drowned girl, Stanton the Little Sugar-Eater, and the trouser-wearing sisters stay with me for a long time. The train races along the Canadian frontier, and I feel unhappy and miss my little friends. The girl withdraws into the well, in a host of green angels, and on the boy's chest the cruel star of the North American police begins to grow, like saltpeter on a damp wall.

And then once again the frenzied rhythm of New York. But it no longer surprises me. I know the mechanism of the streets and talk to people and penetrate a bit deeper into social life. And I denounce it. For I have come from the countryside and do not believe that man is the most important thing in the world. ["New York (Office and Denunciation)."]

Time is passing, and this is not the time to read more poems. We have to leave New York. I won't read the poems about Christmas or the poems about the port.[25] Someday you will read them in the book, if you are interested.

Time is passing, and I am already on the ship taking me away from the howling city toward the beautiful Antilles. My first impression, that that world has no roots, stays with me . . .

Because if the wheel forgets its formula,
it will sing naked with herds of horses;
and if a flame burns the frozen blueprints,
the sky will have to flee before the tumult of windows.[26]

Edges and rhythm, form and anguish, the sky is swallowing them all. No longer does tower battle cloud, no longer do swarms of windows devour more than half the night. Flying fish weave moist garlands, and the sky, like that terrible big blue woman of Picasso, rushes over the sea with open arms.

The sky has conquered the skyscrapers, and from a distance New York's architecture seems prodigious and, no matter what was intended,

25. It is uncertain which poems "about the port" Lorca is referring to.
26. From "Dance of Death."

moves one as much as a spectacle of nature, a mountain, or a desert. The Chrysler Building defends itself from the sun with its huge silver beak, and bridges, ships, railways, and men seem deafened and chained: chained by a cruel economic system whose throat must soon be cut, and deafened by excessive discipline and because they lack a sufficient dose of madness.

At any rate, I was leaving New York with a certain sadness and with profound admiration. I was leaving many friends there, and it had given me the most useful experience of my life. I must thank it for many things, especially for the holograph blues and the British stamp greens given me by the New Jersey shoreline as I strolled with Anita the Portuguese Indian and Sofía Megwinoff the Russian Puerto Rican, and for that divine aquarium and that zoo[27] where I felt like a child and remembered all the children in the world.

But the ship is getting farther away, and we are beginning to come to palm trees and cinnamon, the perfume of the America with roots, God's America, Spanish America.[28]

But what is this? Is it Spain again? Universal Andalusia? It is the yellow of Cádiz, but a shade brighter; the rosiness of Seville, but more like carmine; the green of Granada, but slightly phosphorescent like a fish.

Havana rises up amid cane fields and the noise of maracas, cornets, bells and marimbas. And who should come to welcome me at the port but the dark Trinidad of my childhood, who used to stroll "along the pier of Havana."[29]

And the blacks are there, with rhythms I discover are typical of the great Andalusian people—blacks without tragedy who roll their eyes and say, "We are Latins."

27. The Aquarium in Battery Park (since demolished) and the Bronx Zoo.
28. Lorca seems to be remembering the Nicaraguan poet Rubén Darío, whose ode "To Roosevelt" celebrates "la América católica, la América española." The poem ends on these words: "Y, pues contáis con todo, falta una cosa: ¡Dios!" ("And, as you have everything, only one thing is missing: God!").
29. From a Spanish popular song: "Por el muelle de la Habana, / paseaba una mañana / la morena Trinidad" ("Along the pier of Havana one morning, dark Trinidad was strolling").

Against three great horizontal lines—the line of the cane fields, that of the terraces, and that of the palm trees—a thousand blacks, their cheeks dyed orange, as though running a fever of 150 degrees, dance this *son*[30] which I composed and which comes to us like a breeze from the island: ["Blacks Dancing to Cuban Rhythms"].

30. An Afro-Hispanic dance in syncopated rhythm, antecedent to today's salsa, which originated in Santiago de Cuba (Oriente province) toward the end of the eighteenth century. Lorca borrowed his refrain from a popular *son*. His friend the poet Nicolás Guillén (1902–89) published eight poems inspired by the *son (Motivos de son)* in Havana in April 1930. It was Guillén who had delighted Lorca with the words "We are Latins . . ."

The Poet Writes to His Family from New York and Havana

TRANSLATED BY CHRISTOPHER MAURER

The Spanish text followed here is from FGL, *Epistolario completo*, pp. 614–88. I have enriched the notes from previous editions of this book with new information presented in Christopher Maurer and Andrew A. Anderson, *Federico García Lorca en Nueva York y La Habana: Cartas y recuerdos* (Barcelona: Galaxia Gutenberg, in press).

Lorca's first letter home from New York, June 28, 1929

New York, Friday the 28th [of June 1929]

Dearest family,

Well, here I am in New York, after a delightful voyage, an easy one thanks to Don Fernando,[1] who was so kind to me that everyone took him for my father. One cannot imagine a more affectionate, solicitous person, and you should all feel grateful to him.

I feel content, full of joy, and my one worry is getting news from you soon.

Paris impressed me very much, London even more, and now New York has given me the knock-out punch.

I would have to write two hundred pages to give you all my impressions.

The sea voyage was marvelous.[2] The liner was 46,567 tons, and the ocean was completely calm for all six days. They were like six days of convalescence and I have gotten a real tan: as black as blackest Africa. Life aboard a ship is quite gay, and people confide in each other right away. I had a little five-year-old friend, a lovely boy from Hungary who was going to America to meet his father for the first time (the father had left before he was born). He played with me, and we grew so close that he broke into tears when we said goodbye, and, needless to say, so did I. This is the subject

---

1. Fernando de los Ríos Urruti (1879–1949), who had been one of Garcia Lorca's professors in the Faculty of Law of the University of Granada, later Minister of Education in the Second Republic, was on his way to Columbia University and Puerto Rico to give a series of lectures on sixteenth-century political thought. The poet's close association with the socialist De los Ríos, whose daughter Laura married Federico's brother Francisco decades later, is often cited as one of the reasons for the poet's assassination outside Granada in 1936.

2. García Lorca had arrived three days earlier on the aging White Star liner *Olympic*, sister ship of the *Titanic*. Before embarking in Southampton, Lorca and Fernando de los Ríos had spent a few days sightseeing and visiting friends in Paris and London (Daniel Eisenberg, "A Chronology of Lorca's Visit to New York and Cuba," *Kentucky Romance Quarterly* XXIV [1977], p. 235).

of my first poem, this child whom I will never see again, this rose of Hungary who disappears into the belly of New York, seeking his fortune; life will be cruel or kind to him, and I will be but a remote memory, connected with the rhythm of the huge ship and the ocean.[3]

On arriving in New York, one feels overwhelmed, but not frightened. I found it uplifting to see how man can use science and technology to make something as impressive as a spectacle of nature. It is incredible. The port and the lights of the skyscrapers, easily confused with the stars, the millions of other lights, and the rivers of automobiles are a sight like no other on earth. Paris and London are two tiny villages compared with this vibrant, maddening Babel.

When the ship pulled in, I had a great surprise. A group of Spaniards was there waiting for us: Ángel del Río,[4] the professor Federico Onís, the poet León Felipe,[5] a handful of journalists, the managing editor of *La Prensa*,[6] and . . . brace yourselves! . . . MAROTO!! Maroto, who went crazy hugging and even kissing me.[7] He has just arrived from Mexico, and is earning a lot of money as a painter and commercial artist.

They have been extremely good to me, as has the entire Spanish colony. I can now see what a good thing it is to have become a bit famous: all doors are opened, and everyone treats you with distinction.

Both Federico Onís and his wife have shown me great affection. They are admirers of mine, two *lorquistas* (as they say).

Onís is a professor at Columbia, and it was he who arranged what

---

3. Although the child and his mother can be identified (five-year-old Francis Weisz was being taken by his mother Helena to his father, Joseph Weisz, who lived in New York), no such poem has ever been found.

4. Ángel del Río (1901–62), an excellent literary critic and historian, Federico's closest friend in New York, was a recently appointed professor in Columbia's Department of Spanish and Portuguese, directed by the redoubtable Federico de Onís Sanchez (1885–1966), a disciple of Miguel de Unamuno who had emigrated to New York in 1916.

5. The Spanish poet León Felipe Camino (1884–1968), then teaching at Cornell, made several trips to New York during Lorca's stay, and dedicated a poem to him in his 1929 book *Versos y oraciones del caminante II (Verses and Prayers of the Wayfarer II)*.

6. José Camprubí Aymar (1879–1943), brother-in-law of the Spanish poet Juan Ramón Jiménez.

7. Gabriel García Maroto (1889–1969), Spanish printer, painter, and illustrator, who had published Lorca's first book of poetry (*Libro de poemas*) eight years earlier.

pleases me most: I am now a student at Columbia University and I live in a dormitory here, surrounded by American students.

Federico Onís did not want me to live at the International House because, he said, everyone there is a foreigner, and there are so many South Americans that I would always be speaking Spanish. "We must surround the poet with English speakers," he said, "so that he will have to make an effort."

It is difficult to become a student at the university of New York [*sic*], but because Don Fernando teaches here and Onís is one of its most renowned professors, they have managed to get me in.

The university is marvelous. It is located on the bank of the Hudson River, in the heart of the city, on the island of Manhattan, the best part, and is very close to the great avenues. And yet it is delightfully quiet. My room is on the ninth floor,[8] and it overlooks the playing fields, with their green grass and statues.

To one side, below the windows of the rooms just across the hall, is Broadway, the immense boulevard which runs from one end of New York to the other.

It would be foolish to even try to describe the immensity of the skyscrapers and the traffic. Everything I could say would fall short. All Granada would fit into three of these buildings. Just one of these little "houses" could hold thirty thousand people or so.

I will write and give you my impressions.

But meanwhile you should know that my room is very inexpensive and very lovely, with a splendid view; that I am enrolled in an English language and literature class; and that I feel like working. Know also that I will never be able to thank you for all you have done for me, but that I will repay you with a work and a way of life that will make you proud and happy. But no doubt I am lucky with people. I feel as though I had been here all my life, and I haven't had any problems whatsoever in this sprawling Babel.

In fact, once you get over your first impressions and first sense of fright,

8. Lorca occupied room 617, Furnald Hall.

it is very easy to get around New York: much easier than Paris and infinitely easier than London, for all the streets are numbered, and the entire city is mathematically laid out in blocks, the only way to organize the chaos and motion. In a word, I feel well adjusted. New York is an extremely gay, friendly place. The people are naïve and charming. I feel good here, better than in Paris, which I found a bit old and a bit rotten.

But, as I started to say, what happens to *me* is always unusual.

Last night I went to the heart of immense Broadway with León Felipe, Maroto, and a certain Mr. Flores, who is the editor of an English-language magazine that deals with Spanish things.[9] Broadway at night was breathtaking: the towering skyscrapers are covered with brightly colored illuminated signs that blink and change with the most unheard-of, marvelous rhythms. Streams of blues and greens and yellows and reds changing and leaping into the sky, higher than the moon, blinking on and off with the names of banks and hotels and automobiles and film companies. The motley crowd of bright sweaters and bold scarves rising and falling in five or six different streams, the horns of the cars together with the shouting and the music from the radios, and brightly lit airplanes passing overhead with ads for hats, clothes, and toothpaste, changing their letters and playing great trumpets and bells. It is a magnificent, moving spectacle put on by the boldest, most modern city in the world.

Suddenly, when I was most absorbed and enthralled by all this, I hear a loud voice from the window of a large restaurant, calling "Fede*rr*ico! Fede*rr*ico!" and I see a boy in a red silk shirt leap out the window to the street, almost breaking his leg, and he comes up and hugs me. It was the Englishman Colin Hackforth, who visited me in Granada and became a

9. Ángel Flores (1900–92), literary critic, editor of numerous anthologies of Spanish literature and translator of T. S. Eliot's *The Waste Land* (*Tierra baldía* [Barcelona: Editorial Cervantes, 1930]), a book which Lorca probably saw in manuscript in New York. Flores was also director of the Hispano and American Alliance (Forty-second Street and Fifth Avenue), where Lorca spent some of his free time, and editor of its short-lived magazine *Alhambra*. It was Flores who took Lorca to Columbia Heights, Brooklyn, to introduce him to the American poet Hart Crane. See B. Bussell Thompson and J. K. Walsh, "Un encuentro de Lorca y Hart Crane en Nueva York," *Ínsula* XLI, no. 479 (Oct. 1986), p. 1, and the poem by Philip Levine, "On the Meeting of García Lorca and Hart Crane."

close friend.[10] I felt very happy, for you can imagine how difficult and how unheard-of it is for two people to meet like this in New York. It is as unusual as two fishes meeting in the middle of the ocean.

Maroto was astonished. "The same as ever. This could only happen to you." I was truly lucky, for Colin is a writer, a very good one, and he will be the best possible English teacher. He is going to come to the university and we will translate things together every day at six, after I finish my work, and he his. In fact, last night he was already pointing things out to me in English, and he taught me a great number of words. Between him and Onís, who will introduce me to some American girls, I will be forced to make some progress with my English, and Colin is also going to try to find me a French person to converse with.

Here's another strange thing. Do you remember my telling you about a young American poet who wrote a poem to me in the Residencia after hearing me play the piano?[11] I met him again on the train from Madrid to Paris, and he invited me to spend the month of August (the hottest month here) in his house in Canada. His father is a railroad broker, and he will send me the tickets free.[12] Don Fernando told me not to miss this opportunity to visit one of the most beautiful places in North America; to get there, one passes by Niagara Falls. He is a fine boy; he has studied at Columbia and Onís knows him. Last year, as an exercise in his Spanish class, he translated two of the *Gypsy Ballads* into English. In other words, he knows me and hasn't invited me for just any old reason. I've accepted and,

10. Campbell Hackforth-Jones (1905–88) met García Lorca in Granada during the Christmas holidays of 1926–27. The poet attempted to contact him when he passed through London on the way to New York but, having graduated from Oxford, Hackforth-Jones was in New York serving an apprenticeship in a brokerage firm on Wall Street.
11. Philip H. Cummings (1906–91), writer and teacher whom García Lorca had met at the Residencia de Estudiantes, Madrid, in July 1928. Cummings remembers the train ride from Madrid to Paris: "We stretched out and he [Lorca] talked for hours to the rhythmic click of the wheels over the rails, of what life was for and that man was always playing hide and seek with death . . . 'Felipe, life is laughter, amid a rosary of deaths; it is to look beyond the braying man to the love in the heart of the people. It is being the wind and ruffling the waters of a brook. It is coming from nowhere and going to nowhere and being everywhere with many tears around you.'" See García Lorca, *Songs*, pp. 178–79.
12. In reality, Harry F. Cummings (d. 1934) was a real estate and insurance agent in Hardwick, Vermont (Patricia C. Billingsley, "Philip H. Cummings, a Work in Progress," at www.philipcummings.net/, accessed July 24, 2012).

God willing, if all goes as planned, I'll spend the month of August in Canada.

American customs are nothing like Spanish ones. Here they invite you places at the drop of a hat.

Before I forget, here is my address:

Mister Federico G. Lorca (like that)
Furnald Hall
Columbia University
New York City
E.S.A. [*sic*]

I hope you will write me often. I will do so, too, and (as you can see from this one) I'll write you long letters. But my letters would have to be even longer for me to give you all my impressions and prove how often I remember you.

But the person I can't get out of my head is Paco. Please send me a cablegram as soon as you know the results of his exams.[13] And, needless to say, you shouldn't worry. For even if he fails, he will triumph next year.

Please don't forget this: it's important to me.

I feel perfectly fine, and there is plenty to eat. I am surrounded by friends, by people who take an interest in me. I have tried to be nice to them and, of course, have managed to do so.

Mother must go to Lanjarón,[14] and Father, too. It will be very good for him, and if you don't go, you'll both have an attack of trigeminal neuralgia.

I was greatly saddened by Franco's accident.[15] Such things are doubly sad from afar. He was a very brave man who came to an unfortunate end, but one full of greatness and heroism.

---

13. Federico's younger brother, Francisco (1902–76), who would later write a memoir about Federico's life and work (*In the Green Morning: Memories of Federico*) was in Madrid studying for the qualifying exams for the Spanish diplomatic corps.
14. A spa in the mountainous Alpujarras region of Granada which Lorca often visited with his family. "Strange Berber Andalusia," he calls it in a letter, "where one can understand the wounds of St. Roque, tears of blood, and the taste for the buried knife" (*Epistolario completo*, p. 510).
15. The Spanish aviator Ramón Franco Bahamonde (1856–1938), brother of Francisco Franco, was presumed dead after his plane went down during a transatlantic flight to New York. Two days after this letter was written, he was found alive, together with his crew.

The weather is delightful today. It is beginning to rain, and a cool breeze is riffling the trees and the vaporous shirts of the boys playing tennis.

Lots of hugs and kisses.

You are probably in the Huerta[16] listening to the tinkling bells from the Seminary and the distant bells of the Cathedral. I am listening to the sirens and the murmur of New York.

Give my best to the whole family, and don't forget anyone: Aunt Isabel, Aunt Matilde, Clotilde,[17] Mama-yaya, the girls, and all our friends. All my love.

Federico

Write soon!
Farewell.

June 6 [sic for July 6, 1929]—New York

Dear family:

You have probably already received my first letter, in which I gave you my impressions of New York and my address in this huge city.

I didn't want Father's birthday to slip by without sending him a big hug and warmest birthday greetings.

I have already begun my English classes at the university. I take them in the same building I live in,[1] and the dining hall is also there, so I do everything without any need to go outside and work up a sweat. My room is lovely, and there is always a breeze. It's the highest point in the city, alongside the river, and it is quite cool.

I still haven't felt the heat. It is exactly the same temperature here as it is in Granada, and my room and the whole campus are as cool as a

16. The Huerta de San Vicente, the Lorca family's country house, then on the outskirts of Granada.
17. Matilde García Rodríguez (1865–1955) and her sister Isabel (1876–1973), paternal aunts, and Clotilde García Picossi (1892–1987), the poet's cousin. Mama-yaya was Eduarda Miranda Lorca, a distant cousin of Lorca's mother whom the family employed as a seamstress.
1. Lorca had enrolled in "English for Beginners," taught by Amy I. Shaw and given in room 503, Journalism Building, "a course for educated foreigners who have practically no knowledge of spoken English" (Eisenberg, "Cuatro pesquisas," p. 1).

garden. What is truly dreadful in summer is to go downtown and mingle with the throngs of autos and people, but you have to admit that it is equally dreadful to cross the Embovedado[2] on a July afternoon. Night at Columbia is delightful, here beside the river, and in fact everywhere else in the city.

I think I have a certain talent for English. We'll see!

My friends here continue to be extraordinarily kind to me, and I haven't had a single bad moment. The poet León Felipe, a professor at Cornell University, and his wife[3] have been like parents, and have been keeping me safe and sound. Yesterday I had a visit from the son of the Duke of Tovar, who is studying at Columbia, and who offered to do whatever he could for me. A very nice boy, a believer in democracy, and a great admirer of the United States.[4] I went to a party for some Mexican painters and poets—people I knew of but had never met—and guess who else was there? Miss Adams, the girl I saw so much of in Granada.[5] It's a small, small world! Speaking of strange coincidences, in England I ran into the girl who was staying at Don Fernando's house. She asked me to remember her to you.[6]

These first few days I have been getting to know New York. Last Sunday I went to Coney Island, an island at the mouth of the Hudson, an amusement park with arcades and all sorts of extraordinary things. Like everything else here, it is monstrously huge. According to the newspapers, there were more than a million visitors that day.[7] I can't even begin to de-

---

2. An urban space not far from the Lorca house in Granada, created by the paving-over (which Lorca considered an atrocity) of the Darro River.

3. Berta Gamboa (1888–1957), Mexican teacher and translator.

4. Rafael de Figueroa y Bermejillo, Torres y Martínez-Negrete (1903–82), son of Rodrigo de Figueroa y Torres, third Duke of Tovar, was studying engineering at Columbia and lived in Lorca's dormitory (John Jay Hall) during the fall term, 1929–30.

5. Mildred Adams Kenyon (1894–1979), journalist, translator of Ortega y Gasset, and later author of *García Lorca: Playwright and Poet* (New York: George Braziller, 1977), had met Lorca in Granada in April 1928.

6. The British Hispanist Helen Grant (1903–92), who was then studying Spanish and French at Oxford. Gibson, p. 610.

7. Lorca probably visited Coney Island not on a Sunday but on the Fourth of July, 1929: according to the next day's *New York Times*, there were over a million persons there.

scribe the color and movement on the beach, with throngs of twenty and thirty thousand people. The amusement park is truly a child's dream. There are incredible roller coasters, tunnels of love, music, freak shows, dance halls, wild animals, Ferris wheels and all sorts of rides, the world's fattest women,[8] a four-eyed man, etc. etc., and thousands of stalls selling a fantastic variety of ice cream, hot dogs, French fries, little buns, and candies. The crowd rolls through the island with the sweaty, salty murmur of the sea: a crowd of Jews, blacks, Japanese, Chinese, mulattoes, and blond-haired Yankees.

It is an amazing sight, but it is simply *too much*, and one visit is enough. The people drawn to this island of games are the real *people* of New York, the salt of the earth. One hardly ever sees an automobile: you get there on the subway and on paddle boats, which is how I myself arrived, floating down the river under a lovely blue Sevillian sky.

When night came, all the lights were lit, and it was like a childhood dream—the big golden Ferris wheels, the brilliant towers of wood and glass, with the music and the sound of the rides in the background.

My friends did their best to get me to speak English, and made me ask for things. You wouldn't believe what I went through, but I did very well, to everyone's great amusement.

I haven't yet gotten a letter from you, and you can imagine how I would love to receive one. I hope you will all write me, and that your letters will be long and unhurried, and that the girls will write, too, so I will get news of everyone. As you can see, I'm writing you at greater length than I ever have, and I will continue to do so, so that each seven or eight days you will have news from me.

To give you some idea of the size of Columbia University, let me say that close to 16,000 students have enrolled in the summer session, which

---

8. Among them Etta, whom the *Times* describes as "400 pounds of pulchritude," corollary of "the fat lady" who appears in Lorca's "Landscape of a Vomiting Multitude." In 1929, Coney Island, which was turning "from a tinsel town to a substantial suburb of a great city," complained of "a growing scarcity of dog-faced men, mermaids and many legged livestock . . . On the entire Island this Summer there are only three pairs of Siamese twins and but two editions of the strongest man in the world" ("Coney Enters Its Steel Age," *The New York Times*, June 16, 1929, IX, p. 2).

lasts until August 18.[9] This place is like a fairgrounds. The girls are extremely pretty, a little wild in the way they dress, but full of charm and personality. I'm going to practice my English with one of them, but I want to make sure I get the prettiest, and not commit myself without seeing her first. It would be terrible to end up with some chatterbox who wouldn't teach me anything, and then—well, what a nuisance to get rid of her! But seriously, this is the only way to learn English. Having a conversation partner is useful, for that way one can avoid pure grammar and learn the colloquial expressions for things.

I hope you haven't forgotten my address:

> Mister Federico G. Lorca
> Furnald Hall
> Columbia University
> New York City
> E.S.A. [*sic*]

No harm in repeating it, just in case you forgot or my letter was lost.

I long for news from Paquito. I wrote him at the Residencia de Estudiantes and he must have received my letter by now.

You can't imagine how I miss you all, and I hope you are well. I'm fine, in fact I am rather happy. Would you send me your photos—of Father, Mother, and the girls—to put in my room?

I will send you the latest issue of the *Revista de Estudios Hispánicos*, New York, which has just published an article on my poetry.[10]

On Monday there is a meeting of the Spanish students to plan the Spanish party they will give at the end of the semester. I am in charge of the chorus.[11] I'm going to make these Americans sing the *cachucha* "Por la

9. Almost 14,000 students had enrolled in the summer session. Among them were five hundred foreigners, mostly from China, Japan, Mexico, and Cuba. During the 1929–30 academic year, Columbia had the largest student population in the country (*The New York Times*, June 9, 1929, p. 28, and *Columbia Spectator*, Dec. 16, 1929, p. 3).

10. An intelligent review of *Primer romancero gitano (The Gypsy Ballads)* by Lorca's friend León Felipe had appeared in *Revista de Estudios Hispánicos* II (April–June 1929), pp. 193–97.

11. "Hardly had he arrived in New York, when he adopted a title, and one moreover neither short nor humble: 'Director of the Mixed Choruses of the Instituto de las Españas in the United States of America'" (Daniel Solana [=Gabriel García Maroto], "Federico García Lorca," *Alhambra* [N.Y.] I, no. 3 [Aug. 1929], p. 24).

calle abajito," and some *sevillanas*. It will be hilarious to hear them say *carrrra* instead of *cara*.

Would you believe there are over six hundred students of Spanish language and literature? Take care. I will write again in a few days. But write me soon. Hugs and kisses and much love from your son and brother,

Federico

Sunday, 14 [July 1929], New York

Dear family,

My life in New York goes peacefully on. I'm very good at adapting to new circumstances, and I feel fine in this new environment, which is so different, but, to me, very suggestive.

On Isabelita's saint's day, I sent her a cable using the Acera del Casino address, and the cable was returned to me: "Addressee Unknown." I was furious, for I imagined that Señor Raigón's maids[12] had simply said, "She doesn't live here," and refused to accept the cable. I didn't want to try again, because the cable cost two dollars to send, but this oughtn't to happen again, and you should tell them to accept all the mail that is sent there. It seems very, very sad that Isabelita is an "unknown addressee" at Acera del Casino, 31, Granada.

The telegraph company is a very reliable one. Someone over *there* is to blame. I was extremely angry, for I wanted you to get news from me, and wanted to wish Isabelita a happy saint's day. The important thing is that it not happen again.

My English class at the university is great fun. It includes Japanese, Chinese, blacks, Indians, a heavily made-up sixty-year-old Cuban lady named Ofelia [Díaz Pardo], and me. The teacher speaks only English, and she is excellent.[13]

I have to lug the dictionary around with me all day, for these Americans

---

12. Apparently, the telegram had been returned by the maids of Guillermo Raigón Gómez, Consul of Panama in Granada, who resided in the same building as the Lorca family, on the Acera del Casino.
13. Amy Irene Shaw Abbott (1891–1991), remembers FGL in Eisenberg, *Textos y documentos lorquianos*, pp. 19–20.

are very nice and are always asking me questions and trying to strike up a conversation. In my residence hall there is a Jewish boy, of Russian origin, who has been talking my ears off. He is greatly interested in Spain and is always asking me questions. Naturally, each question and answer require fifteen minutes of word hunting in the dictionary. But it is the only way to learn.

Yesterday I had tea with Miss Adams, and she has invited me to spend next Sunday at her house in the country. The Sunday after that (from Saturday morning on), I am going to Onís's farm, on the banks of the Hudson, three hours from New York, and the Sunday after that (you can see how little free time I have), I'm going to make a trip to the country with two girls who are friends and "old admirers" of mine: two lovely girls from Puerto Rico, home of the most beautiful women in America.

I have also met a famous black writer, Nella Larsen, of the literary avant-garde, and with her I visited the black neighborhood and saw much that surprised me.[14] To my great amazement, everyone understands my French. With this writer I spoke French the whole afternoon, and we managed to say whatever we felt like. Necessity, mother of invention, worked a miracle or two! The little French that I knew came back to me, and I remembered all the words. And that made me very happy indeed.

This writer is an exquisitely kind woman, full of the deep, moving melancholy that all blacks have. She gave a party at her house, and there were only blacks. This is the second time I've gone somewhere with her, for she interests me enormously.

At the last party, I was the only white. She lives on Second Avenue, and from her windows you could see all the lights of New York. It was night and beacons were sweeping back and forth across the sky. The blacks sang and danced.

---

14. In a letter to Carl Van Vechten, who was in Europe, Larsen (1891–1964) writes that her friend Dorothy Peterson "has picked up a charming Spanish musician and poet—or rather Colin Hackforth-Jones picked him up for her. He really is delightful. Sings and plays thats [sic] beautifully fragile old fifteenth- and sixteenth-century things. I won't tell anything about his poetry because it hasn't been translated. We have both received letters from his mother who is Donna Quintero somebody or other Lorchkne [sic!] to visit her in Granada. Very nice of course." Undated letter (ca. July 28, 1929), Carl Van Vechten Papers, Beinecke Rare Book and Manuscript Library, Yale University.

What marvelous songs! Only the *cante jondo*[15] is comparable to them.

There was a little boy who sang religious songs. I sat down at the piano, and I sang, too. And you wouldn't believe how much they liked my songs. They made me sing some of them four or five times: the "Moricas de Jaén," "No salgas, paloma, al campo," and "El burro." The blacks are an extremely kind people. When I said goodbye, they all hugged me, and the writer gave me her books, with warm dedications—they told me this was quite an honor, for she has never done that for any of them.[16]

At the party there was a black woman who was, without exaggeration, the loveliest, most beautiful woman I have ever seen in all my life. It would be impossible to imagine more perfect features, or a more perfect body. She danced a sort of rumba, accompanied by a tom-tom (African drum), and her dance was a sight as pure and as tender as the moon over the sea, or some such simple and eternal thing in Nature. You can imagine how delighted I was by that party. With the same writer, I was in an all-black cabaret, and I kept thinking of Mother: it was one of those places you sometimes see in the movies, and which terrify her.

The most interesting thing about this city is this very mixture of different races and customs. I hope to study them all, and make some sense of this chaos and complexity.

I have also attended the church services of several different religions, and have come out of them with a fresh enthusiasm for our prodigiously beautiful, unequaled Spanish Catholicism. I will say nothing of the Protestant cults, for I simply can't get it into my head—my Latin head—how people can be Protestant. It's the most ridiculous, most odious thing in the world.

Imagine a church where, instead of a main altar, there is an organ, and, in front of the organ, a man in a frock (the pastor) who is speaking. Then everyone sings for a while, and out the door they go. They have suppressed all that is human and comforting and (in a word) beautiful. Even American Catholicism is different. It is undermined by Protestantism, and has the same

---

15. Generic term for a type of Andalusian song, dance, and guitar music also known as flamenco. See Lorca's essay "Deep Song," in C. Maurer, tr., *In Search of Duende.*
16. These would have included *Quicksand* (1928) and *Passing* (1929); both copies are lost.

coldness. This morning I attended a Catholic Mass, said by an Englishman. And I now see how miraculously an Andalusian priest says the Mass. The Spanish people have an innate sense of beauty and a lofty sense of God's presence in the temple. I can now understand the uniqueness of the Spanish Mass, the most fervent of all spectacles. The slowness, the grandeur, the adornment of the altar, the cordiality and fellow feeling in the adoration of the Blessed Sacrament, the cult of the Virgin . . . in Spain all this has a personality of its own, with an enormous poetry and beauty.

I also understand, here in New York, face to face with the Protestant churches, the racial reasons for Spain's great struggle against Protestantism, and the truly Spanish attitude of Philip II, a great king whom history has treated unjustly.

What American Catholicism lacks is solemnity; i.e., human warmth. When it comes to religion, solemnity means cordiality, for it is living proof (proof for the senses) of the immediate presence of God. As though to say, "God is with us. Let us render him homage and glory." It is a great mistake to suppress the element of pure ceremony. That is one of the great things about Spain, these exquisite forms, this sense of nobility in the way God is treated.

And yet . . . as I watched the Catholic parishioners this morning, I saw signs of extraordinary devotion, above all among the men, a rare thing in Spain. Many took Communion, and it was a serious, extraordinarily disciplined group, with no nonsense.

I saw some Japanese children make their First Communion—their little yellow faces, their white clothing, the most delicate, tender thing you can imagine.

The religious problem is important to see and to study in the United States.

I have also been to a Jewish synagogue, the one for Spanish Jews.[17] I heard some extremely beautiful chants, and the cantor was a true prodigy of voice and emotion. But I realize that in Granada almost all of us are

17. Shearith Israel, at Central Park West and Seventieth Street. The congregation's burial ground (Oliver Street and New Bowery) is the "cementerio judío" of Lorca's poem.

Jews. It was amazing—they all looked as if they had been born in Granada. There were more than twenty of them, who ran the gamut from Don Manuel López Saez to Miguel Carmona. The rabbi is named Sola,[18] and has the same pallid complexion as Solá Segura, who is probably his relative. I was doing my best not to laugh. There was a very solemn, beautiful ceremony, but I found it meaningless. To me the figure of Christ seems too strong to deny.

What was truly extraordinary was the chanting. The chants were extraordinary, heartrending, disconsolate. It was a continuous, long, and strikingly beautiful lament.

Some other time I will tell you about other things I've seen. I don't see much of the Spaniards. I prefer to live the life of an American. It isn't hot at all. Two hot days are always followed by two cool ones. Today it is delightful. Much cooler than in Granada. But remember, I live by the side of the river, in the highest spot in the city. I imagine you have already received my letters. Once I get settled, I am going to write you twice a week. You do the same, and give me all sorts of news, and get the girls to write, and mail your letters immediately, so they'll get here soon.

I am feeling fine. The food is good, and I lead a calm, quiet sort of existence. This high and lofty room, full of silence (relative silence), doesn't really give one an idea of New York.

Best to everyone. For you, hugs and kisses from your son (and brother)

Federico

Tell Paco to write.

[c. July 24, 1929]

Dear family,

I have gotten two letters from Mother and a letter from the girls. You can't imagine how happy I am to know you are all well. I'm very sorry you

---

18. David de Sola Pool (1885–1970), an authority on the Sephardic Jews and on the history of Shearith Israel. Lorca also refers to two friends of his father: Manuel López Saez, a conservative Granada businessman and politician, and Miguel Carmona Gutiérrez, of Chauchina.

are feeling bored, but I, too, grow bored when I am all alone in my room around noon when I settle down to work and there is no family silliness and no "illuminated coffee."[1] Write me nice long letters, and tell me all that is happening. That is what *I'm* doing, isn't it? I will always be delighted and amused to hear from you. I want you to have all my news, and not worry about me. But you must write back to me.

The photos of the girls came out very well, they're lovely. I've hung them in my room. But I also want photos of you. Take a picture of yourselves in the Huerta and send it to me. I keep remembering that Mother should go to Lanjarón, without fail.

You ought to help Paquito keep up his spirits, whether he passes or fails his exams. If he fails, it isn't his fault: he has worked hard, *very* hard, and on the next set of exams he will do splendidly. I know there isn't any need to tell you this, for you're a wonderful family, like no other in the world, but there's no harm in everyone putting in his own two cents. Anyway, if Paquito passes, I want you to send me a cable, *ipso facto*. They get here the same day. I got your cable on my birthday, and I suppose you received mine. Since there is a six-hour time difference, you may have gotten mine a little late. But it only takes two or three hours.

I celebrated my birthday and, needless to say, thought of you often. I spent the whole day working, and at night some friends came to get me and we went to visit a certain editor and writer, an important Hispanist named Mr. Brickell.[2] There was a little party, and—I couldn't get out of it!—they made me play the piano and sing. You have no idea how these Americans love Spanish songs. I have a real following here! And since they tell all their friends, Mr. Brickell's house was packed. I have to admit, hardly anyone knows more songs than I. They were simply amazed. This winter, for sure, I am going to give a recital of Spanish popular music at some really fashionable salon.[3] This is great propaganda for Spain and, above all,

1. Family name for coffee laced with liqueur.
2. Henry Herschel Brickell (1889–1952), book reviewer for *The New York Evening Post* and the *North American Review*, and an editor at Henry Holt and Company. For his memories of García Lorca, see "A Spanish Poet in New York," *Virginia Quarterly Review* XXI (1945), pp. 386–98.
3. "Some of the parties given for him were not as successful. A woman's club . . . gave a dinner in his

for Andalusia. So . . . my birthday had a happy ending, although I couldn't have imagined that all of *you* were going to be ferreted away indoors. I thought you would be outside, in the cool, admirable wind of Granada.

Summer is behaving itself. We have had six very cool days—cool enough to wear a vest (imagine me in a vest!). Now it is starting to warm up a bit, and return to normal.

I get up early and study English, then I go to class next door. I eat here at the university, and go back to my room, get freshened up, and sit down to write, or go on with English. At seven o'clock, in broad daylight, I eat dinner and go out for a walk, or go to a party or meeting of some sort until eleven, and then to bed. There are more parties and gatherings here than anyplace else in the world. Americans cannot stand to be alone. I am always turning down invitations. They are getting to be a nuisance, and I have decided to go only to the ones I like, or the ones that seem useful, but no others. If they catch you off guard, the old women intellectuals here will devour you. The day before yesterday, late afternoon or early evening, I went to visit a Peruvian girl, an "admirer" of mine (God deliver us!). Actually, it wasn't as bad as I expected. She had invited me so that I could meet five or six incredibly beautiful South American girls. Some were blond, others dark, others brunette. This woman seems to have invited every shade imaginable, in order to delight her guest. No invitation could have been more exquisite. We chatted away and when dinnertime came (this was about a quarter to eight), she invited us to stay for dinner. I ought to explain that only very rich Americans have maids, and in that pretty little apartment there were none. So we had to cook for ourselves. I took off my jacket and put on an apron. One of the girls made me a paper chef's hat, and I washed the plates and spoons. Everyone worked. They made some sort of dish with corn on the cob and butter and chicken and rice,

honor where he shared attention with a singer of American folk songs named Jack Niles. Folk music was supposed to be a bond between them. Both of them sang for their supper, both were applauded, neither understood the other's language. Had Federico sung in French, he would have been understood. As it was, the audience cheered for his charm; and as he departed the limp that always signaled fatigue showed in his walk" (Mildred Adams, pp. 125–26).

and later fruit and wonderful coffee, since the hostess has spent most of her life in Puerto Rico.

Then we set the table, and the table was beautiful: the glassware was blue, and amazingly delicate. There's democracy for you: the table settings were lovely, but we had to set the table ourselves, for there is no serving class. Yesterday I carefully sewed on my first buttons. They're on so sturdily that if you tried to get them off you'd take a piece of the pants with them. I sewed them on much better than any of *you* ever did, not to mention Castilla,[4] who sticks them on with spit! I have spent some money, but not very much. The first few days, naturally, I wasn't sure where things were cheapest, and had to find out for myself, and ended up paying more. The American diet is very healthy. Mother could live happily here, for she has good taste and enjoys all sorts of food. But when I think of Father in one of these restaurants I die of laughter. I can imagine him trying to catch the first ship that would deposit him, six or seven days later, in Gibraltar or Vigo. Keep writing. I have written this today, and tomorrow, or the day after, I'll write again. And please write long letters. You can write to Don Fernando, c/o Don Federico Onís. Say hello to the whole family for me, and to all my friends, to Manolo Montesinos,[5] and, especially, to the great Manuel de Falla.[6] I have often spoken of him in New York, always with an enthusiasm and admiration he can scarcely imagine. I have seen so many things here, and yet I understand what an extraordinary man he is, and how we should all love him and encourage him in all he does.

Hugs and kisses to you from your son

Federico

---

4. Luis Castilla, one of Lorca's tailors in Granada.

5. Manuel Fernández-Montesinos Lustau, who married Federico's sister Concepción in 1929, Mayor of Granada when the Civil War broke out, was arrested in his office and executed by the Nationalists on August 16, 1936, several days before Lorca himself was murdered.

6. Lorca had known Falla since the composer had moved to Granada in 1920. Relations had been somewhat strained since December 1928, when Lorca published the first two sections of his unorthodox "Ode to the Most Holy Sacrament" in the *Revista de Occidente*, Madrid, with a dedication to Falla. The composer disapproved of the poem, and said so in a pained letter. See Francisco García Lorca, *In the Green Morning*, tr. C. Maurer (N.Y.: New Directions, 1986), pp. 127–28. Lorca completed the poem in New York.

Dearest family,

My stay in New York goes calmly on, and I think I am getting a lot out of it. I am beginning to understand some English, a little bit, anyway, but I am translating, and I think I will win the battle in the end.

I have also begun to write, and think what I am writing is good. But of course I don't want to publish any of it until it is completely finished and polished.

They are typically American poems, and almost all of them deal with the blacks.[1] I think I will return to Spain with at least two books, although I have yet to see and study the most important aspects of all this.

I am deeply interested in New York, and think I can strike a new note not only in Spanish poetry but in all that has been written about these things. But don't tell anyone. It seems likely that once my book on New York is finished, it will be translated into English and published *first* in that language. My friend Brickell, the editor, wants to publish something of mine, and that is fine with me. The next time I write, I will send you two long articles about my poetry from one of the big New York daily newspapers, plus *Alhambra* magazine, which has published six photos of me (one of them of me sitting on the rim of the fountain at the baths in Lanjarón).[2]

Naturally, all this is in English—Paquito will do the translating.

About Paquito, what can I say?[3] I know Father must have been sorely disappointed, for he wanted Paco to be *bolder.* But it must be all over by now, and you are probably feeling happy and thankful. I approve completely of Paquito's attitude. Any honorable, truly conscientious man would feel the same way. I would have done the same thing myself. And besides, next year Paquito will do magnificently on the exams. He will no longer be nervous, and he'll know the subject matter backwards and forwards. I

---

1. The manuscripts of "The King of Harlem" and "Standards and Paradise of the Blacks" are dated August 5 and August 12, respectively.
2. Daniel Solana (=Gabriel García Maroto), "Federico García Lorca," *Alhambra* (New York) I, no. 3, August, 1929. In the same issue, Walker Evans—a friend of the editor, Ángel Flores—published his first photographs. No one has ever located the two newspaper articles.
3. Federico's brother had withdrawn from the examinations.

am very sorry about the whole thing—on his account, not yours, for in the end, of course, he will accomplish whatever he wants to. But I feel sorry for him: perhaps he will begin to feel depressed, and that would be a shame for a boy of his genius, elegance, and extraordinary intelligence. You ought to realize that Paquito is one of the most gifted, sensitive, levelheaded people I have ever met. And you ought to let the matter drop for now, and not badger him. I know that you won't, and that you'll feel happy with him. Tell him to work hard for the next time. I imagine you all feel happy to be back together again, and I would be, too, if I weren't so far from you. If I didn't have the friends I do in New York, this separation would be very sad indeed, but, to be honest, I have hardly had the chance to feel lonely. Maroto, who is a great tease, tells me, "No matter where you go, you're always the spoiled child, always the center of attention. It's no fair. Where you are, no one else exists." To be honest, I have some very good friends, and thanks to them my life has been interesting. Last night I went to a party at the home of Miss Adams, who is from one of the most distinguished families in New York. It was a party in my honor—she wanted to introduce me to her friends. There were a lot of nice Americans. An excellent pianist played music by Albéniz and Falla, and the girls wore embroidered Spanish silk shawls. In the dining room a surprise awaited us: bottles of sherry and Spanish brandy. I had a wonderful time. Naturally, I had to do my "Spanish song" number, and I played the guitar and sang *soleares*[4] with great success. I don't even worry about making a fool of myself, for I have never seen kinder, more innocent . . . and more intelligent people. The Adams family must have spent a small fortune on the party. When I said goodbye to them, and thanked them, they told me, "None of this can compare with all you did in Granada for our daughter." Miss Adams is truly charming. She has begun to make a name for herself, and is one of the most frequent contributors to the *Times*, the most important newspaper in all North America. I think Paquito met her in Granada.

It's interesting to see what prestige Spain enjoys in this country. In good society, a Spaniard is always considered a gentleman. Spain has a cer-

4. A variety of *cante jondo* (flamenco). Lorca had been playing the guitar since 1921.

tain historical prestige and it's quite true that they always distinguish between us and the Spanish Americans.

I had a visit from Cecilio Huertas, a typical character from Fuente Vaqueros,[5] and an excellent person. We went out for a walk and chatted for a while. One of these days I'm going to visit him and have a *paella*, which a friend of his will make. He lives among Italians, and once in a while he lets out an Italian expression. His local accent is unchanged, but he sometimes comes out with things like "una dollare" for one dollar.

He is so affectionate, he came to visit me last Sunday, but I couldn't attend to him, because two girls, friends of mine, had come to take me to the Russian church.[6] The Russian church is admirable. It's almost like the Catholic one. They have the Virgin and the saints, and the ritual is even more splendorous than ours. It is completely Byzantine, and more complicated and primitive than the Roman rite. But it is extremely beautiful, full of emotion. What are simply amazing are the choirs and the hymns. The Mass reaches its climax when the "pope," after consecrating the host, turns toward the audience, holds up the crucifix, and bursts into a loud lament with a beautiful melody. As theater, they really do it well, these "popes," with their long beards and glittering vestments. The ceremony lasted forever—one has to stand or kneel for over two hours, and they purified me with incense twelve or fifteen times.

The church was full of Russians and Greeks. Magnificent types. I saw the same old women one sees in Spain, kneeling before the Mother of

5. Huertas was born in 1890 in Fuente Vaqueros, where Federico was born eight years later.
6. Sofia Megwinoff writes that one Sunday she and her sister Mercedes "took him to the Russian (Catholic-Orthodox) church at the corner of Morningside Avenue and 120th Street . . . Federico was tense and frightened. We went on walking and entered a church in Harlem (black things were in vogue then). We went in when the Mass was beginning. Perhaps it was a Methodist church, I can't remember exactly. There he was *really* frightened. He stared at us and at the solemn black women, with their enormous eyes, many of them dressed in white, giving out papers with the hymns. Although no one seemed very surprised by our presence, Federico was frightened and anxious to escape" (Eisenberg, "Cuatro pesquisas," p. 15; my translation). There was no Orthodox church at Morningside and 120th, and Megwinoff may have been referring to the Russian Orthodox Church of Christ, with its excellent choirs, at 121st and Madison. The rector, when Lorca visited, would have been Rev. Vassily F. Kurdiumoff (see *New York Times*, March 16, 1927, p. 45 and March 12, 1928, p. 29).

Sorrows, or pounding their heads on the floor. The gestures of the faithful are more exaggerated than ours, for they are more Oriental, more vehement. They cross themselves backwards, extremely slowly, and they all carry candles and give evidence of extraordinary devotion. There is a devotion and (especially in the part of the service devoted to the dead) a silence that one does not find in Spain.

But I still say that the beauty and profundity of Catholicism is infinitely superior. If one is going to be a practicing member of some religion, there is none more perfect than Catholicism.[7] What the Byzantine church has, and what I haven't found in Roman Catholicism, is this notion of the patriarch. The "pope" is a superior figure, emanating authority and goodness, a true patriarch, and our priests have none of that. The priest is a simple officiant, and as soon as he leaves the church, he can turn into the worst person imaginable. But, unlike the Catholic priest, the "pope" (whether because of the ritual or his vestments or his eminence) has the appearance of a superior man, one who has been initiated into mysteries.

I tell you all this because I think you will find it interesting. It will give you some idea of the number of different creatures and opposing beliefs that exist in this huge city, where life is so violent and so full of new reactions and secrets. Even so, I have finally begun to understand the layout of New York. I often go places by myself now, the only way to see things well, without hearing someone else's comments and opinions.

Next week my Russian friends and I are going to go to the Chinese theater, something I await with great interest.[8]

In a few days [sic] I leave for the Canadian border, the state of Vermont, where I'm going to spend fifteen or twenty days with a boy I met at the Residencia. He has a farm in the mountains on Lake Eden, and that is where I'm going. I'll write you from there, and you write to me there. Fifteen days is nothing. This trip is like going from Granada to Loja, and yet it in-

7. Lorca finished and dated his poem "Ode to the Most Holy Sacrament of the Altar" on September 17, 1929.
8. Lorca seems to be referring to the Sun Sai Gai Company, who performed in the Grand Street Theater. A packet of postcards of costumes from the Chinese theater (in the Lorca Foundation archives, Madrid) suggests the poet's interest in Chinese theater.

volves a twenty-hour train ride. You simply can't imagine the immensity of the United States.

This boy, who is a poet, was so eager to have me visit him that he sent me the $20 train fare. I've asked my friends if this is normal, and they tell me it is the custom here. When an American invites you, he treats you to *everything*. So, next week I take the train to Burlington,[9] and I expect to have a great time. This boy is extremely kind, and in his house only English is spoken, which will be very good for me. But to give you some idea of the freedom of belief in this country, let me just tell you that the mother of this boy is a fervent Catholic, the father a Protestant, the boy himself a Catholic, and a cousin who lives with them is a complete atheist and a demagogue. They get along like angels.[10]

Mother, you asked how I was spending my time, and how much money I am spending. The first few days I spent more, out of necessity. But by now I'm living very, very simply. Simply but well. I pay seven dollars a week for the room, which is a good one. As for food, that depends. I eat in the dining hall at John Jay for 55 cents, and the food is quite good. When I am hungrier, I spend 75 cents. When I go downtown and eat with friends, it is about a dollar.

Laundry is very expensive, a dollar or a dollar and a half to have my clothes washed, and that's why I'm being so careful with them. I haven't had to make the slightest sacrifice. Of course, people are always inviting me to dinner, and I'm fortunate not to have to invite *them*, for I have no place of my own. The meals consist of soup, a platter of meat with potatoes, peas, beets, and sauces, a piece of cake or apple pie, a glass of iced tea with lemon, and a cup of coffee or a glass of milk. All this for 55 or 60 cents. There is plenty to eat, I couldn't eat more.

9. Cummings told the researcher Daniel Eisenberg: "We met him at Montpelier Junction, after he had ridden all night from New York City" ("A Chronology . . . ," p. 237).
10. Cummings calls this a "fantasy." "My family [were] born Congregationalists, and you can't get much more Protestant than that. Mother was a churchly woman, but other than an occasional funeral or wedding, I don't think my father ever darkened the door of a church. There weren't even any Roman Catholics in the family. We had a cousin, daughter of my mother's sister, Edna Southwick, who with her mother visited us a week at the camp on Lake Eden. As I recall, Aunt Carrie and Edna were both Methodists" (letter to C. Maurer, March 1, 1984).

But I hope Father won't forget to send me my allowance right away, so I don't run short of money. He ought to do this right away. And please tell Paco to wire me whatever money I've earned from my books, so that I have money to go to the theater, which interests me enormously. The theater here is magnificent, and I hope to get a lot out of it for my own work. Goodbye, much love. Hugs and kisses from your son, who loves you and remembers you often.

Federico

Remember me to everyone, even when I forget to say so in the letter. The weather continues to be excellent.

[second week in August 1929][1]

Dearest family,

Today I received Mother's letter, so I know Paco is back at the Huerta. Why doesn't he write me? I wrote him a long letter, and haven't gotten a reply. I asked him to send me books. *I still haven't seen my Canciones,*[2] and to me that doesn't seem right. Of course, I haven't written to the *Revista*, for I thought Paco would send it. But after what happened, I don't suppose he felt like it.

I haven't written to anyone because I haven't had time. In New York there is no time for anything. Since I have a lot of things to do, I spend all my writing time on you.

A moment ago I received a lovely photo, a bird's-eye (or airplane's-eye) view of the Acera del Casino. An American friend clipped it out of a Chicago newspaper and sent it to me right away, thinking our house would be in it. And indeed it is. In the center of the photo you can see the house, and the trees in the Plaza del Campillo. This was a touching little kindness. He also sends me all the articles on Spain which appear in the daily newspapers, and there are many of them.

1. Written before the 20th or 21st of August, the day of his departure for Vermont, and after the arrival of the *Graf Zeppelin*, on August 4. Perhaps August 9 or 16, given the mention of payday (which would probably have been a Friday).
2. The second edition of *Canciones* (*Songs*) was published by *Revista de Occidente* in 1929.

The Americans are friendly, frank, and as open and disarming as children. They are incredibly naïve, and extremely helpful. This morning I was having breakfast with my friend Colin[3] on Wall Street, the center of business and banking, where the Stock Exchange is, and the huge skyscrapers.

It is the spectacle of all the world's money, in all its unbridled splendor and cruelty. I couldn't begin to describe the tumult and hugeness of it all—the voices, the shouts, the running to and fro, the elevators, the poignant, Dionysian worship of money. This is where one sees the magnificent legs of the typist who appears in so many movies, the charming, conniving wink of the gum-chewing office boy, the poor, pallid fellow who turns up his coat collar and timidly stretches out his hand and begs for a nickel. It is here that I have gotten a clear idea of a multitude fighting over money. It is a true world war, with a faint trace of courtesy.

We ate breakfast on the thirty-second floor with the president of a bank, a charming man with a depth of feline coldness and ancient English reserve. People were coming in after being paid. They were all counting their dollars. Their hands were trembling as they always do when we are counting money. Out the window was the skyline of New York, crowned with great trees of smoke. Colin had five dollars in his pocket, and I had three. And he said in a truly charming way, "Just think. We are surrounded by millions. And yet the only two real gentlemen here are you and I." There was a *torrent* of noise on the street. When we left, I saw a man whose legs had been amputated, pushing himself in a little cart down one of the canyons between the buildings, and, a little way off, a madman talking to himself with a paper hat on his head.

Wall Street and its skyscrapers are truly marvelous. Several days ago I saw the Graf Zeppelin anchored beneath them like a green fish, and for a moment I thought I was dreaming.[4] Returning to the university is like

3. Campbell Hackforth-Jones (see letter of June 28, *n.* 9) was working for Beverley, Bogart & Co., with offices in the Equitable Building, 120 Broadway; the breakfast probably took place in the Bankers' Club, on the 38th floor.
4. The German airship flew over Manhattan, on its way to Lakehurst, New Jersey, at nine in the evening on August 4, 1929, after a sixty-seven-hour transatlantic voyage.

returning to another country. It is completely quiet. The grass and the statues of Hamilton and Jefferson soothe me with their color and their broad faces of seventeenth-century revolutionaries.

I listen to the horns of the ships on the river, and if I want, I can imagine I am in the country. You probably think I am in a marvelous place, but I think that you are, too. You really are, you know. When you've seen New York, you've seen almost every city in North America. Everything is uniformly the same. But think of the variety one has in Spain! You travel "further" going from Granada to Gerona than crossing the entire United States.

Today's letter is but a greeting. Write me often. Ask the girls and Paquito to write me. Remember me to the rest of the family, to all my friends, and especially the Amigo family and the charming Joaquín Amigo,[5] who does not belie his name.

I think only you, and no one else, should read my letters. Just the family. But don't show them to *anyone* else, for they are personal letters, written for you and nobody else, and, besides, they have no literary value. They only matter as family letters. It would be ridiculous to think otherwise. Lots of hugs and kisses for all of you from

Federico

[August 23?, 1929]

Dear Mother and Father,

Due to one thing or another, I've let a couple of days slip by without writing, but that doesn't mean I don't think of you constantly.

I got the highest possible grade on my English exams, and we had our evening of Spanish music, which went very well.[1] My role was an impor-

5. Joaquín Amigo Aguado (1899–1936), who had helped Lorca edit the literary magazine *gallo* in 1928; in a letter Federico describes him as "one of the most talented young men in Granada, and with the most purity and enthusiasm" (*EC* 559).
1. Far from getting "the highest possible grade," Federico did not show up for the final, and received a grade of NC (no credit) (Eisenberg, *Textos y documentos lorquianos*, pp. 17–19). As for the "evening of Spanish music," Mildred Adams, with whom Lorca spent time in New York, recalls: "The happiest thing he did in those six weeks was to assemble a chorus in Columbia's Spanish Institute and teach

tant one. In the past none of their concerts were very good. But this time I sat at the piano and directed the whole thing, and it came off with great brio. I wish you could have seen these Americans singing the *Vito, vito!*[2] It was marvelous.

Between that party and this family's inviting me here [to Vermont], much time has gone by. Yesterday I arrived in this village, which is called Eden Mills, meaning *"Paraíso de los molinos,"* in the Green Mountains, on the border of Canada.

I've seen don Fernando de los Ríos, who was to return to Spain today, and we've eaten together four or five times, as befits two old shipmates. The day before yesterday I went to the station and said goodbye to [Gabriel García] Maroto, Mr. [Herschel] Brickell, Ángel del Río, [Ángel] Flores, and others. They were all in stitches. It was my "moment of truth" in English, and the first trip I've made by myself on this enormous continent. Grand Station Central [*sic*] is enough to frighten anyone, but even an idiot could find his way around this country. It is impossible to get lost, even when one wants to. There are signs everywhere, and gruff employees to show you the way (actually, they're very pleasant and nice). This was also my first trip on an American Pullman (which you've seen in the movies), and it is a true prodigy of comfort and technical inventiveness. I lay down, put out the light, and opened the windows. I wanted to sleep, but the sight of the moon and the boats on the Hudson River was so wonderful that it filled my head with ideas and kept me from sleep, which wipes out everything. At times we heard the great eastern express trains, in contrast to the mute little boats nodding at the riverbank with their almost imperceptible lights. I'm now in the prettiest place in the U.S., next to a huge lake in the midst of a northern forest. I live the most "American" life

---

them Spanish folk songs. In its lesser way, the Spanish Institute at Columbia filled for him the place occupied by the Residencia [de Estudiantes] in Madrid. It had a library of Spanish books, a big meeting room, a piano. Its members were mostly Spanish-speaking students, and here they had space for talk and laughter. Out of their number, the homesick Andalusian gathered enough singers to make a chorus. On August 7, 1929, in the last week of summer session, the chorus gave a concert of popular songs [. . .] A program still extant shows the Director of the Chorus of the Institute to have been Federico García Lorca." *Federico García Lorca: Playwright Poet*, p. 93.

2. Spanish folk song used by Lorca in several of his plays.

imaginable. I was really lucky to get this invitation: otherwise, I should never have seen what a small American farm is like. The family is charming. They are three very tall people, Puritans, with blond hair, like the people one sees in Tom Mix movies. But very gentle and very affectionate, in a serious, distinguished way. I am living a life from the movies, as in an adventure film. The ferns, toadstools and moss come spilling down from the mountains to the lake, and the birds (very few of them) sing delicately and distantly above the tangled briar patches. It is cold, and in the dark, leaden water of the lake it is impossible to distinguish the reflection from the things reflected. At night we see and speak to one another by the light of oil lamps. New York is relatively near (the distance from Cadiz to Madrid), but it seems infinitely remote. Everywhere I can hear the water in the abandoned mills, and this afternoon, at the entrance to the forest, I found an old wooden spinning wheel covered with cobwebs. The poignant romantic atmosphere (the shores of the lake are entirely covered with water lilies) seems to chime with the sort of poetry I am now writing. I speak English little by little, and the day is wonderfully long. The house is built from unpainted wood, and the owner, who is from Florida, finds Negroes so odious that he has hung a sign at the entrance saying, "The Charleston is Prohibited Here," and yet, outside, over the totally American-looking portico, with its little columns, is a sign saying "Dew-Kum-Inn," which means more or less *"Venga aquí, por favor."* It is truly naïve and delightful.[3]

This morning, after rowing for a while around the lake, we went to visit two ladies who are unimaginably picturesque and amusing. We found them dressed in pants, doing some plastering. They are two intelligent old maids, and in their old age they are doing something truly extraordinary.

I don't remember whether I mentioned to you that the cruel winters and poor soil have made many of these farmers abandon their farms and move away. Well, here are these two ladies, who bought an old ramshackle wooden house and are fixing it up all by themselves with no help from anyone. They

3. The poem "Tierra y luna" (Moon) (*Collected Poems*, pp. 758–62) is dated several days later, August 28, at the Dew Kum Inn, not an inn but a "camper" or lakeside house the Cummings family was renting. (The name of the "inn" is also a pun on the name of the family.)

are putting on the roof, raising walls, putting down floors, and finding sensible uses for second-hand furniture. From a millstone they have made a stove, and from the bin where bread was once kneaded they have made a kitchen table, and so on. Eventually, they will have a magnificent home. Birds were nesting inside the house, but the two old ladies haven't disturbed them, so that there are ten or twelve under the eaves where the dining room is. "We've made a bird gallery," they said, where the little creatures can rest peacefully. I didn't know whether to laugh or pat them on their fannies. It was strange and very moving. I can tell you that their house is in the middle of the forest and is difficult to get to, but the peace I felt there is a rare experience. The meadows around the house are full of white immortelles.

In Spain this would be considered madness, and people would make pilgrimages to see these ladies, but there is nothing unusual about them here. They amuse themselves and lead their lives the way they want to. For here nothing is frowned upon, and everything is tolerated . . . except social scandal. You can have a hundred mistresses and people know it and nothing happens, but just wait until one of them denounces you and whips up something in public. Then there is no hope for you socially. This is something really appalling. "Appearances" are what they live for, reality matters nothing. The afternoon I spent with these ladies was really wonderful. It taught me of the dream of life and reminded me how differences in character disappear thanks to identical things that lie beneath the surface.

They gave us a truly exquisite Chinese tea with dried jasmine blossoms. And they looked very delicate and very feminine with their silvery hair once they changed into their simple white dresses. We must have had fifteen cups of tea: I lost count. [Philip] Cummings, the young man who is my friend here, translated my poems for them.[4] They understood them very well and were really touched (something I can always judge). I told

---

4. The translation was published in 1976 by Daniel Eisenberg: *Songs*, tr. Philip Cummings, with the assistance of F.G.L. (Pittsburgh: Duquesne University Press). Eisenberg explains (p. 13): The translation "was made . . . with continuous discussion between Lorca and Cummings over the meaning of the Spanish and the appropriate English equivalents. Cummings himself tells in an earlier introduction how 'each poem was a mental wrestling match.' Although Federico's English was limited—not nonexistent—he was able to assist Cummings by exegesis in Spanish, which he was under other circumstances always so reluctant to do . . ."

them I descend from a very ancient Arabic family, and they showered me with all sorts of courtly attention, which I have borne with a certain melancholy and a touch of humor.

Then we went home. In the doorway was the American flag . . . and the Spanish one, and I gave them my thanks. All of this is very American. Poetry and foolery. Power and childishness. Technology and primitivism. Don't forget to send my allowance. I'm doing well and not spending much. Since it's about to get cold, I have moved to John Jay Hall at Columbia, but you should send your next letter to Furnald. I will write to Paquito. Say hello to all my friends and to the family. I don't have to tell you how often I think of you, particularly in these calm, quiet places, so different from Spain. But this trip is extremely important for me. And I find it wonderful to have experienced this totally American, intimate way of life. Just now they are lighting the lights. The atmosphere reminds me of my childhood in Daimuz.[5] Not a single frog can be heard in the lake. The silence is perfect. And from this wonderfully peaceful spot I send you hugs and kisses

Federico

P.S. The Cummings family sends its best wishes. You can feel very good about the affectionate way they're treating me.

5. A country place along the Cubillas River, near Asquerosa, Granada, which the poet's father had purchased in 1895.

Me, on the lake, half sportsman and half altar boy.

[last week in August, 1929]

Dearest Conchita and Isabelita,

Before leaving these woodlands, I am writing to you on a piece of bark which I myself pulled from the tree.[1] Lovely paper, isn't it? I got your letter, and Father's, and I hope you received mine from Eden Mills. I'll send you the drawings.

Say hello to Manolo and everyone else.

Give Mother and Father and Paquito a kiss for me.

Hugs and kisses to you from

Federico

Now I'm going to stay with Ángel del Río, whose wife teaches me more English than anyone else. And then to John Jay Hall, Columbia University, for the semester.

1. The letter is written in pen on both sides of a piece of birch bark, accompanied by a birch leaf.

The Cummings family. Nothing could be more American.

A big hug. I feel great. The meals here are a real challenge. The title of this letter is "Autumn in New England."

[c. September 21, 1929]

Dearest Mother and Father,

I'm writing in pencil, for I'm changing dormitories and my room isn't ready yet. It has been a while since I last wrote.

My summer vacation is over. After leaving Cummings, I spent a few delightful days with Ángel del Río.[1] In the morning I studied English and

1. Del Río has described Federico's adventurous trip from Eden Mills, Vermont, to Bushnellsville, near Shandaken, New York, on August 29: "Lorca, finding himself alone in Kingston, had decided to take a taxi without being able to give the right directions to the driver. They had been going around mountain roads until a kindly neighbor had given them our address. The fare was $15. As

This is the incredibly lovely landscape around Newport, which I visited. The words across the bottom of the card make it look a bit smaller, but you can see its greatness and serenity. The whole country is like this. The mountains are covered with pine trees and the lakes come one after another, giving rise to perspectives and patches of great beauty, though too monotonous. You wander around this place and a certain sweetness comes over you, as though you had fallen asleep in this paradisiacal light. Don't forget to write me. And so should Paquito and everyone else. Goodbye!

in the afternoon I worked.[2] And I have written a great deal: almost a whole book. I don't know why I say "almost": if I go on like this, I will return to Spain with three books. I had a great time with these friends of mine. They're my family here. Ángel's wife mends my clothes, ties my ties, and just about everything else. She's simply charming. She and her South American girlfriends *take care* of me: to them a poet is something fantastic. Then Onís

Lorca had spent all his money, I had to pay the driver and placate his fury. Federico's terror was the outcome of his conviction that he was lost, without money enough to take care of the bill. Immediately he gave the incident a fantastic twist and said that the driver, whom he could not understand, had tried to rob and kill him in a dark corner of the woods" (Mildred Adams, p. 117).

2. Among the poems Lorca worked on during the nineteen days he spent in Shandaken were "After a Walk," "Nocturne of the Void," and the final section of his "Ode to the Most Holy Sacrament of the Order" (*Collected Poems*, pp. 634–37).

came to get me, and drove me to his farm,[3] and I spent a week helping him with the Anthology he is preparing, a very important collection of the whole of Spanish and Latin American poetry. Following my own criteria, I myself selected the poems of Salvador Rueda, José Asunción Silva (a great Colombian poet), Machado, Juan Ramón, and some minor poets.[4]

Once I have moved in, I will have a new address—John Jay Hall, Columbia University—and that is where you should send your letters. All these trips have helped me get to know the admirable banks of the Hudson River. I have often sailed up and down it, and know all its villages and towns. And thus the East of the United States, the region least frequently visited by tourists, has become almost familiar to me. You can imagine how many amusing, and sometimes embarrassing, experiences I have had. I have discovered that I have a sense of humor that allows me to get through difficult situations. And I have a coldbloodedness that comes from belonging to an ancient race, as compared with the "Samsonism" (children of Samson) of this people. My room in John Jay is wonderful.[5] It is on the twelfth floor of the dormitory, and I can see all the university buildings, the Hudson River, and a distant vista of white and pink skyscrapers. On the right, spanning the horizon, is a great bridge under construction, of incredible grace and strength.[6] The sky is magnificent, and the temperature is perfect. Autumn in New York is probably the loveliest season of the year, as it is everyplace else.

The university is full of joy and bustle. I must start to write my lectures. I already have the material for the first one, on "The Virgin in Alfonso the Wise and in Gonzalo de Berceo."[7] I am going to speak about the delightful Gothic Virgin in this place, where there are more Protestants than anywhere else in the world. (To me the word "Protestant" means *"dry" idiot.*[8]) I am

3. Lorca spent September 18–21 at the home of Federico de Onís, Gardnertown Road, Newburgh, N.Y. (Eisenberg, "A Chronology," p. 238).
4. *Antología de la poesía española e hispanoamericana (1882–1932)* (Madrid: Estudios Históricos, 1934). According to Onís, these poets (with the exception of Silva) were the ones whose presence is most noticeable in Lorca's first book, *Libro de poemas* (*Antología*, p. 1101).
5. Room 1231.
6. Construction work on the towers of the George Washington Bridge (then known as the Hudson River Bridge) was approaching completion in the summer of 1929.
7. A few notes for this lecture are in the Lorca archives. See *OC*, Vol. III, pp. 1342–43.
8. A reference to those whom Lorca thought responsible for Prohibition. Cf. "The Birth of Christ,"

amazed, and always chuckle to myself, to see how many sects and fake religious cults there are in this country. I can spot Catholics a mile off by their manner and their intelligence.

My lecture will be an apology for the Gothic faith, as it struggles against the sharp edges of the devil's world. I will write another one on "Adventure in Tirso and in Cervantes," and another, which is already completely thought out, on "The wind, the breeze, and the hurricane in sixteenth-century lyric poetry." A lecture on the breezy landscapes of certain poets, using the air as a touchstone to distinguish their temperaments and qualities.[9]

It seems likely I will soon make my trip as a lecturer, though I shudder to think of the macaws and parrots and rumba dancers that will be pounding on my shoulders and eardrums. But we'll see.

I will write again tomorrow or the day after. I have fallen a bit behind.

Your letters were waiting for me when I got back from Onís's house.

Tomorrow I will write to poor Encarnación.[10] I was greatly saddened to hear of Mateo's death (may he rest in peace). He was extremely kind and affectionate. I plan to write them, but please give them my deepest condolences.

I will send Conchita the drawings she asks for,[11] and write to Paco with all sorts of news. His letter made me realize how beautiful and wild the Monte del Duque must be. When I get back, we must go and see it. What Paco tells me about Estepona fills me with enthusiasm here in New York. How beautiful Andalusia is! And that seaside Andalusia . . . how refined and lovely. It is here that one realizes the beauty and importance of Spain. It is the only strong and vital country left in the world.

It seems likely I am going to Chicago,[12] a nerve center of Yankee dynamism, and there I'll finish learning the value of the sea at Málaga and the

---

lines 19–20: "Idiot clergymen and cherubim in feathers / follow Luther in a line around the high corners."

9. A fragment of this lecture, entitled "Escala del Aire" ("Ladder of Air"), has been found among Lorca's papers and published in *OC,* Vol. III, pp. 1341–42.

10. Apparently, a friend of Lorca's mother, whose husband Mateo had just died.

11. Probably, pillow designs.

12. The trip was never made.

little houses lost in the red mountains and the love and definitive grace of my own country. I have gone to the window. How I would love it if you could see this prodigiously impressive landscape of buildings and rivers, with the aristocratic university in the foreground, and the two magnificent granite fountains, with their cool water jets. And yet . . . I remember Polinario's tavern, with its cypress tree and broken chair.[13]

I feel wonderful. Hugs and kisses

Federico

P.S. I asked you for my October allowance because I must pay three months of the residence fee in advance. The room costs a dollar a day, and another dollar to eat makes two. This is paring expenses to a minimum, but I am getting by. That was the reason I asked for the money: so that I could pay in advance. Also, I've enrolled in an English course which I need to take.

I asked Ángel del Río for thirty dollars because I needed to have some money in the bank. The room is a good one, and this dormitory has a very inexpensive dining hall. Besides, it is the newest, most elegant dorm, and is prodigiously warm in winter. I have managed to live here on the same money as in Madrid. Sometimes, when I feel hungry, I spend a little more on food, but I want to eat less, because *I have put on weight*, and don't want that to happen.

I haven't received the money from the *Revista*. They have a lot of nerve. "Muncha alma," as Ortega y Gasset[14] would say. I will save that money to go to the theater, which is very good and very new, and extremely interesting. So please, send the allowance at the beginning of each month. Send me my November allowance on the first of November.

Farewell.

Remember me to Montesinos and all my friends.

---

13. A famous old tavern on the Calle Real, near the Alhambra, a meeting place for flamenco artists, run by Antonio Barrios Tamayo, *El Polinario*, the father of Lorca's friend the pianist Ángel Barrios.
14. José Ortega y Gasset (1883–1955), the Spanish essayist who had founded the *Revista de Occidente*, publisher of *Lorca's Gypsy Ballads* and *Songs*.

I'm sending you photographs taken by del Río and his wife in the sort of cabin we lived in for a while. I think I look very handsome. In one of them I appear with Helen and Stanton, the children who took me on walks through the woods. One day I asked Stanton: "Are there bears here, too?" and he answered, "Yes, sir, there are bears and hens and frogs and lots of little bugs you can't even see." This shows his charming innocence, which would be unheard-of in Spain from a twelve-year-old like him. In other photos I am with del Río and his wife. And there is one where Amelia caught me writing, lost in thought, and she says this is the one where I look "cutest."

This is the one where they caught me off guard. As you can see, we were living in a typical American cabin, built on stones, where Stanton's family put us up very well indeed.

Dearest Mother and Father,

Today I am nicely settled in. I have enrolled in my English class, and will audit several others. So *here I am*, a Columbia student. I asked you for my October allowance in order to pay for my room in advance, for that is what they require. Anyway, it is the best bargain in New York. I pay a dollar a day for the room. But the room is splendid, better than one could get for the same price in Spain. Clean towels daily, and they change the bed linens twice a week.

I live neatly and simply. They have invited me to give several lectures at universities in the West, and I'll almost surely go, for that way I will earn some money. Were it *enough*, I would write you, and you wouldn't have to send any more. Anyway, if I earn a few extra dollars, I will use them to buy some things and to go to shows, especially the theater.

This morning they began "initiating" the new students in my dormitory. At nine in the morning I was awakened by the shouting, went to the window, and saw them *stripping* the initiates—some of them down to their birthday suits. In five minutes there was a huge mound of shoes on the playing field. Two brave souls who put up a fight were seized without mercy and tossed into the basin of a fountain by the door of the library. The poor boys came out like wet hens; from up here they looked like two broken rag dolls.

It was great fun. Just across from me the eighteenth-century statue of Hamilton, about to break into a minuet or a gavotte, is wearing a paper hat and holding a huge broom. The students greet each other with long handshakes, exactly like the peasants of Asquerosa or Romilla.[1] They grip each other's hands and for a long minute or two they pump them up and down in an almost mechanical way. Others show their affection by feigning punches, and finish off with a big bear hug.

Everywhere, there are dull thuds, shouting, the noise of elevators, and red, blue, and green sweaters.

Here's a surprise for you—my room is number 1231! My neighbor,

---

1. Two villages near Granada where Lorca had spent much time as a young man.

The difference between getting married and not getting married is this: here you have me, fit and handsome, and there you have Angelito del Río, who is my age but is a broken-down old man.

who is a very refined person, a student from Georgia,[2] invited me in for tea a moment ago, and we conversed for the most part in sign language, for what is most difficult about English isn't reading, but listening, and listening is very difficult indeed. Many words which I can recognize when they are written down escape me completely when I hear them, because we say

2. No students from Georgia seem to have been living on the twelfth floor of John Jay. Lorca may be referring to either Francis C. Hayes or John Crow, both Southerners. Crow remembers García Lorca as being "very much out of his element . . . As a matter of fact, he used to annoy me. I didn't realize at the time that he would be such a major figure. Garcia Lorca was somewhat stuck on himself in the first place! He always talked about how great he was, which rubbed us the wrong way. The thing that bothered us most was that he'd come by our rooms saying, *'Vi la luz encendida'* ('I saw the light on'). He would knock on the door at about 2:00 in the morning when we were just getting ready for the next day's classes, and he would come sit down for a couple of hours until we were exhausted!" The two of them solved the problem by taping cardboard over the door to block the light. See Onofre di Stefano and Darlene Lorenz, "Conversations with Three Emeritus Professors from UCLA," *Mester* VIII (1979), pp. 30–31.

"a" and it *is* "a," but they pronounce the "a" in six or seven different ways, so it's a real mess. But I never despair, I only smile and I manage to make myself understood whenever I want. The hard part is getting them to recognize the word one is saying, a rather complicated matter, given the special *head* of the Anglo-Saxon race. Just now the Columbia rugby team has come onto the field, dressed in their black and tobacco-colored uniforms. The players are a little like sandpaper and a little like tree trunks, and they are frighteningly strong and seedy-looking. Soon they will break each other's heads open and no one will care. The same thing holds true for rugby players as for picadors. Everyone secretly hopes the picador will be driven up against the wall, and feels let down if he does a good job with the *pica*—you've probably noticed how people applaud them with a certain anger. I love rugby, for besides being typically American, it is so exciting and has such *incredible* natural beauty that it gives me a lump in my throat. Of course, I could never have been a player. I am sending you some photographs taken by del Río and his wife in the sort of cabin we lived in for a while. I think I look very handsome. In one of them, I appear with Helen and Stanton, the children who took me on walks through the woods.[3] One day I asked Stanton, "Are there bears here, too?" and he answered, "Yes, sir, there are. There are bears and hens and frogs and lots of little bugs you can't even see." This shows his charming innocence, which would be unheard-of in Spain from a twelve-year-old like him.

In other photos, I'm with del Río and his wife. And there is one where Amelia caught me writing and she says this is the one where I look "cutest."

Write me long letters, and give me news. I suppose the Procession of the Virgin is over by now, and all those fairs they hold in the village squares are going on, threatened, as always, by the rains.

I feel fine. Autumn in Lanjarón is wonderful. You must take Mother to

3. Stanton H. Hogan (1917–2008) and his sister Helen Hogan, children of the farmer who rented the house to the del Ríos, would become the protagonists of two poems from *Poet in New York*. Amelia Agostini del Río remembers that, although the children did not understand Spanish, the poet sung to them, told them stories, and conquered them with his charm (*Cartas y recuerdos*, in press). The father suffered from cancer, and the mother, Phoebe M. Stover, died from cancer in 1937. Stanton would have been 13 or 14 when Lorca met him. Helen was transformed into "Mary" in Lorca's 1932 lecture on *Poet in New York*, and into the "Girl Drowned in the Well (Granada and Newburgh)" in the poem. See also Eisenberg, "Cuatro pesquisas . . . ," pp. 11–12.

Lanjarón whether she likes it or not. You must *make* her go, and if she hasn't gone, or isn't going, and has an attack of colitis, Paco and Conchita and Isabelita will be to blame, and I'll be angry with them for the rest of my life. Hugs and kisses.

Federico

[October 21, 1929]

Dearest family,

I have received your letters, and you mine. I'm feeling well, and hope that you are, too.

All this is beginning to change a bit for me, for I now know how to get around this huge city. But it is only now, when I know how to move about and ask questions and shop by myself, that I realize how huge this city and this civilization are. You have to live here for a few months to finally grasp the layout of New York and its immensity, which goes unsuspected in the first few days.

The other day, at *last*, I really got lost. I went out to do some errands, and took the elevated train. But instead of the Sixth Avenue train I mistakenly caught the Ninth Avenue one, which took me in the wrong direction, to a place totally unknown to me. It was a huge city of low, wooden houses, full of Chinese people and signs in Chinese, with the muted music of player pianos and jazz orchestras. I realized I was lost, and I started to look around at the streets and browse in the Chinese stores. Lunchtime came, and I ate at a Chinese restaurant. For sixty cents I had a very strange, totally cold, but undeniably tasty meal. The little Chinese boy who waited on me couldn't have been older than ten, and he looked like a pretty doll. He was wearing a little red smock and he left the plates on the table with an almost reptilian silence, but in an exquisite, aristocratic way. Afterwards I went out and began to explore the city, a neighborhood about four times the size of Granada,[1] and at last, since I knew I was lost, and had almost

---

1. The Ninth Avenue El, now demolished, ran from South Ferry to the Bronx, the sixth most populous city in the U.S. (1,265,258) on the 1930 census. In 1929 Granada had about 100,000 inhabitants.

gotten lost on purpose, I began looking for the subway stops and the elevated train. But the stops I found weren't the ones I needed, and they would have led me even farther astray. I felt a certain anguish, as though I were in a virgin forest or on an island on some planet not my own. And I didn't want to ask directions. I had only to ask a policeman to point me in the right direction . . . and in the end I did have to ask for help. I saw some women going by and questioned them in English. And what a surprise! They answered in perfect Spanish: *"Venga con nosotros, que llevamos el mismo camino."*[2] They were two wealthy women from La Coruña who were passing through New York. You can imagine what a good laugh we all had. At last we took the elevated train and I got off at Columbia. But then I went back to the subway and reached the place I had wanted to go in the first place (a complicated matter), and I did what I had set out to do. By the time I got back to Columbia it was midnight. Until something like this happens to you, you just don't realize where you are, and how immense these streets are, and how many millions of people live here. Anyway, I am beginning to get to know the city. Please don't tell me to carry a map. The map never helps me at all, it's useless. When it comes to maps, I have no sense of direction. When I trust my instinct I reach my destination, but a map only leads me astray. I just don't have the knack for it. I had a terrible time learning which was my right hand, and in fact I still have to make the sign of the cross with it before turning right into a building or down a street. I don't know which is my right hand, just as I didn't understand the mystery of the clock until I was almost twenty years old. A map is just impossible, for me at least: I can't seem to link its abstract lines with the living, noisy reality around me. But I do perfectly well without it, better than most people do with their special maps. My spatial memory is amazing. Once I have been somewhere, I remember it always, and my friends can't believe it when we're on the elevated train at night, and you can see hardly anything, and I tell them, "We're going by Eighth Street." But this isn't at all strange in New York, which, as I told you before, is quite easy to figure out. You don't get lost very often, and if you do, you can pick up the

2. "Come with us. We're going in the same direction."

thread immediately. What *does* cause problems is its size, and it is truly surprising how *long* it takes to get from one place to another.

We are well into autumn now, and the light is very beautiful in the parks and on the avenues. The university is preparing to celebrate its anniversary, and in front of my dormitory they are putting up the speakers' platform. I practice my lousy English with my American friends. I understand *myself*, at least, and I go to their rooms, or they come to mine, to have tea. One of them is very impressed with the Spanish photographs of Isabelita and Conchita. I have never seen more innocent creatures in my life than these Columbia students, or kinder, or more savage ones. This is a totally savage people, perhaps because there is no class system. These boys stretch and yawn with the innocence of animals, they sneeze without taking out their handkerchiefs and are always shouting, everywhere. And yet they are open and friendly, and they truly enjoy doing a favor for you. But how different they are from Spaniards who have been brought up properly.

I have also been going to the rugby games at the stadium of the university. The day before yesterday, four players were knocked out cold.[3] I can understand how excited people get, for it is an amazingly beautiful, graceful, manly spectacle, with special appeal for the weakling who is unfit to participate.

A bullring is nothing compared to this—it is a scandal. What barbarians they are! I have never heard people scream and swear the way they do in these Anglo-Saxon crowds, laced with blacks and old Indians.[4]

Changing the subject, Paco wrote me a letter for which I am deeply grateful. But *I don't owe any money to anyone*, thank God. I haven't asked anyone for money because I have been leading a very frugal life, and don't want to be a burden. I have received my money from the *Revista*, and that was the money I used to register at the university.[5] I asked you to advance me my monthly allowance because I had to pay the residence fee in advance.

---

3. Lorca refers, with his usual exaggeration, to the Columbia-Dartmouth game of October 19, 1929.
4. "Old Indians"? Perhaps Dartmouth fans wearing Indian headdresses. According to the *Times* of October 20, 1929, around forty thousand people attended.
5. On September 27, Lorca paid the fifty-dollar matriculation fee for two English classes in the Columbia University Extension Division, but later withdrew (Eisenberg, "Cuatro pesquisas," pp. 2–3).

I had more than enough money in the bank and was able to pay the fee, and still have money left over to pay for meals.

I asked Don Fernando for thirty dollars, I think, because I didn't remember how much I had, and it came in handy. And come to think of it, I don't believe I've asked you for any money beyond the monthly allowance we agreed upon. A hundred dollars isn't much, but my life is very simple. Don't send more. Well, perhaps twenty dollars more per month, but until now I have managed nicely. Besides, I am going to give some lectures, and will use that money to buy what I need.[6] If I need money urgently for anything, I'll ask for it. What you ought to do is to send the money at the beginning of the month directly to the bank where I have my account: Corn Exchange Trust Company, University Branch, Broadway and 113th Street. And of course, if I succeed as a lecturer, you won't have to send me anything at all. Well, perhaps fifty dollars.

A student can live on less money than anyone else in the United States. Only here could I get by on one hundred dollars. We'll see whether my allowance will leave me enough to go to the theater, in which I am greatly interested. I have been writing a play which might prove interesting.[7] One must think of the theater of the future. Everything that now exists in Spain is dead. Either the theater changes radically, or it dies away forever. There is no other solution.

Write me often, and I will, too. I will end this and get to work. It is three in the afternoon, and the wind is blowing hard and whistling around the twelfth floor. The radiator is on, and it is so hot that I have to leave the top part of the window open a little. The heating system is amazingly good. Not that the old charcoal brazier doesn't have a certain charm, which I love, but it is barbarous when compared to these superb radiators.

Hugs and kisses to everyone.

Federico

---

6. On January 21, 1930, Lorca gave a lecture on Spanish lullabies at Vassar College, and grudgingly accepted an honorarium of $75; he had been promised more (Andrew A. Anderson, "García Lorca at Vassar College: Two Unpublished Letters," *García Lorca Review* XI [1983], pp. 100–109). On February 10, he spoke at Columbia University (301 Philosophy Hall) on "Three Modes of Poetry: Imagination, Inspiration and Evasion."

7. Perhaps *El público* (*The Audience*) or *Así que pasen cinco años* (*Once Five Years Pass*).

[October 22 or 23, 1929]

Dearest Mother, Father, and Conchita,

The problem you mention in your letter has an easy solution. If you want me to return, you have only to send me a cable, and I will do so immediately. I would rather be here, of course, but I could always put my affairs quickly in order and leave. What I really ought to do is stay for at least another two months, if I am to take advantage of this.

But I will do whatever you say. I am willing to leave and, naturally, will be glad to see you. But it seems a good idea, since I'm already here, to stay a while longer, above all if I can earn some money, which seems probable. Conchita's wedding plans seem very natural, and I don't want to do anything to disturb them. They make a happy couple, and everyone is fond of them, and since Conchita will remain in Granada, they won't have the emotional difficulty of separation. Her husband is our close friend, and we know him well enough to know what a good person he is, and what a gentleman. And besides, it seems very good, since Paco and I are such drones and haven't married and had children, that Conchita should form a family. I am very happy with the *rightness* of this marriage, and anyway, that is the way the world is today. Only God knows the truth. If I am not at the wedding (and that is up to you), you should write me and telephone me right away.

Some English friends of mine in New York have begun to see what they can do to have my theater performed here. This might be a good thing for me, and it would be excellent if it really happened.

If something is performed, it would be *Perlimplín* and *The Billyclub Puppets*, translated into English and done with a nice set.[1] There is avant-garde theater here, and it wouldn't be difficult. I don't want to get my hopes up: I'll just wait and see. It is the ladies who are taking an interest in all this. In fact, it is the women who do everything in America. One of them is a millionaire and there are also three or four Jewish women connected with the

1. Mildred Adams had offered to translate *Amor de don Perlimplín con Belisa en su jardín* and the *Títeres de Cachiporra* into English and did, in fact, translate the latter, a puppet play. But none of Lorca's works was produced in New York until February 1935 (*Bitter Oleander* [*Bodas de sangre*] at the Neighborhood Playhouse).

241

world of letters.[2] I haven't done anything, but we'll see. Naturally I would love to be successful here. Not only would it advance my career, it would be beautiful to arrive in New York and have them perform what was shamefully banned in Spain or what no one wanted to put on "because there's no audience for it."[3] But, as I said, I'm not getting my hopes up. We'll see. I will keep you posted. And don't tell anyone about this—as I said, it is still up in the air. But it might happen.

I received, unexpectedly, $140. Many, many thanks! You are too good to me, and Father is extremely generous. But I live simply, and am happy to say I haven't run out of money, and haven't had to ask anyone for a loan. I am more *responsible* than ever. It may seem hard to believe, but I spent more in Madrid than I do here. The life I was leading in Madrid was more dissipated and more pretentious. Here there are days when it is as though I were living in a small town. It is wonderfully peaceful.

Sometimes I go to the theater. I have seen a black revue which is one of the loveliest, most moving shows one can see, and I have become a fervent admirer of the talking pictures, for one can work true miracles. I would love to make a talking picture, and am going to try my hand at it, and see what happens.[4] It is at the movies that I learn the most English. Just last night I went to a Harold Lloyd movie, a talking film that was simply delightful.[5] In the talkies you hear sighs, the breeze, and even the faintest sounds, all faithfully reproduced.

Write me at once and tell me how you are, what is going on, what you are thinking about. I am in good health, thank God.

Tomorrow I will write you a long letter and tell you lots of things.

2. Lorca may be referring to Irene Lewisohn, Edith Isaacs, Aline Bernstein, and Rita Wallach Morgenthau, all of whom were connected with the Neighborhood Playhouse and with the world of theater (*Cartas y recuerdos*, in press).
3. Rehearsals of *Perlimplín* had been shut down by Spanish censors, and Lorca had struggled to find someone who would stage his historical drama in verse *Mariana Pineda* (1927).
4. While in New York Lorca wrote the script for a short surrealistic silent film entitled *Viaje a la luna* (*Trip to the Moon*). The text, partially filmed by Federico's Mexican friend the painter Emilio Amero in the 1930s with collaboration, among others, by photographer Manuel Álvarez Bravo, was edited by Antonio Monegal (Valencia: Pre-Textos, 1994) and filmed posthumously by Frederic Amat (1998). An English translation may be found in *Collected Poems*, pp. 749–55.
5. *Welcome Danger*, Harold Lloyd's first talking picture.

Today's letter is a bit short, not because I don't feel like writing, but because I don't like this paper. I am sending you a lovely photo taken alongside the sundial of the university. It is an enormous ball of porphyry. If you look at the ball very closely, you can make out a landscape of skyscrapers, and the sun.

I think I look pretty good. You can't say I don't send you enough pictures.

Remember me to everyone. Hugs and kisses and much love from your son, who misses you.

Federico

[first week in November 1929]

Dearest family,

How are you? I'm doing fine, thank God, in this enormous country, which seems stranger and stranger, ever more fraught with absurd, incredible things. The fall semester has begun, and New York is full of theater, film directors, opera, and automobiles. Every day they begin a new skyscraper: they are finishing one that is a hundred stories high, a black-and-white building that is truly marvelous.[1] I am still surprised by it all, but by now I've found my bearings, and can get around the city and its six boroughs completely on my own. What a pleasure to discover things by myself, without needing anyone's help. There are moments, amid the urban landscape and all its strange sights, when I really miss you all.

A few days ago I had the pleasure (or the horror) of seeing the stock market collapse. As you know, the New York stock market is the stock market of the entire *world*. The crash means nothing to the international economy. But it was dreadful. Twelve *billion* dollars were lost! The sight of Wall Street, which I've already told you about (it is the center of the world banking industry), was indescribable. I spent more than seven hours mingling with the crowd when the panic was at its height. I just couldn't leave. Everywhere one looked, there were men shouting and arguing like animals

1. The Chrysler building, which was opened to the public in April 1930.

and women crying. Groups of Jews were screaming and wailing on the stairways and on every corner. These were the people who were ruined overnight. The messengers worked so hard running orders that many of them simply collapsed, and no one was able to wake them or get them on their feet. The streets—the terrible canyons between the buildings—were filled with hysteria and chaos, and you cannot possibly imagine the suffering and anguish of the crowd. Obviously, the more everyone panicked, the more stock prices fell. At one point the government and the great bankers had to intervene and try to bring everyone to their senses.[2] In the crowd, the screaming, the unbearable hysteria, I found a friend of mine, a woman who came up to me in tears because she had lost everything she had, about fifty thousand dollars. I tried to console her, as did her other friends. It was the same everywhere—people fainting, cars honking their horns, telephones ringing. Twelve billion dollars lost. It is simply unbelievable.

When I broke away from that inferno, I found traffic cut off on Sixth Avenue. A banker had thrown himself out of the window of his room on the sixteenth floor of the hotel Astor. I got there just at the moment they were removing the cadaver. He was a very tall red-haired man, and all I can remember is his huge floury white hands against the gray cement street.[3] This sight gave me a new vision of American civilization, and I

2. He is probably referring to the meeting that took place on October 24 at the offices of J. P. Morgan & Co. In their report to the press, a group of bankers managed to convey the impression that the government would intervene, thus calming the public and keeping stock prices from falling still further.

3. There is no mention of a death at the hotel Astor (Forty-fourth and Broadway) in the New York papers for October 24 and 25. The death reported by Lorca was probably that of a man who fell or jumped from the fourteenth story of the Roosevelt Hotel (Madison Avenue and Fourty-sixth Street) at 6 p.m. on October 24 (see "Wealthy Vermont Man Falls 14 Stories to Death Here," *New York World*, Oct. 25, 1929, p. 20). Four years later, in Argentina, Lorca told a journalist: "I was lucky enough to see the latest 'crash,' a formidable sight . . . It was a painful, yet great experience . . . A friend of mine told me, and we went to see it . . . That day I saw six [!] suicides . . . We were going down the street and suddenly a man threw himself from the enormous building of the Hotel Astor, and was crushed on the sidewalk" (*OC*, Vol. III, p. 543). Lorca's report of six suicides is not entirely inexplicable. The *Times* reported: "Wild rumors of failures, of suicides and other calamity spread through the district. Ambulances were reported clanging to buildings where men were reported to have shot themselves because of losses. Last night, when the hysteria had ebbed, all [!] of the rumors were demonstrated to have been just rumors" ("Weird Roar Surges from Exchange Floor During Trading," *The New York Times*, Oct. 25, 1929, p. 2).

found it all very logical. I don't mean that I liked it. But I watched it all in cold blood, and I am happy I witnessed it. It was a sight as horrifying as a ship going down, and there was a total absence of Christianity. I thought pityingly about all those people with their narrow, closed spirits, victims of the terrible pressure and cold, calculating refinement of two or three bankers who own the world.

After it was over, I went off in search of my Russian friends, who are so full of spirit, *crazy* almost, but open to all of life's rawness and mystery. One of these Russians (I have never told you about him) is among the most extraordinary men I have ever met.[4] He has twice been sentenced to death for his beliefs, and he lives here at Columbia as a student under an assumed name. He is twenty-seven years old, and knows ten languages. Sometimes he gives me English lessons, and he reads my poems with the enthusiasm only a Russian can feel. It seems he will soon leave, and return to his life as a revolutionary. Here, of course, he hasn't done anything, nor does he intend to. But what a great heart, and what intelligence! I'm enclosing a photograph of me with María Antonieta Rivas, a Mexican millionaire, founder of the magazine *Contemporáneos* and of the Ulysses Theater in Mexico City, a great friend of mine.[5] Also shown are a Hindu ballerina who is extremely pretty and a Hawaiian pianist who is very good and has been a great success in New York.[6] They are three strange birds, to be sure, but all three are intelligent and very artistic.

The photo shows Columbia University, and we took it the same day as the one I sent you showing the ball in the background. You can't see my

<hr/>

4. Perhaps this is Vladimir D. Kazakevich, who lived near Lorca on the twelfth floor of John Jay Hall and who later became editor of the journal *Science and Society*. Ella Wolfe remembered, years later, that her circle of acquaintances in New York thought Kazakevich was "playing footsie with the Russians" and worked for the Soviet secret police. (Letter to C. Maurer in *FGL escribe a su familia*, p. 50, n. 5. Also, *Men's Residence Halls Charge Sheets*, July 1, 1929–June 30, 1930, Columbiana Collection, Columbia University, Administrative Records, Cage 25, Range 3, Section 9).
5. María Antonieta Rivas (1900–31), companion of exiled Mexican statesman José Vasconcelos, committed suicide two years later in Notre Dame Cathedral. See Fabienne Bradu, *Antonieta* (Mexico: Fondo de Cultura Ecnomica, 1991).
6. Neither the Hindu dancer nor the Hawaiian pianist have ever been identified with any certainty, though Rivas reports seeing a concert by Ruth St. Denis that fall. See Maurer, "García Lorca and Spanish Music in New York," *Romance Quarterly* 58 (2011): 258–75.

dormitory, but it's not far away. All the buildings in the photo are part of the university. These people came to get me three Sundays ago and we spent the afternoon together. That day I spent the whole morning at the Metropolitan Museum, which is marvelous, taking notes on the Virgins painted by the fourteenth-century primitives, for my study on Gonzalo de Berceo.

Please write often and write long letters, and send me all the news, above all news of Conchita.

Remember me to all, especially to Manolo Montesino. Hugs and kisses and much love from your

Federico

[To Concha García Lorca and Manuel Fernández-Montesinos]

[December 6 or 7, 1929]

[Telegram]

Congratulations hugs kisses enthusiasm newlyweds consider me present wedding doing fantastic will drink wine for you

Federico

[Early December 1929]

Dearest parents,

I hope that by the time you receive this Conchita[1] will have gotten married and you will have returned to normal despite the bitter taste left by situations like this one. I was really sorry not to be there, because I would have made sure Mother wasn't sad, as she surely must have been. I would have blamed her melancholy on her "liver problem," and she would have had a better time. But everything is fine, and only God knows the truth about these things. One thing for sure: happiness is a very important, utterly necessary thing in this world, and you always come out on top when you face serious occasions with a little laughter in your heart. What would

1. The poet's sister, Concepción, married Manuel Fernández-Montesinos Lustau (1901–36) on December 7 in Granada.

I'm enclosing a photograph of me with María Antonieta Rivas, a Mexican millionaire [. . .] Also shown are a Hindu ballerina who is extremely pretty and a Hawaiian pianist who is very good and has been a great success in New York [. . .] The photo shows Columbia University, and we took it the same day as the one I sent you showing the ball in the background. You can't see my dormitory, but it's not far away. All the buildings in the photo are part of the university.

have become of Clotilde, for example, without the happiness that was always budding in her breast which marked her whole way of life? What goes on *inside* people is another matter. But the person who succeeds at life is the one who is always happy and optimistic.

No doubt [Manuel Fernández] Montesinos is a fine person, as Mother says in her letter, and Conchita is happy, and that's what counts. She is marrying contentedly, and that means a lot. And in reality, she *isn't leaving home.* And if, God willing, they start a family, it will be a great satisfaction for everyone . . . and a great headache . . . only kidding! What's terrible about life is the way some things never change. That's another reason I'm glad she is getting married. And I hope you will look the same way. I wrote her a long letter—I don't know whether it got there yet since I put it in a mailbox on the street, and that doesn't seem to be the safest way to mail letters.

We've had our first imposing snowfall,[2] and New York is displaying its very strangest landscapes in white and gray. I am working and studying English, which I can now read, but which is very difficult to understand, and above all, I spend my time writing. For sure I'm going to bring back two books of poetry.[3] I think I'm writing the best things that have ever come from my pen. And I am certain that the sonnets I'm working on now are really new and well put together.[4]

I've begun to go to the theater, which is extremely important in New York, and I am amazed at the quality of American actors.[5] In some companies, you can't even tell who the leading man or woman is, since they're all so well directed.

What about Paquito? Why doesn't he write me? What is he doing? Here in New York I've visited that idiot Alco[v]er, and I can't stand him. He's such a colossal pedant that at times he makes you throw up. But at least I've gotten to the point of admitting that he *is* an idiot.[6]

Rubio Sacristán[7] has been bouncing around New York and marveling over all this. He's the best, with a great heart, a real straight arrow.

For me it is great to be able to talk about all this with him. I've already introduced him to all my American friends, so they'll invite him to their parties and he'll feel a little happier here.

---

2. On November 23 and 24, 1929.

3. Probably, *Poet in New York* and *Earth and Moon*, later conflated into a single book.

4. "Adam" is dated "December 1, 1929, New York," and the sonnet "I know that my profile will be serene" is dated "New York, 1929, December."

5. For Lorca's experience of the New York theater, see Andrew A. Anderson, "On Broadway, Off Broadway, GL and the New York Theatre, 1929–1930," *Gestos* VIII, 10 (1993), pp. 135–48.

6. The diplomat José Felipe Alcover y Sureda (b. 1903) who began his career as Spanish Viceconsul in New York.

7. José Antonio Rubio Sacristán (1903–95), law professor, historian, and economist, who had been Federico's roommate at the Residencia de Estudiantes, Madrid, was studying economic history at Columbia. According to Mildred Adams, the two shared an apartment on the Upper West Side when Federico moved out of John Jay Hall.

A couple of days ago I spoke at Barnard College, where all the students are girls, and who should greet me—in correct Spanish—but "Julia la morena," a girl Paquito met at the Residencia (in fact, they say she had her eye on him). She doesn't seem very pretty—she is an almost Latin type—but she does have some *good qualities*, to use an expression I'm always hearing from a Mexican friend here who hardly speaks any Spanish.[8]

I've read in the papers that Primo de Rivera is leaving power and calling for general elections.[9] Is that true? What will become of Spain? I was on the subway and was reading the newspaper held by the person sitting beside me. I was so amazed, and pulled up so close to the fellow reading the paper, that he began to get a little annoyed. But I went on reading. And then this fellow—an old man who looked like a butcher—got up and left the newspaper on the seat. I picked up the paper and calmly began to read. I will never forget the amusement on the faces of two boys—messengers from the telegraph company—who were sitting facing me.

Anyway, that might be a very important piece of news.

The other day I went to one of America's great holidays, Thanksgiving. They celebrate the arrival of the first English colonizers and eat the turkey that *we* eat at Christmas. That night I had dinner at the home of [Federico de] Onís, but left early to have dessert with my friends the Brickells, who were putting on a real celebration. You have no idea how much these Americans love me—I'll only say that Miss Brickell and the old lady who lives with them give me a kiss every time they see me or say goodbye, and in America they only do this with family and close friends. They are worried about my being so far from you, and they're so exquisitely polite that there isn't a family occasion or holiday when they don't invite me, with deepest sincerity. These are rich, influential people and at their home I've met really important people in New York art, literature, and finance. Since I had a terrible cold that night, they brought me back to Columbia in a car, which is like going from Granada to Chauchina, and the next day they sent

8. Perhaps the artist and photographer Emilio Amero, for whom Lorca wrote his filmscript *Trip to the Moon.*
9. The dictatorship of Miguel Primo de Rivera came to an end with his resignation on January 28, 1930.

me a vaporizer and some excellent capsules, which have cured me completely. All this with affection and concern that are shown only by these Americans.

I can only tell you to write me, and not to get too serious about the marriage, and to say hello for me to the newlyweds with all due joy and happiness.

God knows I'm sorry not to be there. But we'll see each other soon. Before you know it. I'm going to earn a little money and spend a long time with you, and then I want to go to Russia, *at my own expense*, without depending on Father's magnificent (thank God) generosity. Goodbye. Hugs and kisses to everyone, from your son who loves you always

Federico

[Third week of December 1929]

Dearest family,

I imagine that Conchita and Manolo are back at home after their honeymoon, and that they had a great time and saw lots of beautiful things. How sorry I feel not to have been with you, and not to have witnessed all the preparations for the wedding. You know I would have made some scathing comments about the gifts, for you know how much I love to *criticize*. I suppose the gifts were fine, at least the ones from certain people, and I suppose everything went well. I can imagine how much Laurita and Isabelita[1] must have enjoyed the comings and goings. By the way, I haven't been able to send a gift, but I hope to take them something on my return.

No, come to think of it, if I bring back any gift at all it will be for Mother and Father, and the newlyweds will get the *leftovers*. Write me a long letter and tell me all about the wedding, and who was there, and get Conchita and Manolo to write, too.

It's been rather cold, but the heating here is so good that one hardly

1. The poet's sister Isabel and her friend Laura de los Ríos Giner, who later married his brother, Francisco (Paquito).

feels anything: it's so warm indoors that it's almost excessive. I'm going to spend Christmas Eve with [Federico de] Onís and Ángel del Río and [José Antonio] Rubio [Sacristán]—we're going to eat together and then I'm going to see my friends the Brickells, and go to Midnight Mass at the Church of St. Paul,[2] where the music is magnificent. I've received five or six invitations for dinner on Christmas Eve, all from Americans insisting that I not be alone. These people may have their faults, but they're incredibly friendly and affectionate. Christmas in New York has an extraordinary gaiety; not that it can compare with Christmas in Granada, which has a popular poetic atmosphere unique in all the world.[3]

The popular spectacle is very, very lively. Everywhere one looks—stores, theaters, cafés, façades, store windows, private houses—there are wreaths of mistletoe with red ribbons, to bring good luck. And everywhere there are Christmas trees—in the stations, bookstores, pharmacies, subway . . . And, as if that weren't enough, on Times Square, which is the center of the city, the meeting place of all its electrical madness, mechanical rhythms, grating metal, and incredible tremors—right there, in the middle of the street, they've put up a huge pine tree covered with electric lights and signs wishing Merry Christmas to all the people of New York, and all *foreigners*, too. The tree is full of loudspeakers playing band music by all the best orchestras. This is a really nice touch—putting a Christmas tree, a symbol of domesticity and intimacy, in the middle of this huge city for those who have no home, no land, no anything. New York is full of these contrasts. There is more bustle in the streets, and you can really tell that Christmas is near. I think that the Christians celebrate the birth of Christ with special intensity in order to express their scorn for the Jews. Here in New York there are *two and a half million* Jews.[4] It is they who bear the brunt of business, and the Americans hate them deeply.

On New Year's the Brickells are giving a Spanish party, and will be

2. St. Paul the Apostle, at Sixtieth and Columbus.
3. The manuscript of "Christmas on the Hudson" is dated December 27, and "Birth of Christ" is probably from the same period.
4. The New York metropolitan area had approximately 7 million inhabitants in 1930. The Jewish population would not reach two million until the 1950s.

observing our tradition of swallowing the grapes—and playing Spanish games like *estrechos*.[5]

These are the friends who have been trying to help me put my dramas on in New York. They are very influential, and maybe it will happen—*The Billyclub Puppets* is already being translated.[6] We'll see. I'm going to keep my mouth shut, but you may be getting a nice surprise. *Don't say a word* about this. It would be a real triumph for me.

I received the hundred dollars just when I had run out of money and badly needed them. Still haven't given those lectures, and was completely broke. No matter. A couple of times I have had to cut back, especially on food, but it has been fun. Needless to say, I haven't gone *hungry*, for New York is marvelous when it comes to choices and prices, all with great cleanliness and quality.

In any event, Ángel [del Río] and José Antonio [Rubio Sacristán] are here in case I run into difficulty, but it's better for you to send me my January allowance plus forty dollars, since I have to buy socks, some shoes, and other things that have perished in the fearful washing machine.

I'm working hard on lots of different things and remember you constantly, all the time. I know this stay in New York is going to bear fruit. Hugs and kisses to all of you. And special hugs and kisses to Mother and Father from your son, who loves you

Federico

[January 1930]

Dearest family:

The Christmas season has gone by, with excellent weather and all its usual sparkle and glitter. I received your letters and the ones Manolo and

---

5. On New Year's, at the stroke of midnight, Spaniards everywhere swallow twelve grapes, one at each stroke of the clock. *Estrechos* is a parlor game played on the night of January 5, the eve of the Fest of the Epiphany.
6. By Mildred Adams, to whom he had also entrusted the translation of *The Love of Don Perlimplín for Belisa in Their Garden*, which he read to a small group at the home of the Brickells on Christmas Eve. See Adams, *Federico García Lorca*, p. 124. Adams finally returned the manuscript of *Don Perlimplín* to Lorca, declaring she was unable to translate its poetry to her satisfaction.

Conchita sent me from Córdoba and Barcelona, which I deeply appreciate. They ought to celebrate their wedding now, since they weren't able to before. With a family as large as ours, it is hard to get everyone together long enough to celebrate *anything*. You see how Eloísa[1] recovered; so I hear from Conchita. Naturally, I'm delighted to hear she is better, and I'll feel even happier when she is back to normal. I hope you've had a very merry Christmas, the one you deserve.

On Christmas Eve I went to Onís's house for dinner. José Antonio Rubio was there, and Ángel and Amelia del Río, and the great Italian critic Prezzolini,[2] and his son Alessandro. The dinner was delicious, and there was plenty of wine and good cheer, but I had to leave them at ten o'clock to visit the Brickells, who had put up a Christmas tree and had invited all their closest friends. There I had an even better time, for it is another, very different society, and there I feel like a foreigner. They gave me an infinite number of presents, and I took part in a ceremony that is very English, but full of charm and warmth. They had set up a little altar and on some Talavera tiles they placed as many candles as there were guests. One by one, we lit them, and as we lit each candle, we had to make a wish for another person. Naturally, I wished for your health and happiness. One wish for the five of you (for you seem only one to me). The Americans take these superstitions quite seriously, for they are like children.

Afterwards we went to Midnight Mass at St. Paul's Church, where they sang a magnificent, stunningly solemn Mass with a choir of children. And there I could see how alive Catholicism is in this country, for it must battle the Protestants and Jews, who have their churches right across the street. Hundreds and hundreds of people took Communion. You might say that the entire cathedral took Communion. And it was a typical New York crowd: blacks, Chinese, Americans, etc.

But I know the best Christmas Eve I have ever seen was the one with

1. Federico's first cousin, Eloísa Palacios García.
2. The Italian scholar Giuseppe Prezzolini (1881–1982) was a member of the Committee on Intellectual cooperation at the League of Nations, and a visiting professor in the Columbia University Italian Department.

the nuns at the convent of St. Thomas, or that unforgettable Christmas Eve in Asquerosa, when they put a flat red hat on St. Joseph and a mantilla on the Virgin Mary.[3] But the excitement in the streets is the same. In all the city squares they put up Christmas trees covered with lights, and loudspeakers, and the people came and went, among drunken sailors.

The next day *The New York Times* reported that there were eighty cases of extremely serious alcohol poisoning, many of whom died, naturally.[4] Thanks to Prohibition, people drink more in New York than in any city in the world. There are hundreds of companies that try to sell alcohol and poison people, for they make wines from wood and from chemical substances that leave people blind or corrode their livers. It is dreadful! Of course, all this was imposed by the odious Methodist Church, which is much, much worse than the Spanish Jesuits ever were. In fact, the whole state of New York has never been "dry," but always wet, *very* wet, and all they have done is to make normal, clean drink a new, artificial paradise, longed for by everyone, and the number of drinks has risen sharply. Of course, I myself drink nothing without first making sure it is good. Besides, the homes I'm invited to are distinguished ones, and they offer high-quality drinks.

I am going to Cuba for sure in March. Onís has arranged the trip. I will give eight or ten lectures there. Would you please send me my lecture on Góngora? If you don't have a copy, I think Arboleya[5] does. I don't want to give it the way it is now, but will use it as a rough draft for the new one I'm writing. Also, please send the lecture on *cante jondo*. Not to deliver it as is, but to gather the ideas from it.[6] This business of *cante jondo* and Andalusian

3. Federico told Brickell that St. Paul's was "'the most beautiful church in the world, and the music, too, much better than anything he had ever heard in Spain.' Then he was taken to the Columbus Circle Childs for hotcakes and maple syrup, which invoked more ecstatic expressions, and he described another Christmas Eve in Spain, when he and Maestro Falla had gone together to a little church somewhere in the hills near Granada, where the nuns danced stately dances before the high altar, playing castanets and tambourines" (Brickell, "A Spanish Poet," p. 391). Lorca was referring to the nuns known as Agustinas Recoletas de Santo Tomás de Villanueva.
4. See "75 Felled by Liquor, No Holiday Deaths," *The New York Times*, Dec. 26, 1929, p. 1.
5. Enrique Gómez Arboleya (1910–69), a friend who had helped Lorca launch the literary magazine *gallo*.
6. In New York, Lorca rewrote his 1922 lecture and delivered it under a new title—"Arquitectura del Cante Jondo"—in Spain and Latin America, 1930–34.

poetry is an extremely important subject, and I am going to present it *po-lemically* not only in Cuba but afterwards in Madrid.

I am working hard. I am writing a book of poems, an interpretation of New York, and its forcefulness has made an impression on my friends. I think everything of mine pales alongside these latest poems, which are, so to speak, *symphonic*, like the noise and complexity of New York.

Greetings to everyone, the whole family, Eduarda, and especially Aunt Isabel. Hugs and kisses for the girls and you.

Federico

You promised to tell me about the wedding, but you haven't told me anything I couldn't imagine for myself, or didn't know already.

Hugs and kisses.

22 January 1930

Dearest family,

Naturally I felt very bad about the death of Eloísa. Give my condolences to her poor husband and to Aunt Eloísa and Matilde.[1] There is no way, *morally*, that Aunt Eloísa can surrender to despair, though she has reason to. She ought to devote herself to taking care of her grandchildren, for she is their only support. That's the advice you must give her; it will make her stronger and she will be able to calm herself by remembering her duty to be strong and face up to the situation. The other path leads directly to madness and annihilation, in humane solutions devoid of religious meaning. I am convinced that the truly noble, humane position in life is to fight off all such unhappy events, no matter how terrible, with great serenity and love, and bestow our help on *the living*, for the dead cannot be helped. Willpower and awareness of one's duty can work miracles. And, in the last analysis, this is logical and it's what we have to do.

I felt sorry, also, that Conchita had to spend her honeymoon dressed in mourning, which is sad for a newlywed, but I hope she'll hang on to her

1. Lorca's paternal aunt Eloísa García Rodríguez (1868–1953), her sister Matilde García Rodríguez, her daughter Eloísa Palacios García (who died in 1930), and Eloísa's husband.

new clothes and wear them later. In fact, it would be far better to follow American custom, where there is no such thing as mourning clothes, even at a funeral. To tell the truth, these people have less feeling than we do: they scarcely have souls. I cannot believe there is a single American in heaven (ah, but there are none in hell, either!). They have no spirit. They are good in a superficial way, and even when they are bad, they have no sort of personal distinction.

Andrés Segovia has been here, and came looking for me, and has been as refined and as affectionate as ever.[2] He has taken me to the homes of a couple of millionaires I didn't know, where I have witnessed some hilarious scenes from American life, all of which are very valuable to me.

In New York, it is a very complicated thing to enter "society," for invitations rain down on you until your life becomes impossible. I've met a whole gaggle of Americans and their families, from multimillionaires to the poorest employees of the subway and sailors on the Hudson, and I have carefully chosen wherever I wanted to go, and the people I need to deal with for my own affairs. I'm almost sure my theatrical works can be put on in New York; everyone thinks so, and these are influential people. But don't say a word about this to anyone. I've also eaten dinner these days with maestro Arbós,[3] and with "eminent" musicians and singers from the Metropolitan.

But this is only at night. The days I spend working, and very hard, and I'm getting nervous about all the things I want to—and must—do, and have no time for. I am preparing lectures, studying English, and above all writing. I think the poem I'm writing about New York, with prints,

2. The great Spanish guitarrist (1893–1987), who had participated in the 1922 Cante Jondo festival organized by Lorca, Falla, and others, arrived in New York around the middle of January 1928 and performed a memorable solo guitar recital at Town Hall. Segovia's amusing memories of García Lorca are collected in Alberto López Póveda, Andrés Segovia, *Vida y obra* (University of Jaén, 2009), vol. I , p. 239.

3. Enrique Fernández Arbós (1863–1939), orchestral director, violinist, and composer; a close friend of Manuel de Falla, remarked in January 1930 that music-loving New York was witnessing an "hora española." Among Spanish musicians who had attracted critical attention in New York, 1928–30, were Fernández Arbós, Segovia, pianist José Iturbi, the Aguilar Quintet, Pablo Casals, soprano Lucrecia Bori, and the dancers Argentina and Argentinita. See Christopher Maurer, "García Lorca and Spanish Music in New York," pp. 274–75.

words, and drawings, is something really intense, *so intense* that *they won't understand it* and it will provoke arguments and scandal. But I am certain it is the most accomplished part of my work, and my intelligent American friends are looking for someone to translate it: whether they will find anyone, I don't know.

I'm working on other things, too, but it is hard to manage different things at the same time. I hope you're all well, that you're facing all your tragedies with serenity, and that you *reject* all bad thoughts. God help you.

Write me lots, and send me my allowance on the first day of each month. I've already received the one for January. Yesterday I gave a lecture in Vassar, which is the most distinguished college in all America, with the richest girls.[4] About three hundred of them went to the lecture, and some were very pretty. I ate and slept there, and danced with the girls. They've invited me to the big party the college gives in February. They had great fun listening to my lecture, which was really a joke, and many of the girls studying Spanish asked me to sign books for them. They paid me 75 dollars, on top of all that admiration, for my silly little speech. But those 75 dollars will go for a suit and some shoes, because I'm now *stark naked*. Naked! I have no clothes, and have only managed to look presentable thanks to my "combinatory fantasy," but I can't go on this way. That's why I asked you to send me $40 more. Hugs and kisses and fond remembrances from your son who loves you deeply,

Federico

[New York, end of January 1930]

Dearest Mother and Father,

I'm fine, and I'm working hard on my lectures. I've been reading in the American newspapers about all the disturbances in Spain, wonder what will happen, and feel uneasy.

---

4. He gave his lecture on "Spanish Cradle Songs" (for the text, see *Deep Song and Other Prose*, pp. 7–22) at Vassar on January 21, 1930.

Just today I received the lectures. The one on deep song will give me some details I need [for the new version], but the one on Góngora will be more useful. So please do me a favor and mail me the pages—from page 20 to 26—which you didn't send. And please do this right away: that's why I've answered by return mail. I know that the part about Góngora's death will make an impression on those *sentimental* Cubans.[1] I know that my lectures are strong. Not that I pander to the public, but that page is pretty, and since I'm giving a number of lectures, they have to have some variety.

I was really happy to hear the good news about Paquito's exams, and believe he will triumph and win a position. I feel incredibly eager to see you. God willing, if things go well, it will be easy to return to this country, and that would be great: not to live here forever, of course, but for another stay like this one, for here I can earn what in Spain would surely be impossible.

Anyway, look for those five or six pages. Or better, ask [Enrique Gómez] Arboleya to copy them out on the typewriter and you send them to me.

I hope things will go well in Cuba. Needless to say, I'll send you telegrams from every place I go and you'll always have my address and know, without missing a day, where I am and what I'm doing. On February 10 there's going to be a reception for me at Columbia, with an introduction by Onís. I'm going to talk about modern poetry.[2] I'm looking forward to it not only because of the number of people planning to attend but because of who they are.

I didn't want to do this, since it's something entirely *too serious*, but I've got to get used to things of this sort if I'm going to go to Cuba. Anyway, I have to feel grateful, since this is an honor given to only a few people.

But it doesn't go with my character, and it seems useless.

Yesterday I ate with two illustrious Spaniards, La Argentina[3] and Lucrecia

---

1. See *Deep Song and Other Prose*, pp. 84–85.
2. The lecture, now partially lost, on "Imagination, Inspiration, Evasion," was delivered on February 6 at Columbia University and, weeks later, in Cuba (*Sebastian's Arrows*, pp. 153–62). Spanish text in *Conferencias*, ed. C. Maurer (Madrid: Alianza Editorial, 1984), pp. 13–31.
3. The dancer Antonia Mercé Luque (1890–1936), born in Buenos Aires of Spanish parents. Federico

Bori the singer, one of the public idols of New Yorkers, who love the opera above all else.[4] They are absolutely charming. They treated me to dinner and the three of us ate in a little restaurant near the Hudson. We drank Anís del Mono and they raved about it, but I noticed they were giving us a substitute, Anís del Topo. When I told them at the end of our meal, they made such a huge scandal that I think they were about to come to blows with the owner of the restaurant, a wily fellow from Galicia who was very funny.

On February 5 there is a party at the most important women's club in New York,[5] and the only males invited are [Andrés] Segovia, the pianist [José] Iturbi,[6] and me. Ah, the thought of kissing the hands of those old ladies, those lunatics!

This letter is merely to thank Father for patching up my finances. I feel very bad about how expensive dollars are, and don't want to be a burden, less now than ever. I hope the situation improves in Spain,[7] but to me it seems this is something that will follow its own course toward a dramatic, definitive solution, and no doctor will be able to head off what is destined to happen.

Hugs, kisses, and good health from your

Federico

[March 8, 1930]

Dearest Mother and Father,

As you know from my telegrams, I'm in Havana, about to begin my lectures.[1] I've been working very hard lately and have let a few days slip by

read a speech in her honor at the Cosmopolitan Club on February 5, 1930 and participated in another homage at Columbia University. For the text, see FGL, *In Search of Duende*, pp. 63–65.

4. Professional name of the popular lyric soprano Lucrecia Borja González del Rianebro (1887–1960).

5. A homage to La Argentina at the Cosmopolitan Club.

6. José Iturbi Báguena (1895–1980), the Valencian pianist, composer, and orchestral director, had enjoyed a huge success in his December 1929 New York premiere at Carnegie Hall.

7. Primo de Rivera had stepped down as dictator on January 28.

1. Lorca had left New York by train on March 4 and arrived in Havana (on the ferry *Cuba* from Key West) on March 7.

without writing. But here I am, back again, with the same happiness and pleasure as ever.

My arrival in Havana was a real event, for these people are very exaggerated. But Havana is truly a marvel, both the old city and the new. It is a mixture of Málaga and Cádiz, but much livelier, and much more relaxed because of the tropics. The rhythm of the city is a suave, sensual caress, full of an absolutely Spanish—or rather, Andalusian—charm. Havana is basically Spanish, but it comes from the very most characteristic, deepest part of our civilization. Naturally, I feel right at home. You know how much I like Málaga, and this is richer and more varied. I don't know what else to tell you. I always have the impression that my friends are right around the corner, and have to remind myself that I'm in the Caribbean, in the lovely Antilles, rather than in Vélez or Motril.[2] The sea is a prodigy of light and color. It looks like the Mediterranean, but its shades are more violent.

I came here by train, crossing the United States: North and South Carolina, Georgia, Charleston and Florida. In Florida I stopped for a day with my friend [Victor Andrés] Belaúnde, an important political exile from Peru who lives in Miami,[3] and spent some time with the pianist Julián Decrey, an American who specializes in Bach.[4] Miami is a human effort only the Americans could have managed. The beach is the largest in the world, naturally, and it functions principally in winter, since the temperature is always around 75 or 80 degrees. Right now it is filled with millionaires, and the umbrellas and cars and naked women make up one of the richest spectacles you can imagine. The next town is—get ready—*Coral Gables!*—which you know from that imbecile Molina, who I think lives here.[5] I burst out laughing to think I was in Coral Gables: *Coral Guy-bls*, as the Americans say. This is a garden city that was an economic disaster for its founder, since it's a bit far from the sea and too close to Miami, which has

2. Coastal towns in Málaga and Granada.
3. Belaunde (1883–1966), from Arequipa, Perú, who would become an important lawyer, diplomat, and statesman, was teaching at the University of Miami.
4. Julian H. DeGray (1905–95), who taught piano at the University of Miami, would also coincide with García Lorca in Havana.
5. Fernando Molina (born *ca.* 1881 in Granada), Vice Consul of Spain in Miami.

everything. I ate in Coral with some Americans. The climate of Miami is unexpected and surprising after you get here from New York. As for the effort made here by the Americans, I need only say they have constructed forty magnificent artificial islands to build their palaces on, and they are crisscrossed by canals with white yachts flying the American flag.

When I went through Miami, the president of the university came to see me[6], and in the evening I had to improvise a little speech for the Spanish students. I don't know what I said, but in America you can say anything you want to, since, with a few exceptions, they're a little slow.

I've had a visit, just now, in my hotel room. The person left, and just as I was sitting back down I received your telegram. I'm happy to know you're all well, thank God. I have so many things to tell you. Tomorrow is my first lecture in the Teatro de la Comedia.[7] The crowd will be the largest I have ever faced in my life, but I feel sure of myself.

Tomorrow I'll write telling you how it went, and will send newspaper clippings.

I'm in great health. Hope you are, too.

Hugs and kisses from your son

Federico

(I've just had another visit.)

I didn't have time to write you from New York telling you about the reception at Columbia University.[1] It went admirably well. Onís made a speech and it was all very pleasant.

I'm sending you two invitations to save, and a clipping from the Spanish newspaper of New York, *La Prensa*, which is run by the brother of Zenobia, Juan Ramón's wife.[2]

These will reach you late, but better late than never, and I almost didn't

6. Bowman F. Ashe (1885–1952). Lorca's friend Ángel del Río had been teaching at the University of Miami and arranged the visit.
7. He read his lecture on "Imagination, Inspiration, Evasion" on March 9, 1930.
1. The reception mentioned on p. 258.
2. Jose Camprubí (1879–1942).

want to send them at all because of the photo. The photo was made the day before by a friend of mine who is a photographer,[3] and it's terrible. You can see I look much uglier than I am in reality.

Two days before I left New York, Sánchez Mejías gave a very pretty little lecture about bullfighting, and I introduced him.[4] A lady (an *old* one, naturally, for in New York there are only old ladies) told me: "How handsome you look in a tuxedo!" But that didn't save me in the photo.

Also, the day before I left, I went into the baptism of Onís's little boy. La Argentinita and I were godmother and godfather (loveliest of godmothers, in her black *mantilla!*).

The child we baptized is two and a half years old and when they gave him the salt he licked his lips and said "That's good!" He is a very handsome little boy, and they named him Juan Federico in my honor and his father's. As is the custom, I paid for the baptism and now I'll buy a medal for my new godchild.

I hated to leave New York, for by now I have a truly charming group of friends there.

In Havana I met up with [José María] Chacón [y Calvo],[5] who, as you know, is from one of the best families in Cuba. It was he who made me send you the cable saying I was with him, "so your parents will know you are here with true old friends."

Hugs and kisses

Federico

[Spring 1930]

Here I am, against this admirable background of sugar cane and, as the Cuban newspapers say, "*aplatanado*," as completely at home as a banana! I'll spend tomorrow cutting out newspaper and magazine articles, and I'll send them to you. Every day I read with greater interest about the situation in

3. Perhaps Emilio Amero. The photo, from *La Prensa*, New York, is reproduced in *CR*.
4. Ignacio Sánchez Mejías (1891–1934), to whom Lorca dedicated his "Lament for the Death of a Bullfighter" in 1934, had given a lecture on February 20. Lorca's introduction was so impressive that Sánchez Mejías complained: "Instead of preparing the bull for me, you've ruined it!"
5. Cuban critic (1892–1969), whom Federico had met in Seville in 1922 and who had become a close friend.

Lorca with Cuban children, spring 1930. On the back of the photograph is a message to a friend, José María Chacón y Calvo, who was about to undergo surgery: "This joyful photograph will clue you in to the smile you need to be wearing after the 'operation.' These three charming children from Matanzas are ready to hurl themselves against the cruel demons of the scalpel. The smallest, standing at respectful attention, awaits your orders, as do I, though I'm sorry to say I am less of a rascal and less elegant than they are!"

Spain. It seems a volcano. I was in the house of the composer [Eduardo] Sánchez de Fuentes, who wrote that habanera—"*Tú*"—that you used to sign to me as a child: "The palm tree gently rocking in the forest . . ." He gave me an autographed copy for Mother.[1]

Stay healthy. I am. Hugs and kisses from your brother and son.

Federico

A hug and a kiss for Manolo [Fernández-Montesinos].

1. Eduardo Sánchez de Fuentes y Pelaez (1874–1944), Cuban composer of habaneras, operas, and symphonies. The dedicated copy of "Tú" is in the Lorca Foundation, Madrid.

Dearest Mother and Father,

My lectures have been very successful. Tomorrow I give the one on *cante jondo*, using gramophone records for the musical selections. The one on lullabies was a great hit. I played the piano myself, and the young actress María Tubau (niece of the old actress of the same name) sang the songs admirably.[1] Everyone is looking forward to the lecture on *cante jondo*. Many people have joined the Institute[2] just to hear me, and many others have asked me for tickets (which I am unable to supply). I have given tickets to two young sailors from Seville who came to the hotel to see me and to an old woman who sells lottery tickets—she was born in Córdoba and once sang in the flamenco cafés. I have written a new lecture on this subject, and consider it very stimulating and very polemical.

I have already been to two Cuban towns, Sagua and Caibarién, where I witnessed a crocodile hunt. I can see you all opening your eyes very wide. But it's true. And I had one of the best times of my life . . . though I must say it was a bit scary, and very dangerous. I saw dozens of crocodiles four or six meters long. The swamp at Zapata is teeming with these little creatures. There is a booming crocodile industry, with factories to tan the hides. This was an exciting and very amusing expedition—exciting because, if the boat had tipped over, I wouldn't be here to tell about it. Anyway, I made it through in fine shape, and the people I was with praised me for my calmness.

As is my custom, I did not take part in the hunt, and was only a spectator. There was a wonderful moment when I saw forty or fifty of those monsters leap nervously into the water. A beautiful experience.

I will send you the newspapers. But it would take three or four hours to clip out all that has been written, and is still being written. Some of it is very nice, and all of it is extremely affectionate. I am going to give more lectures than I thought, and that is the proof of my success here.

1. Actress and singer María Tubau Castillo (n. 1896), niece of renowned Spanish actress María Álvarez Tubau (1854–1914).
2. The Institución Hispano Cubana de Cultura, which sponsored García Lorca's lectures on Góngora, Spanish lullabies, the baroque poet Pedro Soto de Rojas, *cante jondo*, and "The Mechanics of Poetry: Imagination, Inspiration, Evasion."

The day before yesterday, I was given a reception at the Lyceum Club by all the most distinguished ladies of Havana. There I saw the most beautiful women in the world. This island has some extremely original, beautiful women, due to the drop of Negro blood that all Cubans have. And the blacker the better. The mulattas here have a superior beauty, distinction, and delicacy. This island is a paradise. Cuba! If you can't find me, look for me in Andalusia or in Cuba. The other day I went into a huge baroque patio, full of tiles and fountains, and began to chat with some very poor black children, to whom I gave a few coins. When I was about to leave, the mother of these children, a huge good-natured black woman, offered me a cup of tea, which I had to accept and which I drank, surrounded by all the blacks in the neighborhood. You can see how well I've been treated. But often I go off on my own through the streets of Havana, chatting with people and observing life in the city. Chacón[3] has been wonderful to me, and in Caibarién it was he who introduced me to the public. Don't forget that, in America, being a poet means more than being a prince in Europe.

I'm feeling well. Hugs for everybody. And hugs and kisses for you from your son and brother,

Federico

3. Chacón's introduction, "Lorca, poeta tradicional," was published in *Revista de Avance* (Havana) V, no. 45 (April 15, 1930), pp. 101–102.

Notes on the Poems

CHRISTOPHER MAURER

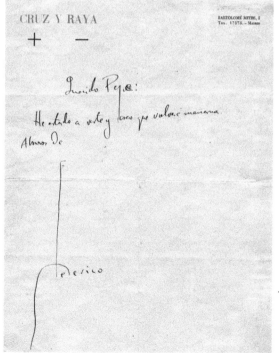

Letter to José Bergamín, ca. July 1936: "Dear Pepe. I was here to see you, and I think I'll be back tomorrow. A hug from FEDERICO."

The textual history of *Poet in New York* is extraordinarily complex, in part because of García Lorca's conviction that poetry, like theater, is as much an *oral* phenomenon as a written one.

The poet's generosity and impulsiveness, his habits as a writer, his inability to date his letters, keep his appointments, and take proper care of his papers, are factors which have had long-lasting effects on the publication of almost all his works. His reluctance to have his poems and plays published is well known, almost legendary. He thought of his plays as works in continual evolution; when a play is published, that evolution is interrupted or broken off entirely. "Plays are meant to be heard in the theater. They ought to last as long as the performance lasts . . . This is what makes theater so beautiful. Scarcely has a play been created than it vanishes."[1] He had no wish, either, to see his poems "dead on the page"; even large public readings seemed to threaten them, making his poems "stiffen and tremble like the dirty cats which children stone to death on the outskirts of villages."[2] In preparing his poems for publication, Lorca was both painstaking and unmethodical. He often gave away the autograph manuscript of a poem without making a copy, and he sometimes relied on others to type his manuscripts, decipher his difficult handwriting, prepare handwritten fair copies, and add punctuation. He did not always check typewritten fair copies against the originals, and when he did he sometimes left glaring errors (e.g., *lavado* for *lavabos*), and more than once he gave the originals to the typist (usually a friend rather than a professional copyist) as a reward for his labor. When his poems were published in magazines, he did not always keep a copy of the printed version. Furthermore, his statements to the press and to friends about work in progress, "completed" collections, and books "ready to be published" are not always easy to reconcile with the known facts. His sudden death in 1936, the political climate of postwar Spain (where Lorca was both exalted and reviled), the temporary exile of his family and some of his closest friends, the dispersion of part of his papers—all this has made it difficult to produce faithful editions of his works. The textual history of *PNY* is complicated still further by García Lorca's changing, sometimes contradictory, intentions between 1930 and 1936 as to which poems to include, how to structure the book, what to title it, and where to publish it.

Poet in New York was published in 1940, four years after Lorca's death. There were two "first" editions: a bilingual one, with translations by Rolfe Humphries, published by W. W. Norton (New York) on May 1, 1940, and an edition in Spanish brought out by one

1. From an interview in 1935. *OC*, Vol. III, p. 572.
2. *OC*, Vol. III, p. 175.

of Lorca's closest friends, the writer José Bergamín, at Editorial Séneca, Mexico, approximately one month later.

Lorca had spoken at times, in the 1930s, of his plans to publish two separate books based on his New York experience: *Tierra y luna* and *Poeta en Nueva York.*[3] By August 1935, however, about a year before his death, these two collections had been combined into one and, with the assistance of a typist (probably his companion and lover Rafael Rodríguez Rapún), Lorca did his best to prepare the manuscript of *PNY* for publication. In the spring of 1936, he gave the still incomplete manuscript to Bergamín, who had expressed interest in publishing it at Cruz y Raya, the publishing house he directed in Madrid. Presumably, the two were to meet to discuss the project. But in mid-July, a month before his death, Lorca left Madrid for Granada without having gone over the details of punctuation, spacing, and spelling, the nature of the illustrations, and other important matters.

Bergamín took the manuscript with him into exile, and in Paris, in 1938, in the midst of the Spanish Civil War, made plans for a French edition, in collaboration with the poet Paul Éluard (who prepared a French translation), Spanish writer Juan Larrea, and the publisher Guy Lévis Mano. That project failed, and *PNY* was not published until after Bergamín reached Mexico, founded Editorial Séneca, and began to publish the works of writers sympathetic to the Republican cause: for example, García Lorca, Antonio Machado, and Miguel de Unamuno.

The manuscript of *PNY*—the one given by Lorca to Bergamín in 1936—contains three kinds of texts: 1. Three autograph manuscripts, one of which is a heavily corrected rough draft, and the others fair copies. 2. Typewritten fair copies with corrections, some made by FGL and others made posthumously by other hands. 3. Printed versions (page proofs) of four poems ("Vaca," "Muerte," "Ruina," and "New York: Oficina y denuncia") previously published in the magazine *Revista de Occidente*. There are also several notes by Lorca which indicate that, when he delivered the manuscript to Bergamín, he did not have copies of individual poems. For example, on the title page of section I, "Poemas de la soledad en Columbia University," the poet writes to his editor: "The fourth poem in this section is the one entitled 'Ribera 1910' published in *Héroe*. The new title is 'Tu infancia en Menton.'" In the case of another missing original, the poet remarked helpfully that he had given it to Miguel Benítez Inglott, "from the Fiat Company, Barcelona"! Lorca trusted that Bergamín would find the texts of the missing poems and insert them in the places he had indicated.

What this means is that the Bergamín manuscript (*B*) is not, by any means, a final,

---

3. For the texts of four poems that would have been included in Tierra y luna—"Tierra y luna" (Earth and Moon), "Pequeño poema infinito" (Little Infinite Poem), "Omega (Poema para muertos)" (Omega, [Poem for the Dead], and "Canción de la muerte pequeña" (Song of a Little Death)—see the translations by Simon and White in *Collected Poems*, pp.756–67; and *Selected Verse*, pp. 296–99. For the history of the two books, see Andrew A. Anderson, "The Evolution of Lorca's Poetic Projects 1929–36 and the Textual Status of *PNY*," *Bulletin of Hispanic Studies* LXI, pp. 221–46.

fully revised one.[4] Judging from his editorial habits, Lorca would probably have made further changes to the poems missing from the manuscript and would have retouched the entire book during the proofreading stage. Despite its indeterminacy, manuscript *B*, which was unavailable to scholars between 1940 and 2003 when it was purchased at auction by the Fundación Federico García Lorca,[5] is the copy-text followed here, as edited by Andrew A. Anderson (Barcelona: Círculo de Lectores / Galaxia Gutenberg, in press), though I sometimes differ from Anderson on questions of punctuation, capitalization, and spacing. Both in the extant autograph manuscripts and in *B*, Lorca's punctuation is much more sparing than in this edition. In *B*, some poems contain almost no punctuation at all.

I thank Rosa Illán and Sonia González of the FFGL for help in consulting both *B* and the rough drafts in the FFGL, and Anderson and Mario Hernández for sharing their knowledge of textual matters. Specific textual problems, and the history of each poem, are discussed in the notes that follow.

ABBREVIATIONS

AAA Federico García Lorca, *Poeta en Nueva York*, ed. Andrew A. Anderson (Barcelona: Círculo de Lectores/Galaxia Gutenberg, 2012 [in press].

AFFGL Series of manuscripts (P-24) in the archives of the Fundacíon Federico García Lorca, Madrid.

B Manuscript given by Lorca to José Bergamín in 1936; *AFFGL* (P-13). Used for Séneca edition and copied, also, for Rolfe Humphries for the W. W. Norton edition. Followed by *AAA*.

GP Federico García Lorca, *Obras completas*, Vol. 1, Poesía, ed. Miguel García-Posada (Valencia/Barcelona: Círculo de Lectores, 1996).

MH FGL, *Manuscritos neoyorquinos: Poeta en Nueva York y otras hojas y poemas*, ed. Mario Hernández (Madrid: Tabapress/Fundación Federico

4. The manuscript also contains a "List of Photographs" which Lorca had thought of including in this book: 1. Statue of Liberty; 2. Students dancing, dressed as women; 3. Burnt Negro; 4. Negro in formal dress; 5. Wall Street; 6. Broadway, 1830 [*sic*]; 7. Crowd; 8. Desert; 9. African Masks; 10. Photomontage of a street with serpents and wild animals; 11. Pine trees and lake; 12. Rural American scene; 13. Slaughterhouse; 14. Photo of the stock exchange; 15. Photo of the Pope with feathers; 16. Photomontage of the head of Walt Whitman with his beard full of butterflies; 17. Photo of the ocean; 18. Landscape of Havana. In one of the letters included in this book, Lorca speaks of a book with "prints, words, and drawings" (p. 276), and in 1936 in an interview he says that his book will be published with "*ilustraciones fotográficas y cinemafotográficas.*" Bergamín remembers that at one point the poet wanted to use both postcards which he had brought back from America and his own drawings. Four of the latter were included in the Séneca edition: "Young Man with Pyramids," "Self-Portrait in New York," "Sexual Forest," and Bust of a Dead Man," in Mario Hernández, *Libro de los Dibujos*, p. 230, nos. 285–88. Only the first two relate specifically to *Poet in New York*. A good discussion of the illustrations, and their correspondence to the poems, is found in Anderson's edition and in his article "The Evolution of Garcia Lorca's Projects . . . ," pp. 231–33.
5. For the history of the Bergamín manuscript, see Dennis and Hart.

García Lorca, 1990). Facsimiles and transcriptions of *AFFGL* P-13 and related mss.

N   Federico García Lorca: *The Poet in New York and Other Poems of Federico García Lorca*, tr. Rolfe Humphries (New York: W. W. Norton, 1940).

S   Federico García Lorca, *Poeta en Nueva York*, ed. José Bergamín (Mexico: Editorial Séneca, 1940).

Vuelta de paseo / After a Walk. Unpublished during Lorca's lifetime. Untitled first draft, *AFFGL* (P13-13), dated Sept. 6, 1929, in Bushnellsville, NY. On the back are the title for an unwritten poem, "Baco en New England" (Bacchus in New England), and some lines from another unidentified composition.

1910 (Intermedio) / 1910 (Intermezzo). Unpublished during Lorca's lifetime. Rough draft (*AFFGL* P13-1) dated New York, August 1929, before the trip to Vermont.

Fábula y rueda de los tres amigos / Fable of Three Friends to Be Sung in Rounds. Undated rough draft (*AFFGL P13-5*) contains the rejected title "Primera fábula para los muertos" (First Fable for the Dead). Unpublished during Lorca's lifetime. His friend Rafael Martínez Nadal believes Lorca is remembering his love affair with Emilio Aladrén (Emilio) and adds coyly that he could identify the other two "friends" without difficulty. See *Cuatro lecciones sobre Federico García Lorca* (Madrid: Fundación Juan March/Cátedra, 1980), p. 30. The rough draft is more overtly autobiographical than *B*: the speaker addresses himself ("~~Oh Federico!~~") and captures himself studying "~~a duck-nosed English~~" (~~estudié un inglés de narices de pato~~) among "~~a hundred thousand students who trample the anemones~~" ~~(con cien mil estudiantes que chafan las anémonas)~~ or counting "~~every coin in the U.S. with the patience of cork and the innocence of a duck~~" ~~(y que cuente todas las monedas de los Estados Unidos / con paciencia de cocho y simplicidad de pato)~~.

Tu infancia en Menton / Your Childhood in Menton. The title refers to the town on the French Riviera, and the epigraph is from Jorge Guillén's poem "Los jardines" ("The Gardens") in section 3 of *Cántico*, 1928. Published in *Héroe* (Madrid) 4 (1932), pp. 4–5, and in *Sur* (Buenos Aires) VII, no. 34 (July 1937), pp. 29–31, with various errata and with the title "Ribera de 1910" ("Shore of 1910"). The poem does not appear in *N*: Humphries was unable to locate the text. A rough draft, published in facsimile and studied by Nigel Dennis and Andrew Anderson in 2005, is dated Jan. 3, 1930.

Norma y paraíso de los negros / Standards and Paradise of the Blacks. Unpublished during Lorca's lifetime. Along with *B* (P24-9), a typewritten copy with autograph corrections, there is an autograph fair copy (P13-8) in the *AFFGL*, dated August 12, 1929, on the back of which Lorca wrote: "para componer" (ready to be typeset). In P13-8, Lorca rejects two titles: "La luna desierta y as de bastos" (Deserted Moon and Ace of Clubs) and "Paraíso quemado" (Burnt Paradise). The word "Paradise" might have evoked the "peanut gallery" (*paraíso*, in Spanish) to which blacks were consigned in the theater (the "heaven" of Carl Van Vechten's 1926 novel *Nigger Heaven*). Lorca may have been thinking of the black cabaret, Smalls Paradise, mentioned in the lecture on *PNY* (p. 185), and the title "Burnt Paradise" might connect with a photo by which Lorca was deeply impressed and wanted to include in the book, a scene of "people burning a Negro" (see p. 271, n. 4); possible reference to a widely circulated photo of the lynching of Jesse Washington.

El rey de Harlem / The King of Harlem. First published in *Los Cuatro Vientos* (Madrid) 1 (Feb. 1933), pp. 5–10 (*LCV*), as "Oda al Rey de Harlem." The rough draft (Biblioteca Nacional de España RES/276 (35–42) and the typewritten copy with autograph corrections in *B* (P24-10) are dated August 5, 1929. The figure of the King was probably suggested by a prose poem, "Alta noche" (Deep Night), in Juan Ramón Jiménez's *Diario de un poeta recién casado (Diary of a Newlywed Poet)*.

Iglesia abandonada (Balada de la Gran Guerra) / Abandoned Church (Ballad of the Great War). First published in *Poesía* (Buenos Aires) I, nos. 6–7 (Oct./Nov. 1933), pp. 28–29. *Ms. AFFGL* (P13-11), entitled "Iglesia abandonada (Recuerdo de la Guerra)"—Abandoned Church: Memory of the War—is dated November 29, 1929. Regarding this poem's inclusion in the section devoted to the blacks, John K. Walsh notes that "Lorca might well have known the glowing legend of the Harlem blacks in the Great War: the record in Europe and the great parade of the 269th regiment (the 'Hell-fighters') up Fifth Avenue . . ." (J. K. Walsh, "The Social and Sexual Geography of Lorca's *PNY*," unpublished ms., 1986). Lorca's awareness of World War I was heightened by Erich Maria Remarque's *All Quiet on the Western Front*, which he read in Spanish translation in New York, according to Ángel del Río (introduction to translation by Ben Belitt, p. xxx.)

Danza de la muerte/ Dance of Death. One of the most often revised poems in *PNY*. First published in *Revista de Avance* (Havana) V, no. 45 (April 15, 1930), pp. 107–109 (*Av*) dated December 1929. *AFFGL* P13-27 is a clipping from *Av* corrected by Lorca. *AFFGL* P13-31 a typewritten manuscript contains further revisions as does *B* (P24-13). Following *Av*, *GP* and *MH* give *perfiles* in line 27; *AAA* follows *B* and *S*, with *desfiles*. In line 52, *ventana* (window) is crossed out in *B* by someone else—Lorca's typist—and *terraza* is added in ink.

Paisaje de la multitud que vomita / Landscape of a Vomiting Multitude. Published in *Poesía* I, nos. 6–7 (Buenos Aires, Oct./Nov. 1933), pp. 25–6, and in *Noreste* (Zaragoza) II (1935), p. 6, with the subtitle "(Anochecer de Coney Island)." First draft in *AFFGL* (P13-12) dated December 29, 1929, long after a July visit to Coney Island.

Paisaje de la multitud que orina / Landscape of a Pissing Multitude. Unpublished during Lorca's lifetime. Neither the *AFFGL* first draft (P13-24), nor the typewritten copy in *B* (P24-15), corrected by Lorca, is dated. In line 32 "Fachadas de orín" (Façades of rust or urine) appears in *B* as "Fachadas de ~~cal~~ crin, de humo . . ." (Façades of ~~lime~~ of horse's mane, of smoke); in P13-24 as "Fachadas de cal, de humo" (Façades of lime, of smoke); in *S:* Fachadas de crín, de humo. Believing *crin* a copyist's error, *AAA* corrects to *orín* (rust or urine), which is consistent with the poem's title and imagery.

Asesinato / Murder. There are no fewer than six versions of this poem: *N, S, B* (P24-16, a corrected typewritten copy), *AFFGL* (P13-22), the text included in the lecture on *PNY* (which Lorca crossed out at an unknown date), and the text in *Cristal* (Orense) II, no. 7 (Jan. 1933). For a comparison of all versions except *B*, see *EM*, pp. 261–62. P13-22, titled "(Asesinato) '—Dos voces en la calle 42'—," "(Murder) '—Two Voices on 42nd Street,'" with the mention of "42nd St." and the word "Murder" added later in pencil, show the poem was written at the same time as "Girl Drowned in a Well." Study of P13-22 with its cancelled title "~~Niña en el pozo~~" (~~Girl in the Well~~) suggests that this little poem may once have formed part of "Girl Drowned . . ."

Navidad en el Hudson / Christmas on the Hudson. Unpublished during Lorca's lifetime. Like *S*, the *AFFGL* rough draft (P13-20) is dated December 27, 1929. In *B* (P24-17), a typewritten copy with autograph corrections, another hand—that of Lorca's typist?—has crossed out the title "~~Poema de Navidad~~," substituting "Navidad en el Hudson."

Ciudad sin sueño / Sleepless City. Published in Gerardo Diego, *Poesía española. Antología: 1915–1931* (Madrid: Signo, 1932), pp. 320–22. *AFFGL* draft (P13-26) with the original title (crossed out by Lorca) "~~Vigilia~~" (~~Vigil~~) is dated October 9, 1929. That draft also contains the title and two crossed out lines from "Infancia y muerte."

Panorama ciego de Nueva York / Blind Panorama of New York. Unpublished during Lorca's lifetime. The undated *AFFGL* draft (P13-19) was originally titled "~~Templo del cielo (canto del espíritu interior)~~": ~~Temple of the Sky (Chant of the Inner Spirit)~~. On a separate sheet, Lorca seems to have made notes for the poem (MH 114): "Pájaros / gemidos / cielo interminable / ~~y el verdadero dolor alejado para siempre de nosotros~~" (Birds / moans / endless sky / ~~and true pain forever withdrawn from us~~).

Nacimiento de Cristo / The Birth of Christ. Unpublished during Lorca's lifetime. Undated first draft in *AFFGL* (P13-25) and typescript heavily corrected by Lorca in *B* (P24-20). Three additional stanzas are added to the first draft by *GP*, p. 944, though I doubt they belong to this poem.

La aurora / Dawn. Unpublished during Lorca's lifetime. Published with stanza breaks after each four lines in some editions, but there are none in *B* (typed copy P24-21). In the *AFFGL* draft (P13-3) Lorca has rejected two titles: "~~Obrero parado~~" (~~Unemployed Worker~~) and "~~Amanecer~~" (~~Daybreak~~). The manuscripts are undated, but the first title alludes to the crash of the stock market in October 1929. *N* mistakenly gave this poem as the third poem in section I.

Poema doble del Lago Eden / Double Poem of Lake Eden. First published in *Poesía* I, nos. 6–7 (Oct./Nov. 1933), pp. 26–28. A manuscript submitted in 1930 to the *Revista de Avance* (Havana), but not published, is reproduced in *MH*, pp. 119–21. That version contains autobiographical references omitted in the later versions: e.g., lines 37–48: "I want to cry speaking my name, / Federico García Lorca, on the shore of this lake; / to speak truly as a man of blood / killing in myself the mockery and the suggestive power of the word. // Here, before the very naked water, / I search for my freedom, my human love, / not my future flight, light or quicklime, / my present time, which lies in ambush for me on the ball of crazed air. // Pure poetry. Impure poetry. / Vain pirouette, torn newspaper. / Tower of saltpeter, where words collide / and a smooth dawn which stays afloat with the anguish of exactitude." The epigraph is line 1146 of the Second Eclogue of Garcilaso de la Vega (1501?–36). The version in *B* (P24-23) is a handwritten fair copy, and the meaning of several lines hinges upon how one deciphers Lorca's handwriting. In line 3, the poet clearly writes *la vino*, meaning *la [que] vino* "the one [the voice] which came"). Both *N* and *S* change this to *la adivino* ("I divine it," "I sense it"). Line 11: *N, S* and *AAA* read *niño pasado* in Lorca's hand in *B* ("the child I was"); I read *pesado* ("heavy"). Lines 14, 17: Lorca writes the singular command *Déjame* in *B*, but then, incongruently, the plural *hombrecillos* in line 17.

Cielo vivo / Living Sky. Published posthumously by Lorca's friend Adolfo Salazar in *Carteles* (Havana), January 23, 1938, p. 30, from a first draft which Lorca left in Cuba in 1930.

An autograph draft in the *AFFGL* (P13-23) is dated "Cabaña de Dew-Kum-Inn. Edem Mills—Vermont—24 de Agosto—1929," referring to the "camper," the lakeside cottage rented by the Cummings family. Cummings, always eager to connect Lorca's production to Vermont realities, told the Hispanist Kessell Schwartz that the poem (or perhaps only the title?) was "inspired by a night of brilliant aurora borealis activity as the lake reflected the lights against a pitch-black Mount Norris" (K. Schwartz, "García Lorca and Vermont," *Hispania* XLII [1959], p. 52).

El niño Stanton / Little Stanton. Unpublished during Lorca's lifetime. When published for the first time by Adolfo Salazar (*Carteles*, Havana, January 23, 1938), Salazar thanked the Cuban poet Dulce María Loynaz, a close friend of Lorca, for providing him with a manuscript, but that copy has not been found. Comparison of the *Carteles* version with extant manuscripts bears out Anderson's observation (*AAA*) that this is one of the most heavily revised poems in the book. There are two *AFFGL* drafts: a handwritten one titled "Stanton" and dated January 5, 1930 (P13-29), and a typewritten copy with the final title which must have been intended for a magazine, filled with interesting autograph revisions (see *MH*, 130, 132) along with the first few verses from "Dawn." In line 28, "un hermano bajo los arcos" (one brother under the arches), *N* and *S* read *arcos*, but *AAA*, following B, *arces* (maples).

Vaca / Cow. Published in the prestigious *Revista de Occidente* (Madrid) XXXI, no. 91 (Jan. 1931), pp. 24–25, with a dedication to Lorca's friend the architect Luis Lacasa (1899–1966). The first draft has not been found.

Niña ahogada en el pozo / Little Girl Drowned in the Well. First published in Gerardo Diego's anthology *Poesía española*, 1932. Published in 1937 in the Chilean literary magazine *Ercilla* V, no. 138 (1937), p. 17. The autograph *AFFGL* draft is dated in New York, December 8, 1929, with the subtitle, "Granada y Newbarg" (sic) added at a later date. In B (P24-28), line 1 reads *"Las estatuas sufren por los ojos con la oscuridad"*: an error by Lorca's typist? *N* and *AAA* offer *"con . . . por . . ."* (which makes better sense) and *S*, *"por . . . con . . ."*

INTRODUCCÍON A LA MUERTE / INTRODUCTION TO DEATH. Pablo Neruda suggested this title to Lorca, who, in 1934–35, was thinking of using it for the entire book of New York poems (see AAA for the history of the title). In B (P24-29), in a note to Bergamín on the title page of this section (VI), indicative of the incomplete nature of the entire manuscript, Lorca writes: "The second poem in this section is the 'Nocturno del Hueco' published in *Caballo Verde*. Altolaguirre has the third [poem] and it is titled 'Paisaje con dos tumbas y un perro asirio.' The fifth is a poem entitled 'Amantes asesinados por una perdiz' and it is in an issue of the magazine *Dos* [sic] of Valladolid. You will have to look for this magazine because I don't have the original." The section is dedicated to Rafael Sánchez Ventura (1897–1980), a friend of Lorca, Buñuel, and Dalí in the Residencia de Estudiantes.

Muerte / Death. First published in *Revista de Occidente* XXXI, no. 91 (Jan. 1931), pp. 21–22, with a dedication to the physician Luis de la Serna (1907–74). That dedication does not appear in B (P24-30), a page proof from *Revista de Occidente* on which the poet pencils in a dedication to Isidoro de Blas, about whom little is known. Neither dedication is found in *S*. The autograph manuscript is missing. *S* follows B but gives the *Revista de Occidente* version in an appendix.

Nocturno del hueco / Nocturne of Emptied Space. First published in *Caballo verde para la poesía* (Madrid), 1 (Oct. 1935), pp. 6–8 (*CVP*), the text followed here. The text in *B* (P24-31) is a heavily corrected and sometimes nearly indecipherable first draft, dated "New-York–Sept[iembr]e (campo) 1929," written during Lorca's visit with Ángel del Río in Newburgh. Lorca probably included this rough draft in *B* as a reminder to himself to replace it with *CVP*. *N* and *S* both did a poor job transcribing this poem. *S* follows *B*, as always, but includes *CVP* in an appendix.

Paisaje con dos tumbas y un perro asirio / Landscape with Two Graves and an Assyrian Dog. First published in *1616* VII (1935), pp. 4–5, a poetry magazine published in London by Lorca's friend the printer and poet Manuel Altolaguirre. That is the version followed here (the original has never been found.) *B* (P24-32) is a posthumous typewritten copy. Following *AAA*, I have differed from *1616* and separated the last three lines with a stanza break.

Ruina / Ruin. Published in *Revista de Occidente* XXXI, no. 91 (Jan. 1931), p. 22, and in Gerardo Diego, *Poesía española*, 1932, pp. 318–20. The text in *B* (P24-33) is a page proof from *Revista de Occidente*, on which Lorca has crossed out stanza 6: "~~Las nubes en manada / se quedaron dormidas contemplando / el abrazo de las nubes con el alba~~" (~~The herd of clouds / fell asleep watching / the duel between rocks and dawn~~). The original is missing.

Amante asesinados por una perdiz / Two Lovers Murdered by a Partridge. Despite stylistic and thematic differences between "Two Lovers . . ." and the rest of *Poet in New York*, *B* offers unassailable proof that Lorca wanted to include this piece, which was written in 1927 or 1928, revised—in Cuba?—and published in the literary magazine *Ddooss* (Valladolid) 3 (March 1931), pp. 13–16, together with one of his New York drawings, "Self-Portrait." It was omitted from *S* and *N* and not included in *PNY* until Ben Belitt's edition of 1955. For the complicated textual history of "Amantes asesinados . . ." see *AAA*, whom I have followed.

Luna y panorama de los insectos (Poema de amor) / Moon and Panorama of the Insects (Love Poem). Unpublished during Lorca's lifetime. The *AFFGL* rough draft (P13-17) contains references to a mysterious "Captain John" and, as Anderson points out, bears the canceled title "~~El poeta pide ayuda a la Virgen~~" (~~The Poet Asks Help from the Virgin~~).

Nueva York (Oficina y denuncia) / New York (Office and Denunciation). First published in *Revista de Occidente* XXXI, no. 91 (Jan. 1931), pp. 25–28, with a dedication (later omitted from *S*) to Fernando Vela, a staff member of that journal. Lorca gave the original to his friend the musicologist Miguel Benítez Inglott, who, upon moving from Barcelona to the Canary Islands, gave it to the Spanish poet José María Millares Sal, whose brother Agustín Millares Sal asked American Hispanist Joseph Schraibman to sell it for the Millares family in New York. It was acquired at auction there by musicologist Hans Moldenhauer and is now in the Library of Congress, Washington. That manuscript (Box 117, Non-Musical Materials, 1700–1987, Moldenhauer Archives), the only one known, contains some striking lines crossed out by García Lorca. Where the known text reads "y me ofrezco a ser comido por las vacas estrujadas . . ." (and I offer myself as food for the cows wrung dry), etc., the earlier draft reads: "~~y me ofrezco a ser devorado por los campesinos españoles / en las escuelas nacionales para sabiduría y ejemplo de los niños~~" (~~and I offer~~

~~myself as food for Spanish peasants / in the national schools, as wisdom and example for the children.~~) *B* (P24-36) includes page proofs from *Revista de Occidente*—Lorca had not kept a copy of the magazine!—with handwritten revisions which may or may not be in the poet's own hand.

Cementerio judio / Jewish Cemetery. Unpublished during Lorca's lifetime. *AFFGL* (P13-28), entitled "Sepulcro judio," is dated January 18, 1930.

Crucifixión / Crucifixion. When Lorca was preparing *B* he found he had given away his only copy of the manuscript of this poem. Omitted from *B, S,* and *N,* it was published for the first time by Miguel Benítez Inglott in the poetry series *Planas de Poesía* (Las Palmas, Canary Islands) IX, 1950, pp. 20–23. The manuscript, reproduced in *MH*, pp. 166, 168, and now in the Biblioteca Nacional de España, Madrid (MSS 23213), reached that institution in deplorable condition, with faded script, foxing, multiple tears, missing pieces, and illegible, barely legible, or missing words. It is reproduced by Mario Hernández (*MH*, pp. 167, 169) and is online at 193.146.129.13/es/Micrositios/Exposiciones/BNE300/documentos/300anos_358-361.pdf (retrieved 8/20/2012). *AAA* indicates in brackets (reproduced here) and in extensive notes conjectural readings for missing words (e.g., *los* in line 12) or truncated ones (e.g., *corazón* in line 22).

Grito hacia Roma / Cry to Rome. Unpublished during Lorca's lifetime. The *AFFGL* ms. (P13-19), entitled "Roma," is undated. Bergamín, Juan Larrea, and other Spanish exiles were drawn to this poem during the Spanish Civil War and World War II because of its condemnation of the Vatican's alliance with fascism: when he wrote the poem, Lorca was reacting to the Lateran Accords of 1929, between the Vatican and Mussolini. On the list of photographs to be included in *Poet in New York* (p. 271) is one of the "Pope with Feathers," which would have shown the Pontiff on the thronelike *sedia gestatoria.* If, by "diamond telephones" Lorca is alluding to a jewel-studded phone presented to the Pope with much publicity by International Telephone and Telegraph, the poem would have been written after October 1930.

Oda a Walt Whitman / Ode to Walt Whitman. Given the homoerotic theme, Lorca chose to publish this poem quietly in an edition of fifty copies at Ediciones Alcancía, Mexico, August 15, 1933. A fragment was reprinted in Gerardo Diego's *Poesía española: Antología (Contemporáneos)* (Madrid: Signo, 1934), pp. 552–54. An autograph manuscript now in the Biblioteca Nacional de España (RES/276/h.28-34) is dated June 15 [1930] and must, therefore, have been finished aboard the *Manuel Arnús,* the ship that took Lorca from Havana to Cádiz.

Pequeño vals vienés / Little Viennese Waltz. First published in *1616,* no. I (1934), by the poet's friend Manuel Altolaguirre. A copy of the poem made by another friend, the Mexican diplomat Genaro Estrada, is dated February 13, 1930, and dedicated "Para L.A." (*MH,* pp. 191–92). *AAA* points out that in the version in *1616* and the version published posthumously in *Taller, Revista Mensual,* no. 1 (December 1938), 34–35 and reproduced in an appendix in *S,* the last stanza reads "Olvidaré mi boca con la tuya" (I will forget my mouth with yours). The Estrada copy reads "Olvidaré mi boca entre tus piernas" (I will forget my mouth between your legs) and *B* (P24-42 an autograph fair copy) and *S,* p. 136, "Dejaré mi boca entre tus piernas" (I will leave my mouth between your legs). This poem and the next were to have formed part of a book which Lorca was planning in 1933: *Porque te quiero a ti solamente (Tanda de valses): Because I Love Only You (Set of Waltzes).* In October 1933 Lorca told the Argentine critic Pablo Suero: "In this book I speak of many things I like but which people say are out of fashion. Fashion I detest. Why shouldn't I admit that I like Zorrilla, that I like Chopin, that I like waltzes? . . . The book is written in waltz time . . . like *this,* sweet, lovable, vaporous" (*OC,* Vol. III, p. 436). Anderson has shown that by January 1934 the poem had been incorporated into the canon of *PNY* (then known as *Introduction to Death*) and that the idea for the waltz collection had been dropped ("Lorca's 'New York Poems',", p. 266). The poem was freely translated and popularized in 1986 by singer Leonard Cohen (*Poetas en Nueva York,* CBS 450307-1).

Vals en las ramas / Waltz in the Branches. First published by Manuel Altolaguirre in his poetry magazine *Héroe* (Madrid) no. 1 (1932), pp. 7–8, with dedication to Aleixandre, whose poem had been published in *Espadas como labios (Swords Like Lips),* that year. There is a manuscript version dated August 21, 1931, Huerta de San Vicente, to which Lorca added, later, the dedication and the indication that it formed part of a series or book (never realized), "Poemas para los muertos" (Poems for the Dead). While preparing *B,* Lorca did not have a copy of this poem, and reminded his editor in a note: "The second waltz is the one entitled 'Waltz in the Branches,' published in *Héroe.*"

Son de negros en Cuba / Blacks Dancing to Cuban Rhythms. This *son* (a Cuban song form combining African and Hispanic influences which Lorca and Salazar helped popularize in Spain) was dedicated to the Cuban anthropologist Fernando Ortiz, who, while in New York studying the culture of Harlem, had invited Lorca to Cuba. First published in *Musicalia* (Havana) 11 (April–May 1930). There are several autograph and typed versions of this poem, including one reproduced in facsimile in *Bohemia* 60:22 (31 May 1968), pp. 22–27, dated "Habana abril 1930." The poem alludes to a rail trip (the *"coches de agua"* are rail cars) Lorca took to Santiago de Cuba. The images in lines 12–16 refer to the cigar boxes he had seen as a child in Spain: thus Romeo and Julieta, the blond hair of Fonseca, the paper sea and silver coins on the lids. Two of the labels are reproduced in Marcelle Auclair, *Enfances et mort de García Lorca* (Paris: Éditions du Seuil, 1968), p. 216 and in *CR.*

Works Cited

WORKS BY FEDERICO GARCÍA LORCA

Collected Poems. Ed. Christopher Maurer. 2nd ed. New York: Farrar, Straus and Giroux, 2001.

Conferencias. 2 vols. Ed. Christopher Maurer. Madrid: Alianza Editorial, 1984.

Deep Song and Other Prose. Ed. and tr. Christopher Maurer. New York: New Directions, 1982.

Epistolario completo. Eds. Andrew A. Anderson and Christopher Maurer. Madrid: Cátedra, 1997.

Federico García Lorca escribe a su familia desde Nueva York y La Habana (1929–1930). Special issue of *Poesía* (Madrid) 23–24 (1986).

Gypsy Ballads. Tr. Jane Duran and Gloria García Lorca. London: Enitharmon Press, 2010.

In Search of Duende. Ed. Christopher Maurer. New York: New Directions, 1997.

Manuscritos neoyorquinos. Poeta en Nueva York y otras hojas y poemas. Ed., transcription, and notes by Mario Hernández. Madrid: Tabapress/Fundación Federico García Lorca, 1990.

Obras completas. Ed. Miguel García-Posada. 4 vols. Barcelona: Círculo de Lectores/Galaxia Gutenberg, 1996–1997.

The Poet in New York and Other Poems of Federico García Lorca. Tr. Rolfe Humphries. New York: W. W. Norton, 1940.

Poet in New York. Tr. Ben Belitt. Intro. Ángel del Río. New York: Grove Press, 1955, 1985.

Poet in New York. Tr. Pablo Medina and Mark Statman. Intro. Edward Hirsch. New York: Grove Press, 2007.

Poeta en Nueva York. Ed. José Bergamín. Mexico: Editorial Séneca, 1940. **(S)**

Poeta en Nueva York. Ed. Andrew A. Anderson. Barcelona: Galaxia Gutenberg, 2013.

Sebastian's Arrows. Letters and Mementos of Salvador Dalí and Federico García Lorca. Ed. and tr. Christopher Maurer. Chicago: Swan Isle Press, 2004.

Selected Letters. Tr. David Gershator. New York: New Directions, 1984.

Songs. Tr. Philip Cummings, ed. Daniel Eisenberg. Pittsburgh: Duquesne University Press, 1976.

Viaje a la luna. Ed. Antonio Monegal. Valencia: Pre-Textos, 1995.

Line of Light and Shadow. The Drawings of Federico García Lorca. Ed. Mario Hernández, tr. Christopher Maurer. Durham, N.C.: Duke University Press/Duke University Museum of Art, 1991.

BIOGRAPHY, CRITICISM, RELATED WORKS

Adams, Mildred. *García Lorca: Playwright and Poet.* New York: George Braziller, 1977.

Anderson, Andrew A. *América en un poeta. Los viajes de Federico García Lorca al Nuevo Mundo y la repercusión de su obra en la literatura americana.* Sevilla: Universidad Internacional de Andalucía / Fundación Focus-Abengoa, 1999.

———. "García Lorca at Vassar College: Two Unpublished Letters." *García Lorca Review* XI (1983): 100–109.

———. "The Evolution of Lorca's Poetic Projects 1929–36 and the Textual Status of *Poeta en Nueva York.*" *Bulletin of Hispanic Studies* LXI (1983): 221–46.

———. "On Broadway, Off Broadway, García Lorca and the New York Theatre, 1929–30." *Gestos* VIII:10 (1993): 135–48.

——— and Nigel Dennis. "The Manuscript of Lorca's 'Tu infancia en Menton.'" *Bulletin of Spanish Studies* 82:2 (2005): 181–204.

Binding, Paul. *Lorca: The Gay Imagination.* London: GMP, 1985.

Bonnadio, Federico. *A Companion to Federico García Lorca.* London: Tamesis Books, 2007.

Bradu, Fabienne. *Antonieta.* Mexico: Fondo de Cultura Económica, 1991.

Brickell, Herschel. "A Spanish Poet in New York." *Virginia Quarterly Review* XXI (1945): 396–98.

Buñuel, Luis. *Obra literaria.* Ed. Agustín Sánchez Vidal. Zaragoza: Ediciones de Heraldo de Aragón, 1982.

Costa, Dennis. "¿Cuánto falta para Jerusalén?: Lorca's Apocalyptic and the Paradigms of Peace in *Poeta en Nueva York* and *El público.*" *Literature and Theology* 22:1 (2008): 64–87.

Dennis, Nigel. *Vida y milagros de un manuscrito de Lorca: En pos de "Poeta en Nueva York."* Santander: Sociedad Menéndez y Pelayo, 2000.

Di Stefano, Onofre, and Darlene Lorenz. "Conversations with Three Emeritus Professors from UCLA." *Mester* VIII (1979): 29–42.

Eisenberg, Daniel. "Cuatro pesquisas lorquianas." Bogotá: Thesaurus, 1975.

———. *Poeta en Nueva York: historia y problemas de un texto de Lorca.* Barcelona: Ariel, 1976.

Eliot, T. S. *Tierra baldía.* Tr. Ángel Flores. Barcelona: Cervantes, 1930.

García Lorca, Francisco. *In the Green Morning.* Ed. Mario Hernández. Tr. Christopher Maurer. New York: New Directions, 1986.

Gibson, Ian. *Federico García Lorca,* vol 1: *De Fuente Vaqueros a Nueva York (1898–1929).* Barcelona: Grijalbo, 1985.

———. *Federico García Lorca,* vol. 2: *De Nueva York a Fuente Grande (1929–1936).* Barcelona: Grijalbo, 1987.

Harris, Derek. *García Lorca: Poeta en Nueva York.* London: Grant and Cutler, 1978.

Hart, Stephen. "Poetry on Trial. The Strange Case of Lorca's *Poet in New York.*" *Hispanic Research Journal* 4:3 (October 2003): 271–84.

Jerez-Farrán, Carlos. "El sadomasoquismo homoerótico como expresión de homofobia en el cuadro 2 de *El público* de García Lorca." *Modern Philology* 93:4 (1996): 468–97.

Maurer, Christopher, and Andrew A. Anderson. *Federico García Lorca en Nueva York y La Habana: Cartas y recuerdos.* Barcelona: Galaxia Gutenberg, 2013, in press.

———. "García Lorca y las formas de la música." *Lecciones sobre Federico García Lorca.* Ed. Andrés Soria Olmedo. Granada: Ediciones del Cincuentenario, 1986. Pp. 235–50.

———. "García Lorca and Spanish Music in New York." *Romance Quarterly* 58:4 (2011): 258–75.

Morand, Paul. *New York.* Tr. Hamish Miles. Ilustraciones de Joaquín Vaquero. New York: Book League of America, 1930.

Predmore, Richard L. *Lorca's New York Poetry: Social Injustice, Dark Love, Lost Faith.* Durham, N.C.: Duke University Press, 1980.

Simon, Gregory. "Geometry & Anguish: García Lorca 1929." *Fake-City Syndrome: American Cultural Essays.* Ed. Kate Gale and Charles Rammelkamp. Los Angeles: Red Hen Press, 2002.

Solana, Daniel. "Federico García Lorca." *Alhambra* [N.Y.] I:3 (August 1929): 24–25.

Valente, José Ángel. "Pez luna." *Obras completas, II: Ensayos.* Barcelona: Círculo de Lectores / Galaxia Gutenberg, 2008. Pp. 1221–35.

Von Koppenfels, Martin. *Introducción a la muerte. La poesía neoyorquina de Lorca y el duelo de la lírica moderna.* Kassel: Edition Reichenberger, 2007.

Walsh, John K. "*Las cintas del vals*: Three Dance-Poems from Lorca's *Poeta en Nueva York.*" *Romanic Review* 79:3 (1988): 502–16.

White, Steven F. "Miseria y esplendor en la traducción de *Poeta en Nueva York,*" *Boletín* (Fundación Federico García Lorca) (Madrid) 10–11 (February 1992): 37–39. Revised and reprinted, in Lilianet Brintrup, Juan Armando Epple, and Carmen de Mora, eds., *La poesía hispánica de los Estados Unidos.* Sevilla: Universidad de Sevilla, 2001, pp. 161–67.

Young, Howard. "La primera recepción de Federico García Lorca en los Estados Unidos (1931–1941)." In Andrew A. Anderson, *América en un poeta*, 105–18.